THE SUPERMAN CHRONICLES Volume 5 Published by DC Comics. Cover and compilation Copyright © 2008 DC Comics.
All Rights Reserved.Originally published in single magazine form in ACTION COMICS #32-36, SUPERMAN #8-9 and WORLD'S BEST COMICS #1.
Copyright 1940 DC Comics. All Rights Reserved. All characters, their distinctive likenesses and related elements featured in this
publication are trademarks of DC Comics. The stories, characters and incidents featured in this publication are entirely fictional.
DC Comics does not read or accept unsolicited submissions of ideas, stories or artwork.

DC Comics, 1700 Broadway, New York, NY 10019
A Warner Bros. Entertainment Company
Printed in Canada. First Printing.
ISBN: 978-1-4012-1851-5
Cover art by Joe Shuster

THE SUPERMAN

CHRONICLES

VOLUME FIVE

SUPERMAN CREATED BY JERRY SIEGEL & JOE SHUSTER
All stories written by Jerry Siegel and illustrated by Joe Shuster and the Superman Studio, unless otherwise noted.

*These stories were originally untitled and are titled here for reader convenience.

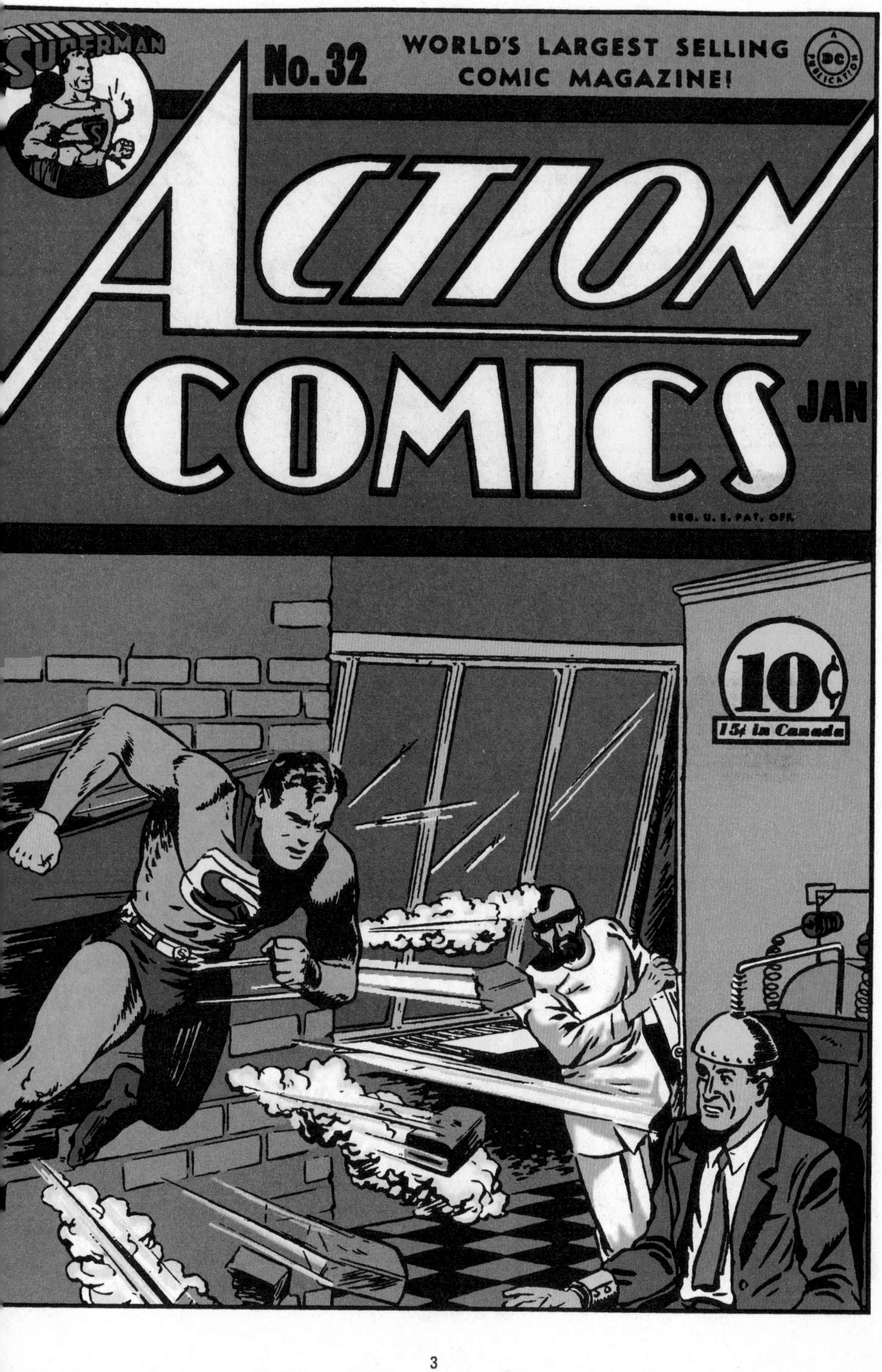
SUPERMAN
No. 32
WORLD'S LARGEST SELLING
COMIC MAGAZINE!
A DC PUBLICATION
ACTION
COMICS
JAN
REG. U. S. PAT. OFF.
10¢
15¢ in Canada

SUPERMAN

REG. U. S. PAT. OFF.

by JERRY SIEGEL and JOE SHUSTER

OF ALL EVILS, GAMBLING IS ONE OF THE MOST VICIOUS-- ITS TOLL OF HUMAN SUFFERING IS ALMOST BEYOND BELIEF! TO SMASH THE GAMBLING RACKET IN *METROPOLIS* IS *SUPERMAN'S* GOAL, IN THIS THRILLING NEW ADVENTURE OF THE MAN OF TOMORROW!

AT THE OFFICES OF THE *DAILY PLANET*--

CALLING ALL CARS! MAN ABOUT TO ATTEMPT SUICIDE JUMP OFF GERARD BRIDGE!

HEAR THAT, CLARK?

YOU BET I DO!

DON'T JUMP!

HE'LL BE KILLED!

AS CLARK ARRIVES ON THE SCENE--

CAN'T YOU DO SOMETHING? HE'S GOING TO JUMP!

WE'RE DOING OUR BEST TO STOP HIM!

NO TIME TO WASTE-- I'LL HAVE TO CHANGE TO MY SUPERMAN IDENTITY IN ORDER TO SAVE THE FELLOW!

-- A FEW SECONDS LATER--

I WANT TO DIE!

BUT AS THE WOULD-BE SUICIDE PLUNGES OFF THE TOWERING STRUCTURE AND PLUMMETS DOWN TOWARDS THE RIVER BELOW--

I WON'T LET HIM THROW HIS LIFE AWAY!

SUPERMAN SNATCHES UP THE FALLING FIGURE--

JUST IN TIME!

WHAT-?

THE MAN OF STEEL CARRIES THE INTENDED SUICIDE AWAY FROM THE CROWD TO A LONELY SPOT-

NOW, TELL ME-- WHY DID YOU WANT TO COMMIT SUICIDE?

I-I'VE LOST MY LIFE SAVINGS! I GAMBLED AWAY MY LAST PENNY AT THE PRESTON CLUB —A GAMBLING RESORT! I DON'T DESERVE TO LIVE, I TELL YOU! AND AFTER THE WAY MY WIFE SKIMPED FOR THE KIDS!

HOW CAN YOU EVEN CONSIDER ABANDONING YOUR WIFE AND FAMILY? NOW PROMISE ME YOU WON'T TRY SUCH A FOOLISH THING AGAIN!

I--I PROMISE!

LATER-- AS CLARK ONCE AGAIN DONS HIS CIVILIAN CLOTHES--

THERE MUST BE NO MORE INCIDENTS OF THAT KIND-- **THE PRESTON CLUB MUST GO!**

KENT MAKES A BEE-LINE FOR THE POLICE CHIEF'S OFFICE --BUT--

GAMBLING ISN'T PERMITTED IN METROPOLIS-- WHY ISN'T THE LAW ENFORCED AT THE PRESTON CLUB?

WHY BOTHER ME I'M HELPLESS TO ACT WITHOUT INSTRUCTIONS FROM THE MAYOR!

NEXT-- AT MAYOR WORTH'S SUMPTUOUS OFFICE--

I'VE LEARNED THAT THE PRESTON CLUB IS A GAMBLING DEN! WHAT ARE YOU GOING TO DO ABOUT IT?

ER--GAMBLING, DID YOU SAY? --UH-H--I WAS UNDER THE IMPRESSION IT WAS AN---ER-SOCIAL CLUB!

WELL, YOUR IMPRESSION IS WRONG! ARE YOU GOING TO ORDER THE PLACE RAIDED, OR MUST I WRITE AN ARTICLE CALLING ON THE CITIZENS TO--

WAIT! YOU SAY THERE'S GAMBLING GOING ON AT THAT CLUB? COME WITH ME! I'LL LEAD THE RAID MYSELF!

LET US IN, OR--

COME RIGHT IN! NO ONE'S STOPPING YOU!

THE PRESTON CLUB

AS THEY ENTER THE CLUB--

NOW WE'LL SEE IF YOU'RE RIGHT ABOUT THIS BEING A GAMBLING RESORT!

YOU STATED THERE WAS GAMBLING HERE, KENT! WELL-- SHOW ME-- **WHERE IS IT?**

I--I DON'T SEE ANY-- I'M AFRAID I OWE MR. PRESTON AN APOLOGY!

THIS IS AN OUTRAGE! RAIDING A RESPECTABLE SOCIAL CLUB LIKE THIS!

--AS CLARK DEPARTS--

CAN IT BE POSSIBLE THAT THE MAN WHO ATTEMPTED SUICIDE LIED TO ME?--I WONDER--

CHANGING BACK TO **SUPERMAN,** HE TRAILS THE MAYOR'S CAR--

SOMEHOW I CAN'T GET OVER THE BELIEF THAT GAMBLING **DOES** GO ON AT THE PRESTON CLUB-- SO I'LL TRAIL THE MAYOR BACK TO HIS OFFICE!

OUTSIDE THE MAYOR'S OFFICE WINDOW, THE MAN OF STEEL OVERHEARS A PHONE CONVERSATION!

JUST AS I SUSPECTED! THE MAYOR IS PHONING THE PRESTON CLUB!

WHAT **SUPERMAN** OVERHEARS--

THANKS FOR THE TIPOFF, MAYOR! A **REAL** RAID WOULD HAVE PROVED EMBARRASSING-- FOR **BOTH OF US!**

THIS HAS GOT TO END, PRESTON! I WANT NOTHING TO DO WITH YOUR FILTHY RACKET!

NEXT MORNING AT THE *DAILY PLANET* OFFICE--

SORRY, CHIEF-- WHEN WE CRASHED THE PRESTON CLUB, THERE WAS NO GAMBLING IN EVIDENCE!

ARE YOU SURE YOU WERE WEARING YOUR GLASSES?

I'VE GOT AN IDEA! IF BOTH OF YOU DROP IN UNEXPECTED AT THE CLUB, YOU **MIGHT** CATCH PRESTON OFF HIS GUARD!

4.

GRANTED THAT THESE GAMBLERS MAY BE THUGS AND--(GULP) KILLERS, DON'T BE FRIGHTENED, LOIS-- I'LL BE WITH YOU!

I'D FEEL MUCH SAFER IN YOUR PRESENCE IF YOUR TEETH WOULD STOP CHATTERING!

TALK RIGHT UP TO HIM, CLARK!

IF--IF YOU DON'T LET US IN, WE'LL ASSUME YOU HAVE SOMETHING TO HIDE!

OH--IT'S YOU BACK AGAIN, EH? BEAT IT! WE DON'T WANT ANY REPORTERS AROUND HERE!

THE PRESTON CLUB

LOOK OUT, CLARK!

I SAID-- SCRAM!

YOU'RE HOPELESS!

--BUT I DON'T DARE GO BACK AND--ER-- SLUG HIM! HE'S LIABLE TO ATTACK ME AGAIN!

RETURNING TO HER APARTMENT, LOIS ALTERS HER APPEARANCE SLIGHTLY--

--IF THIS ONLY WORKS!

SHE TELEPHONES SEVERAL FRIENDS --AND FINALLY--

CAN YOU GET ME IN THE PRESTON CLUB? YOU CAN? FINE!

SHORTLY LATER, A DISGUISED LOIS ENTERS THE PRESTON CLUB WITH A GENTLEMAN FRIEND--

(GOOD-- SO FAR I HAVEN'T BEEN RECOGNIZED!)

LOIS IS THRILLED TO SEE THE INTERIOR OF THE PRESTON CLUB LOADED WITH GAMBLING EQUIPMENT. SHE APPROACHES A TABLE--

GOODY! THIS LOOKS LIKE FUN!

HAVE SOME CHIPS!

SHORTLY AFTER--

TOO BAD, LADY! YOU'VE LOST A SMALL FORTUNE!

SO I HAVE-- BUT I'LL LET YOU IN ON A LITTLE SECRET--

--I HAVE NO MONEY!

WHAT! YOU'D BETTER SEE PRESTON!

LOIS IS TAKEN TO PRESTON'S PRIVATE OFFICE--

I'M FLAT BROKE! PITIFUL, EH?

SHE'S LOST HEAVILY--THEN TRIES TO WELCH!

LET'S SEE HER PURSE! I'LL SOON SEE IF SHE'S LYING!

PRESTON SEES LOIS' REPORTER'S CARD, WHICH SHE FORGOT TO REMOVE FROM HER BAG!

GRAB HER! SHE'S A DAILY PLANET REPORTER!

6.

LET ME GO! YOU'D BETTER-- BECAUSE THERE'S NOTHING YOU CAN DO TO STOP ME FROM REPORTING EVERYTHING THAT HAPPENS!

SO I CAN'T PREVENT YOU FROM TALKING, EH? THAT'S WHERE YOU'RE MISTAKEN, MY GIRL! I CAN STOP YOU-- AND I WILL!

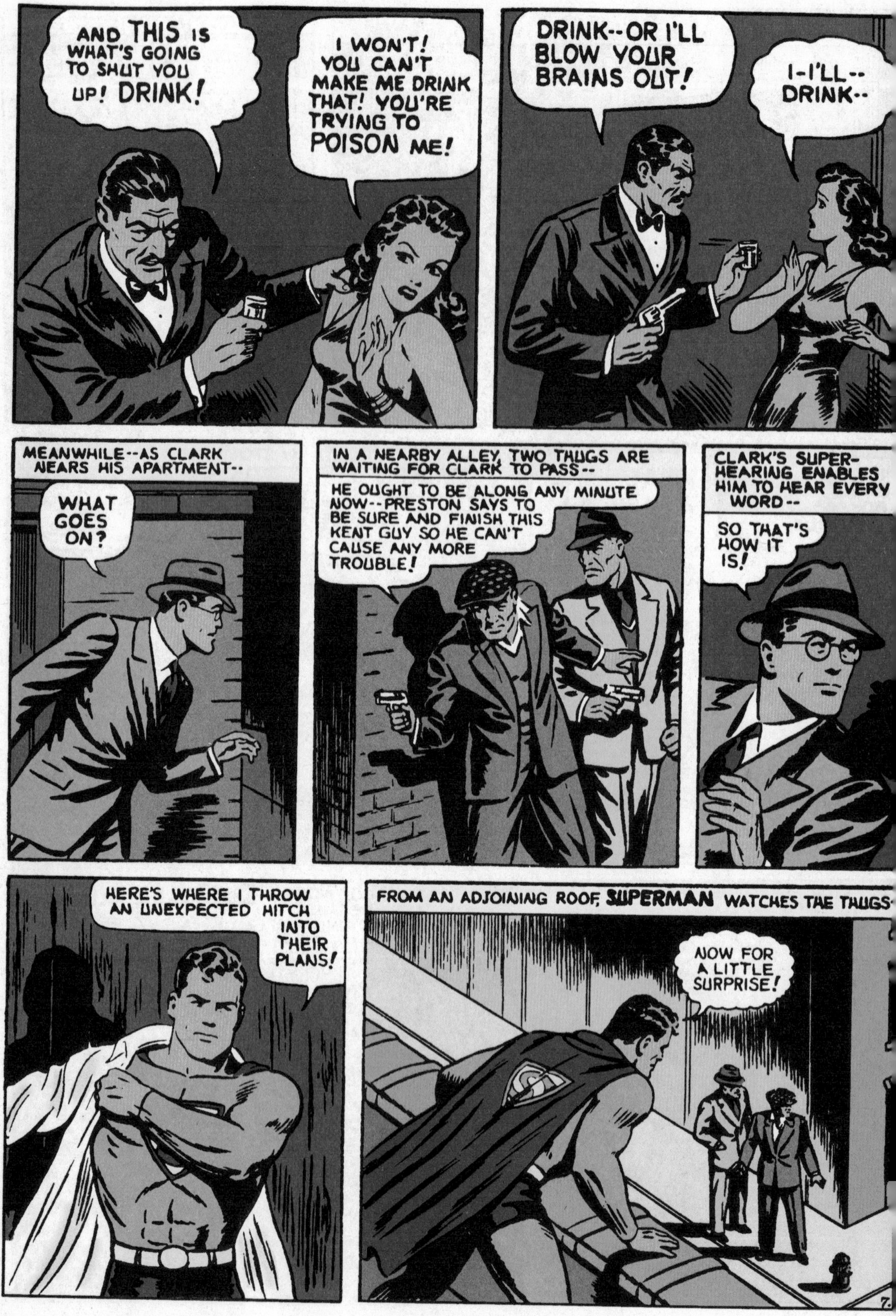
AND THIS IS WHAT'S GOING TO SHUT YOU UP! DRINK!
I WON'T! YOU CAN'T MAKE ME DRINK THAT! YOU'RE TRYING TO POISON ME!
DRINK--OR I'LL BLOW YOUR BRAINS OUT!
I-I'LL--DRINK--
MEANWHILE--AS CLARK NEARS HIS APARTMENT--
WHAT GOES ON?
IN A NEARBY ALLEY, TWO THUGS ARE WAITING FOR CLARK TO PASS--
HE OUGHT TO BE ALONG ANY MINUTE NOW--PRESTON SAYS TO BE SURE AND FINISH THIS KENT GUY SO HE CAN'T CAUSE ANY MORE TROUBLE!
CLARK'S SUPER-HEARING ENABLES HIM TO HEAR EVERY WORD--
SO THAT'S HOW IT IS!
HERE'S WHERE I THROW AN UNEXPECTED HITCH INTO THEIR PLANS!
FROM AN ADJOINING ROOF, SUPERMAN WATCHES THE THUGS-
NOW FOR A LITTLE SURPRISE!
7.

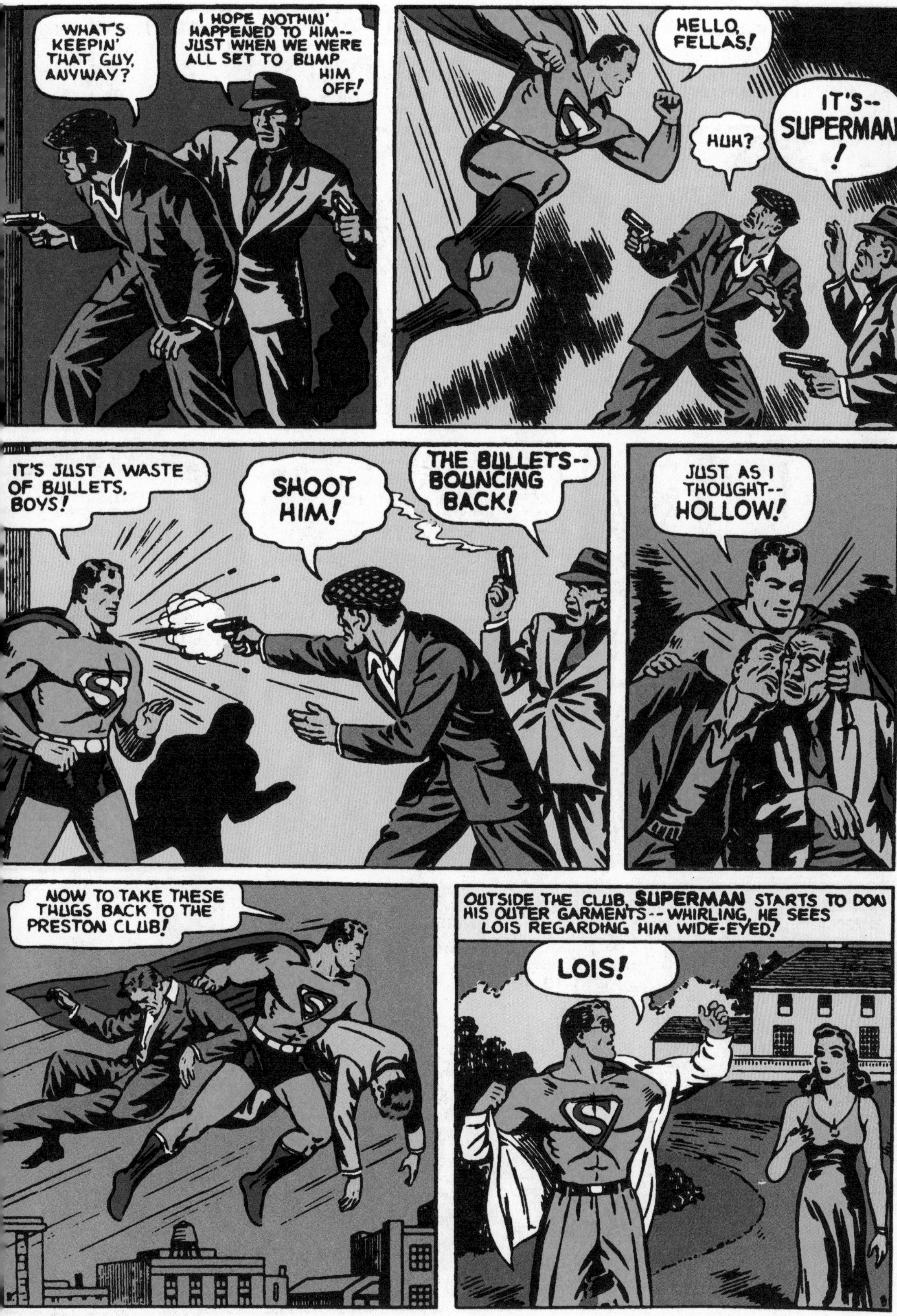

WHAT'S KEEPIN' THAT GUY, ANYWAY?
I HOPE NOTHIN' HAPPENED TO HIM-- JUST WHEN WE WERE ALL SET TO BUMP HIM OFF!
HELLO, FELLAS!
HUH?
IT'S-- SUPERMAN!
IT'S JUST A WASTE OF BULLETS, BOYS!
SHOOT HIM!
THE BULLETS-- BOUNCING BACK!
JUST AS I THOUGHT-- HOLLOW!
NOW TO TAKE THESE THUGS BACK TO THE PRESTON CLUB!
OUTSIDE THE CLUB, SUPERMAN STARTS TO DON HIS OUTER GARMENTS--WHIRLING, HE SEES LOIS REGARDING HIM WIDE-EYED!
LOIS!

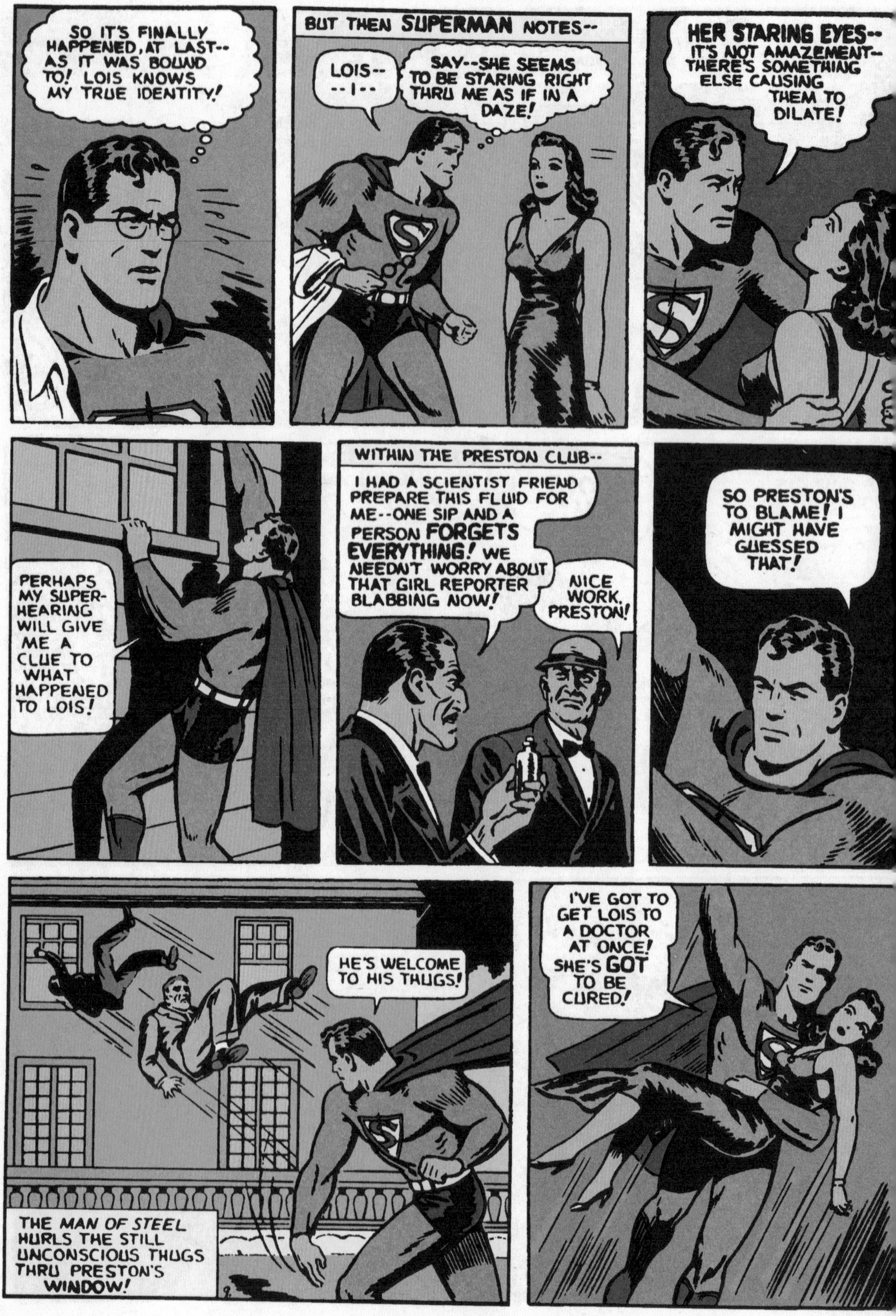

SO IT'S FINALLY HAPPENED, AT LAST--AS IT WAS BOUND TO! LOIS KNOWS MY TRUE IDENTITY!
BUT THEN SUPERMAN NOTES--
LOIS----I--
SAY--SHE SEEMS TO BE STARING RIGHT THRU ME AS IF IN A DAZE!
HER STARING EYES--IT'S NOT AMAZEMENT--THERE'S SOMETHING ELSE CAUSING THEM TO DILATE!
PERHAPS MY SUPER-HEARING WILL GIVE ME A CLUE TO WHAT HAPPENED TO LOIS!
WITHIN THE PRESTON CLUB--
I HAD A SCIENTIST FRIEND PREPARE THIS FLUID FOR ME--ONE SIP AND A PERSON FORGETS EVERYTHING! WE NEEDN'T WORRY ABOUT THAT GIRL REPORTER BLABBING NOW!
NICE WORK, PRESTON!
SO PRESTON'S TO BLAME! I MIGHT HAVE GUESSED THAT!
HE'S WELCOME TO HIS THUGS!
THE MAN OF STEEL HURLS THE STILL UNCONSCIOUS THUGS THRU PRESTON'S WINDOW!
I'VE GOT TO GET LOIS TO A DOCTOR AT ONCE! SHE'S GOT TO BE CURED!

IN HIS IDENTITY AS CLARK KENT, HE TAKES LOIS TO A PROMINENT DOCTOR--

TELL ME, DOCTOR--CAN YOU BRING HER OUT OF IT?

HM-M--INTERESTING-- VERY INTERESTING!

SORRY--I CAN DO NOTHING FOR HER! HER CASE IS HOPELESS! SHE WILL HAVE TO SPEND THE REMAINDER OF HER DAYS IN A SANITARIUM!

AS THEY LEAVE THE DOCTOR'S OFFICE--

I'VE GOT TO HELP HER! BUT WHAT CAN I DO?

(MENTAL HYPNOSIS! -- IF THIS FAILS TO WORK, I'LL HAVE TO GIVE UP!)

(IT WORKED! BUT IF SHE REMEMBERS ME CHANGING FROM SUPERMAN TO--)

MY HEAD! WHAT-- ??

THINK BACK! WHAT CAN YOU RECALL?

HOW DID I GET HERE? I DON'T REMEMBER A THING THAT OCCURRED AFTER PRESTON FORCED ME TO DRINK THAT HORRIBLE LIQUID!

WITH RELIEF, CLARK REALIZES THAT LOIS DOES NOT KNOW HIS SECRET-- HE URGES HER TO KEEP HER INFORMATION ABOUT PRESTON A SECRET, UNTIL SHE HAS PROOF-- THEN-- HOURS LATER IN CLARK'S LABORATORY-

THE KRYPTO-RAYGUN-- A STARTLING INVENTION WITH WHICH I CAN SNAP PICTURES--THEY ARE DEVELOPED RIGHT IN THE GUN--AND CAN BE FLASHED UPON A WALL!

LATER--WITH HIS NEW INVENTION, HE HEADS FOR THE PRESTON CLUB--

OUTSIDE THE CLUB WINDOW, HE SNAPS PICTURES OF THE GAMBLING MACHINES IN ACTION!

PICTURES DON'T LIE!

THEN--AS SUPERMAN TRIES TO ENTER THE CLUB THE DOOR IS SLAMMED IN HIS FACE!

I SAID-- STAY OUT!

SLAM!

THE MAN OF STEEL EASILY SMASHES HIS WAY THRU THE PRESTON CLUB'S LOCKED DOORS!

AND I SAID-- I'M COMING IN!

AWK!

AS THE PLAYERS SCATTER, SUPERMAN STARTS TO DEMOLISH ALL THE GAMBLING EQUIPMENT--

I'LL PUT AN END TO THIS ILLEGAL RACKET!

THEN AS STRONG-ARM MEN TRY TO OUST SUPERMAN--

NO MORE HARD-EARNED SAVINGS WILL BE WASTED HERE! OUT OF MY WAY!

THE PANIC-STRICKEN PRESTON FLEES IN TERROR!

AWAY--I'VE GOT TO GET AWAY!

PRESTON SPEEDS OFF IN HIS CAR-- UNAWARE THAT **SUPERMAN** TRAILS HIM OVERHEAD!

MEANWHILE-- LOIS APPROACHES THE MAYOR--

IT'S WITHIN YOUR POWER TO STOP THE GAMBLING AT THE PRESTON CLUB! WHY DON'T YOU? **WHY?**

I'LL TELL YOU! PRESTON GAVE MY SON SOMETHING TO DRINK THAT HAS AFFECTED HIS MIND. UNLESS I DO AS PRESTON BIDS, HE THREATENS NEVER TO CURE MY BOY!

AS PRESTON ENTERS THE MAYOR'S OFFICE--

YOU!

MY MEMORY HAS RETURNED! AND I ASSURE YOU I REMEMBER **PLENTY!**

I CAN'T STAND ANY MORE OF THIS DECEIT, PRESTON! I REFUSE TO OBEY YOU ANY LONGER! **I'LL EXPOSE YOU,** IF IT'S THE LAST THING I DO-!!

AT THE WINDOW, THE MAN OF *STEEL* SNAPS THE SCENE-

NICE GOIN', MAYOR!

THE INFURIATED PRESTON FORCES THE MAYOR AND LOIS INTO HIS CAR, AT THE POINT OF A GUN--

YOU CAN'T GET AWAY WITH THIS, PRESTON!

YOU'RE MAD!

INTO THE CAR, BOTH OF YOU! I'LL FIX IT SO THAT NEITHER OF YOU TALK, **EVER!**

ENTERING THE ROOM, **SUPERMAN** CURES THE MAYOR'S SON BY MEANS OF HYPNOTISM--

THERE! YOU'RE ALL RIGHT NOW!

WHERE'S MY DADDY?

PRESTON HAS LOIS AND THE MAYOR IN THAT CAR, AND HE'S DESPERATE!

PRESTON LEAPS FROM HIS CAR A MOMENT BEFORE IT STREAKS OFF A CLIFF!

DIE, BLAST YOU!

OUT YOU GO!

SUPERMAN PLUCKS THE TWO PASSENGERS FROM THE FALLING CAR!

--AS PRESTON TRIES TO FLEE--

IN A HURRY? COME ALONG WITH US!

SECONDS LATER, **SUPERMAN** DEPOSITS LOIS, THE MAYOR AND PRESTON IN FRONT OF A POLICE STATION--THEN--

HERE'S THE KRYPTO-RAYGUN WITH THE EVIDENCE PROVING PRESTON'S GUILT!

I CAN NEVER THANK YOU ENOUGH!

LATER--CLARK ARRIVES, AS LOIS FLASHES THE PHOTOGRAPHIC EVIDENCE FOR THE POLICE--

THIS EVIDENCE SETTLES PRESTON'S HASH!

YOU'LL BE CLEARED, MAYOR, WHEN I TESTIFY THAT PRESTON FORCED YOU TO BETRAY YOUR OFFICE AGAINST YOUR WILL!

BUT IT INVOLVES ME ALSO-- I'M RUINED-- RUINED!

THE END

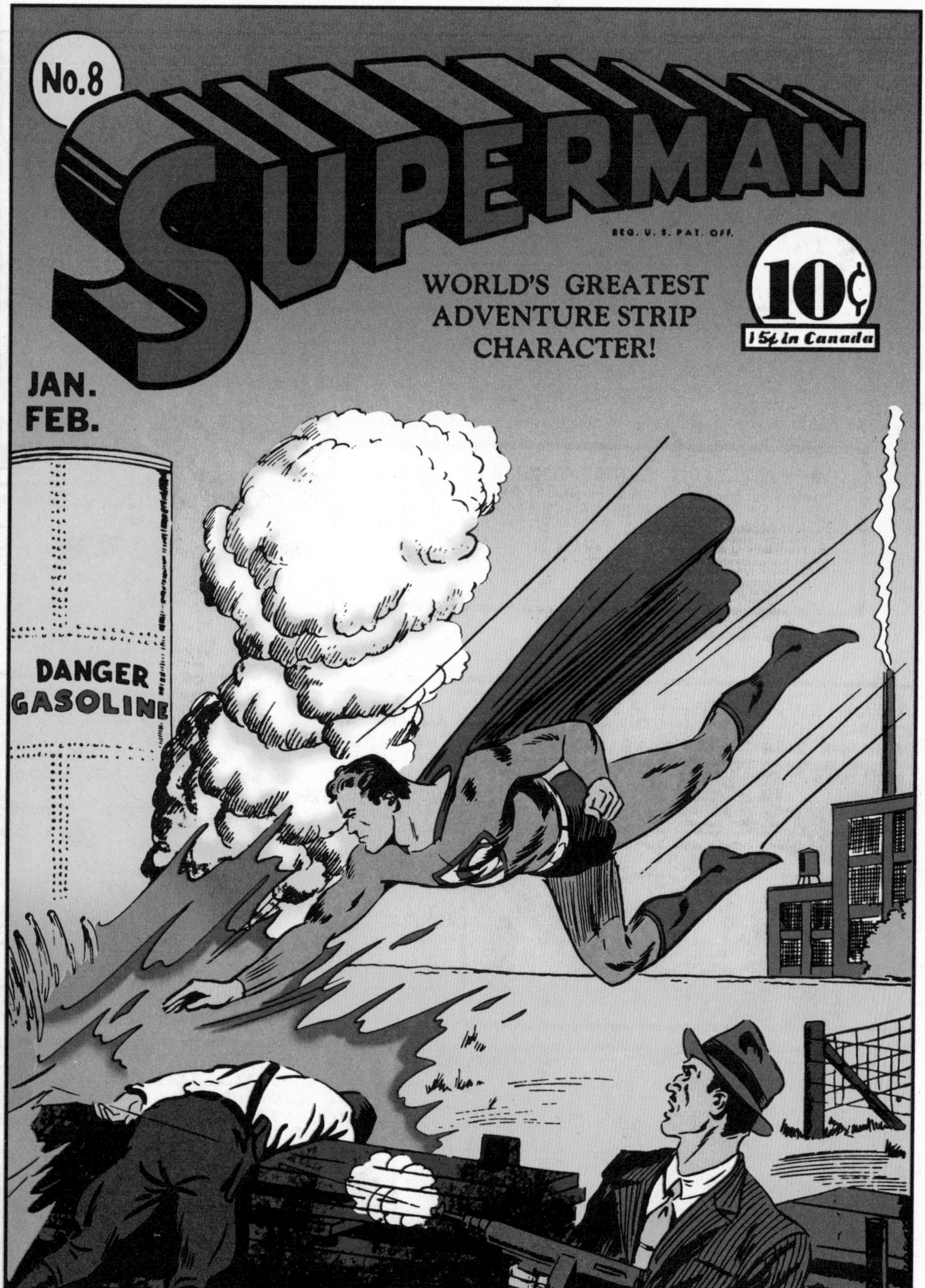
No.8
SUPERMAN
REG. U. S. PAT. OFF.
10¢
15¢ in Canada
WORLD'S GREATEST
ADVENTURE STRIP
CHARACTER!
JAN.
FEB.
DANGER
GASOLINE

SUPERMAN

by Jerry Siegel and Joe Shuster

When civilization is threatened by invading giants, mere police forces are inadequate to meet the menace. A champion steps forward to battle in mankind's behalf, a relentless foe of all criminal intrigue —the mighty, the sensational

A hidden retreat within a semi-extinct volcano somewhere in the mountains of a far-western state.......

And within the laboratory, two hard-faced men work feverishly at their revolting experiments....

Splendid, Professor Zee --- Splendid!

A scientific triumph, Dr. Cardos!

It took countless experiments to achieve it--but at last we've succeeded in increasing the size of living organisms!

A tribute to your scientific genius, Professor!

No time to pause for congratulations! Our work has only begun! We must try the process on human beings! And if it works...

...then we shall have the honor of launching a new, a great civilization!

MONTHS LATER--COLOSSAL SHADOWS ARE CAST, AND THE EARTH TREMBLES AS A **"THING"** LURCHES ACROSS THE COUNTRYSIDE....

GOOD HEAVENS! THIS MUST BE A NIGHTMARE!!

A COLOSSAL HAND RENDS THE U.S. MINT ASUNDER....

...SCOOPS OUT GREAT HANDFULS OF LOOT....

KEEP FIRING!

WE HAVEN'T A CHANCE!

THE GUARDS ARE RUTHLESSLY DESTROYED BY A GIANT RUNNING AMUCK....

HELP!

AAAAAAA!!

THEN OFF LURCHES THE MASSIVE BEING, ITS DEED ACCOMPLISHED...

②

THE SAN PEDRO SPECIAL NEARS A TRESTLE, UNAWARE OF ANY DANGER....

BUT AHEAD.....

HA-HA- HO HO HO!

A POUNDING FIST MAKES SURE THE DESTRUCTION IS COMPLETE....

ELSEWHERE, ANOTHER GIANT CRASHES THRU A FOREST, RUTHLESSLY SMASHING THE TIMBER....

WHEN MORNING DAWNS....

WHA--?

THE WOODS-- DESTROYED!

EDITORIAL OFFICE OF THE DAILY PLANET...

THE MINT LOOTED--TRAINS DELIBERATELY SMASHED--HUGE FOOT-PRINTS SIX FEET LONG SUB-STANTIATE STRANGE REPORTS THAT GIANTS ARE RESPONSIBLE!

IF THAT'S CORRECT, THEN THIS IS A MENACE EVEN TOO BIG FOR SUPERMAN TO COMBAT!

THAT IN ITSELF WOULD MAKE A GOOD STORY!

ASSIGN BOTH OF US TO THIS YARN, WHITE! I'D LIKE TO BE THERE AND OBSERVE CLARK'S FACE WHEN SUPERMAN CLEANS UP ON THESE "GIANTS".

DODGING LOIS, CLARK RETIRES TO A STOREROOM, WHERE HE CHANGES INTO HIS **SUPERMAN** GARMENTS...

GIANTS, EH?

LOOKS LIKE I'M GOING TO GET SOME REAL OPPOSITION FOR A CHANGE!

ANOTHER NEWS FLASH! CITIZENS ARE FLEEING FROM THE WEST COAST AS THE GIANTS AGAIN RUN WILD!

NO SIGN OF CLARK... WHERE CAN HE HAVE DISAPPEARED TO?

PROBABLY HE'S TAKEN FRIGHT AND HIDDEN HIMSELF SOMEWHERE. THAT WOULD BE TYPICAL OF HIM!

FLY YOU TO THE WEST COAST? LADY, WITH THOSE GIANTS ROARIN' AROUND, THAT'LL TAKE A LOT OF PERSUASION!

AND HERE IT IS! MONEY!

THE PLANE TAKES OFF, CARRYING LOIS TOWARD ONE OF THE MOST TERRIFYING EXPERIENCES IN HER CAREER AS REPORTER....

NEARING HIS DESTINATION IN RECORD-BREAKING TIME, **SUPERMAN** IS STARTLED AT WHAT HIS TELESCOPIC VISION UNEXPECTEDLY REVEALS....

WHAT--!

④

WHAT SUPERMAN SEES--! WITHIN AN ALMOST EXTINCT VOLCANO. HUGE GIANTS ERECTING GREAT HOMES!

THE ROADS ARE JAMMED WITH TERROR-STRICKEN REFUGEES FROM THE BROBDINGNAGIANS!

MEANWHILE--AT THE HOME OF THE GOVERNOR....

WHAT'S THE MATTER, LILLIAN? YOU LOOK APPREHENSIVE!

I DON'T KNOW JUST WHAT IT IS, DAD. BUT I FEEL AS THO' SOMETHING **TERRIBLE** IS ABOUT TO HAPPEN!

E E E E E E

A GIANT!

OFF LURCHES THE COLOSSAL MONSTROSITY WITH ITS TWO HELPLESS CAPTIVES--!

SUPERMAN'S SUPER-ACUTE HEARING PICKS UP A RADIO NEWS BROADCAST.....

FLASH! LATEST REPORT IS THAT GOVERNOR CARLSON AND HIS DAUGHTER LILLIAN HAVE BEEN SEIZED BY ONE OF THE INVADING GIANTS!

AT THAT MOMENT, A CAT OF TREMENDOUS SIZE POKES ITS HEAD THRU MASSED TREES...AND CROUCHES FOR THE ATTACK AS IT SIGHTS AN ONCOMING AUTO...!

A SUDDEN LEAP....

A **GIANT CAT**! MORE SPEED, HENRY!

I--I'M PUSHING THE CAR TO THE LIMIT!

AS THE CAT ALIGHTS, THEY COMMENCE TURNING OVER INTO A DITCH....

FORWARD RACES **SUPERMAN**, FASTER THAN THE WIND!

ONLY SECONDS...

CATCHING THE FALLING AUTO, HE SETS IT UPRIGHT, BACK ON THE ROAD...

...TO ACT!

AS THE CAT CLAMPS ITS GREAT JAWS UPON **SUPERMAN'S** ARMS, THE MAN OF STEEL REACTS UNEXPECTEDLY...

UP--!

...AND AWAY!

WE OWE OUR LIVES TO HIM!

BUT LOOK! HE'S **RACING UP THE SIDE OF THE MOUNTAIN**! HENRY, THIS IS **TOO MUCH**! I--I'M GOING TO FAINT!!

REACHING THE TOP OF THE RANGE, **SUPERMAN** LOOKS DOWN THRU A HEAVY FOG AT THE SMOKING VOLCANO AND THE ACTIVITY OF THE GIANTS.

IF I HAD ONLY REMEMBERED TO BRING A CAMERA!

THE MAN OF TOMORROW'S TELESCOPIC VISION REVEALS A SNOW COVERED GLACIER NEARBY!

RACING DOWN THE SIDE OF THE CRATER, **SUPERMAN** LEAPS ACROSS GREAT CREVICES.

I'LL SOON KNOW WHAT THIS DEVILTRY IS ALL ABOUT!

SUDDENLY, HE LEAPS DOWN INTO A CRACK IN THE GLACIER....

I'D BETTER MAKE MYSELF SCARCE-- TEMPORARILY!

FROM HIDING, THE MAN OF STEEL OBSERVES SEVERAL GIANTS LURCH PAST...

I CAN HARDLY WAIT TO TANGLE WITH THOSE BABIES!

SUDDENLY, FROM THE LABORATORY, A MAGNIFIED VOICE BLARES...

BACK, SUPERMAN --BACK, IF YOU WANT TO CONTINUE YOUR ALTRUISTIC EXISTENCE!

SUPERMAN SHOUTS BACK JUST AS LOUD, BUT WITHOUT THE AID OF MECHANICAL CONTRIVANCES....

SORRY--I'VE QUITE BECOME ATTACHED TO THIS SPOT! I'M STAYING!!

IN ANSWER -- A GIANT HAND GROPES DOWN INTO THE CREVICE IN SEARCH OF HIM!

DON'T TRY TO TELL ME HE JUST WANTS TO SHAKE HANDS!

THE STUPID LOOK ON THAT GIANT'S FACE—IT'S PLAIN TO SEE THAT HIS INTELLECT DOESN'T COMPARE WITH HIS SIZE!

CHANGING TACTICS, THE GIANT STAMPS DOWN...

MIND IF I DON'T STAY PUT?

STRIKING THE OPPOSITE WALL, SUPERMAN SOMERSAULTS BACK...

I THINK I'LL GIVE THAT GUY—

—A LITTLE MEMENTO!

HOW'S THAT? I CALL IT "THE OLD SQUEEZE PLAY"!

GET HIM!! GET HIM!! GET HIM!!

AS THE GIANT JUMPS WITH PAIN, SUPERMAN HANGS ON GRIMLY...

YIPPEE! RIDE 'EM—!

YOUR MASTER MUST MEAN "GET HIM"!

8

25

WHIRLING, SUPERMAN TEARS AT THE SIDE OF THE GLACIER....

WHAT SAY WE MAKE THIS AN EVEN BATTLE?

DOWN CRASHES A GREAT PORTION OF THE GLACIER INTO A CRUSHING AVALANCHE!

UP IN THE SKY--A PLANE!

WHAT SUPERMAN'S TELESCOPIC X-RAY VISION REVEALS TO HIM! LOIS LANE-- BESIDE THE PILOT...

D-DON'T YOU TH-THINK WE'D BETTER CLEAR OUT OF HERE?

NOTHING DOING! THIS IS THE STORY OF A CENTURY! FLY LOWER!

HIS ATTENTION DIVERTED, SUPERMAN IS UNEXPECTEDLY CAUGHT BY ONE OF THE GIANTS' FLAILING HANDS!

WHAT--??

NEXT INSTANT, THE MAN OF TOMORROW IS PULLED BENEATH THE AVALANCHE OF ICE WITH THE OTHERS...

THUS PERISHES SUPERMAN- BEFORE THE FURY OF THE MIGHTY PROFESSOR ZEE!!

THE ICE HARDENS REMORSE-LESSLY UPON **SUPERMAN'S** FIGURE, ENCASING HIM IN A RELENTLESS GRIP. BUT THE MAN OF TOMORROW'S MIND IS NOT UPON HIS OWN PREDICAMENT....

LOIS--UP THERE--VENTURING INTO TERRIBLE DANGER..!

THE MAN OF TOMORROW'S X-RAY VISION ENABLES HIM TO WITNESS THE FOLLOWING DRAMATIC EVENTS...

I TELL YOU--WE'RE FLYING TOO LOW!

LOOK OUT!

THE TINY PLANE IS SAVAGELY GRIPPED BY ONE OF PROFESSOR ZEE'S MONSTROUS CREATURES!

NOT THE GIRL! DO NOT DESTROY HER! BRING HER TO ME!!

NO! NO! EEEE-EEE!!

SUPERMAN STRAINS HIS MUSCLES FOR A GIGANTIC EFFORT....

I'VE GOT TO BREAK LOOSE--FOR LOIS' SAKE--!

GREAT RENTS APPEAR IN THE PACKED ICE'S SURFACE...

THEN--UP STREAKS... **SUPERMAN !!**

MADE IT!

AS MORE GIANTS RUSH HIM, THE MAN OF TOMORROW LEAPS HIGH OVER THEIR HEADS....

NOW TO RECONNOITER!

ATOP THE CRATER, **SUPERMAN** ONCE MORE MAKES USE OF HIS TELESCOPIC VISION....

SOMETHING DOING DOWN THERE IN THE LABORATORY!

EITHER YOU INSTRUCT YOUR MEN THAT ALL INTERFERENCE END--OR WATCH YOUR DAUGHTER GROW INTO A GIANTESS!

YOU WOULDN'T DARE!

GET IN THERE!

YOU'RE CARLSON'S DAUGHTER, AREN'T YOU?

YES! OH-- WHAT DO YOU THINK THEY'RE GOING TO DO WITH US?

I'VE HEARD ENOUGH! A LEAP THROUGH THE SIDE OF THE LABORATORY AND.....

11

BUT THE TRANSPARENT WALLS OF THE BUILDING PROVE TO BE UNEXPECTEDLY ELASTIC! **SUPERMAN** BOUNCES BACK FROM THE TERRIBLE IMPACT!

WHAM!

...AZED, **SUPERMAN** IS EASY PREY FOR A GIANT!

DR. CARDOS AND PROFESSOR ZEE CONFRONT THE HELPLESS MAN OF STEEL....

JOIN FORCES WITH US--

--AND WE WILL FREE THE GIRLS UNHARMED!

I DON'T TALK TERMS WITH RATS!

VERY WELL --YOU HAVE MADE YOUR DECISION!

THE GIRLS-- **INCREASING IN HEIGHT!**

YOU--YOU FIENDS!

(--"ODD HOW UNCONCERNED THE GIRLS APPEAR, DESPITE THEIR INCREASING HEIGHT!--") WILL YOU FREE THEM?

NOT UNLESS YOU AGREE TO MY TERMS!

UNEXPECTEDLY TWISTING FREE OF HIS CAPTOR'S GRIP, **SUPERMAN** LEAPS UP--UP --TO THE CRATER'S EDGE!

MOMENTS TO ACT!

RAISING HIGH A BOULDER AS LARGE AS A HOUSE, **SUPER-MAN** HURLS IT INTO THE HEART OF THE SMOULDERING VOLCANO ...

GO TO IT!!

THE ENTIRE MOUNTAIN TOP EXPLODES...

MELTED BY THE LAVA, THE GLACIER RUSHES ON IN A RAGING FLOOD...

I'VE -GOT- TO -BEAT-IT- TO -THE- LABORATORY!

AS THE GIANTS FLEE IN MAD PANIC, PROFESSOR ZEE AND DR. CARDOS ATTEMPT TO RETAIN CONTROL OVER THEM....

STOP! STOP, DO YOU HEAR?

I, PROFESSOR ZEE, **COMMAND** YOU!

BUT ARE CRUSHED IN THE RUSH, FOR THEIR PAINS...

YAAAAA-A-A!!

THE LAVA NEARING--AND THIS STRANGE GLASS REFUSES TO YIELD!

HURRY! HURRY!

A SUPREME EFFORT, AND...

THERE! THAT DOES IT!

YOUR AMAZING STRENGTH IS BEYOND ALL BELIEF!

SUPERMAN!

WHY--- YOU'RE BOTH OF **NORMAL SIZE!**

YOU --YOU'RE NOT EVEN FRIGHTENED!

SUPERMAN LEAPS OFF WITH ALL THREE--AND BARELY IN TIME...

THIS ISN'T THE FIRST TIME I'VE SOARED THRU THE AIR IN **SUPERMAN'S** ARMS. AFTER A WHILE YOU GET TO LIKE IT!

FOR ALL THE GIANTS ARE ENGULFED AND DESTROYED BY NATURE'S UNLEASHED FURY!

13

BUT HOW WERE THE GIRLS RETURNED TO NORMAL SIZE?

THEIR SIZE NEVER ACTUALLY WAS INCREASED. THE MAGNIFYING GLASS ON THE WALL OF THEIR ROOM MERELY GAVE THAT ILLUSION!

LATER--AT THE STATE CAPITOL, LOIS MEETS CLARK KENT

SO YOU'VE SCORED ANOTHER GREAT SCOOP! HOW DO YOU DO IT?

I ATTRIBUTE IT TO MY SUPERB QUALIFICATIONS AS A REPORTER --AND 99% TO THE ASSISTANCE OF **SUPERMAN!**

THE END

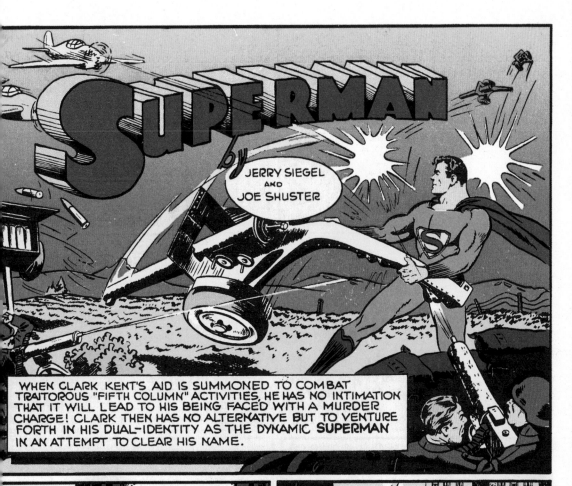

SUPERMAN

JERRY SIEGEL AND JOE SHUSTER

WHEN CLARK KENT'S AID IS SUMMONED TO COMBAT TRAITOROUS "FIFTH COLUMN" ACTIVITIES, HE HAS NO INTIMATION THAT IT WILL LEAD TO HIS BEING FACED WITH A MURDER CHARGE! CLARK THEN HAS NO ALTERNATIVE BUT TO VENTURE FORTH IN HIS DUAL-IDENTITY AS THE DYNAMIC SUPERMAN IN AN ATTEMPT TO CLEAR HIS NAME.

IN THE PRIVACY OF HIS MIDTOWN APARTMENT, CLARK KENT SURREPTITIOUSLY PEERS THRU A WINDOW!

ACROSS THE STREET...A MAN...HIS EYES TRAINED UPON THIS WINDOW!

SWIFTLY THE DAILY PLANET REPORTER REMOVES HIS OUTER GARMENTS, TRANSFORMING HIMSELF TO SUPERMAN..!

HE'S UP TO NO GOOD, I'LL WAGER! AND HERE'S WHERE I FIND OUT FOR CERTAIN!

BUT AS THE MAN OF STEEL IS ABOUT TO CATAPULT HIMSELF THRU THE OPEN WINDOW...

SOMEONE KNOCKING AT THE DOOR...

QUICKLY, CLARK SLIPS A DRESSING GOWN OVER HIS **SUPERMAN** COSTUME, AND DONS TROUSERS....

WHO CAN IT BE?

HOPE YOU DON'T MIND MY DROPPING IN LIKE THIS, CLARK.— I NEED YOUR HELP.

FRANK MARTIN! STEP IN! GLAD TO SEE YOU! ARE YOU STILL CONNECTED WITH THE ANTI-ESPIONAGE SERVICE?

I CAN'T TELL YOU VERY MUCH EXCEPT THAT WE'VE A TIP THE LEADER OF A DANGEROUS FIFTH COLUMN ORGANIZATION IS ENTERING METROPOLIS BY BOAT TODAY. YOU'VE BEEN QUITE SUCCESSFUL AT DETECTIVE WORK IN THE PAST. IF YOU UNCOVER ANYTHING, WILL YOU LET ME KNOW?

CERTAINLY! IF ANYTHING OF INTEREST COMES TO MY ATTENTION I'LL TELEPHONE YOU AT ONCE!

AFTER MARTIN DEPARTS, CLARK SWIFTLY STRIPS OFF THE SCREENING GARMENTS. ONCE AGAIN STANDING REVEALED AS THE DARING **MAN OF TOMORROW**...

THE MAN I WAS GOING TO INVESTIGATE. NOW HE'S FOLLOWING MARTIN!

I'LL TRAIL THE TWO OF THEM AND SEE TO IT THAT FRANK COMES TO NO HARM!

NOW I RECOGNIZE THE OTHER MAN! HE'S JEFF CARLTON—FRANK'S ASSISTANT—PROBABLY ACTING AS MARTIN'S BODYGUARD! —I CAN SET MY MIND TO EASE ABOUT THAT!

BUT AS MARTIN'S TRAILER JOINS HIM....

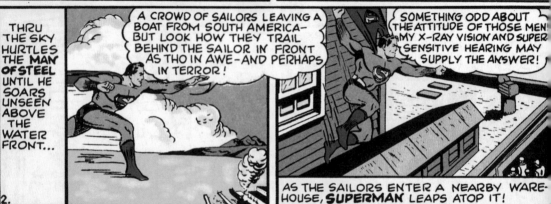

THRU THE SKY HURTLES THE **MAN OF STEEL** UNTIL HE SOARS UNSEEN ABOVE THE WATER FRONT...

A CROWD OF SAILORS LEAVING A BOAT FROM SOUTH AMERICA—BUT LOOK HOW THEY TRAIL BEHIND THE SAILOR IN FRONT AS THO IN AWE—AND PERHAPS IN TERROR!

SOMETHING ODD ABOUT THE ATTITUDE OF THOSE MEN MY X-RAY VISION AND SUPER-SENSITIVE HEARING MAY SUPPLY THE ANSWER!

AS THE SAILORS ENTER A NEARBY WAREHOUSE, **SUPERMAN** LEAPS ATOP IT!

2.

WITHIN THE WAREHOUSE, THE SAILOR WITH THE HAUGHTY BEARING ADDRESSES HIS COMPANIONS AND OTHER MEN WHO HAVE BEEN AWAITING THEM....

AS YOU ALL KNOW, I AM ERIC REIBEL, SENT TO THIS COUNTRY TO CO-ORDINATE OUR ACTIVITIES. ALSO, I BRING PAYMENT TO YOU. IF YOU'LL KINDLY LINE UP....

CONSULTING A LIST OF THE INDIVIDUALS PRESENT, REIBEL SEES TO IT THAT EACH RECEIVES THE SUM ALLOTTED...

BAH! IT'S A MERE PITTANCE!

NO COMPLAINTS. ON THE DAY THE UNITED STATES IS CONQUERED YOU WILL RECEIVE REWARDS BEYOND YOUR HIGHEST DREAMS!

HOLD YOUR TONGUE!

WHAT WE'D PREFER IS MORE THAN PIN MONEY RIGHT NOW!

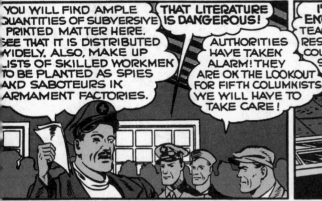

YOU WILL FIND AMPLE QUANTITIES OF SUBVERSIVE PRINTED MATTER HERE. SEE THAT IT IS DISTRIBUTED WIDELY. ALSO, MAKE UP LISTS OF SKILLED WORKMEN TO BE PLANTED AS SPIES AND SABOTEURS IN ARMAMENT FACTORIES.

THAT LITERATURE IS DANGEROUS!

AUTHORITIES HAVE TAKEN ALARM! THEY ARE ON THE LOOKOUT FOR FIFTH COLUMNISTS. WE WILL HAVE TO TAKE CARE!

I'VE HEARD ENOUGH! NOW TO TEACH THEM A LITTLE RESPECT FOR THE COUNTRY THEY'RE SEEKING TO DESTROY!

WE HAVE A BRILLIANT FUTURE BEFORE US! WE MUST CONTINUE OUR COURAGEOUS EFFORT TO UNDERMINE THE UNITED STATES—OUR REWARD WILL COME WHEN WE ARE ITS MASTERS!

LET'S SEE JUST HOW COURAGEOUS THEY ARE!

FRAGILE

USE NO HOOKS

BURN!

DESTROY!

BEFORE THE AMAZED EYES OF THE CONSPIRATORS, THE HEAVY BOX CRASHES THRU THE WALL...!

WHAT—?

MUST BE AN EARTHQUAKE!

RUN!

RUN!

CRASH!

FOLLOWED AN INSTANT LATER BY THE MAN OF STEEL HIMSELF!

WHERE'S ALL THAT BRAVERY WE WERE HEARING SO MUCH ABOUT!

3.

I'LL TAKE THAT LIST, IF YOU DON'T MIND!

GET HIM! HE'S TAKING THE LIST THAT CAN SEND US ALL TO JAIL!

THE MENACE OF EXPOSURE CONFRONTING THEM, THE OTHERS CLOSE IN UPON **SUPERMAN** LIKE CORNERED RATS....

KNIVES, CLUBS, CHAIRS—YOU DON'T SEEM TO HAVE MUCH CONFIDENCE IN YOUR FISTS!

GET THAT LIST!

DESTROY HIM!

BUT NEXT INSTANT THEY ALL FLY BACK AS THO THEY HAD STRUCK A SOLID WALL!

GIVE ME ROOM!

GOT YOU COVERED! NOW EITHER YOU HAND OVER THAT LIST, OR....

I'LL TAKE THAT!

SO YOU WERE GOING TO SHOOT **ME**, EH? JUST FOR THAT, I'M GOING TO SHOOT **YOU**!

NO! NO! THAT WOULD BE **MURDER**!

DISREGARDING REIBEL'S PLEAS, THE **MAN OF TOMORROW** FIRES....

YIII II—IIII!

BANG!

BUT BEFORE THE BULLET CAN REACH HIM, SUPERMAN'S OTHER HAND DARTS OUT AND CATCHES IT!!

UNLESS YOU QUIT YOUR SUBVERSIVE ACTIVITIES, NEXT TIME I WON'T BOTHER TO CATCH IT!

4.

THAT OUGHT TO THROW A SCARE—AND MAYBE A LITTLE SENSE—INTO THEM! NOW TO RETURN TO MY APARTMENT!

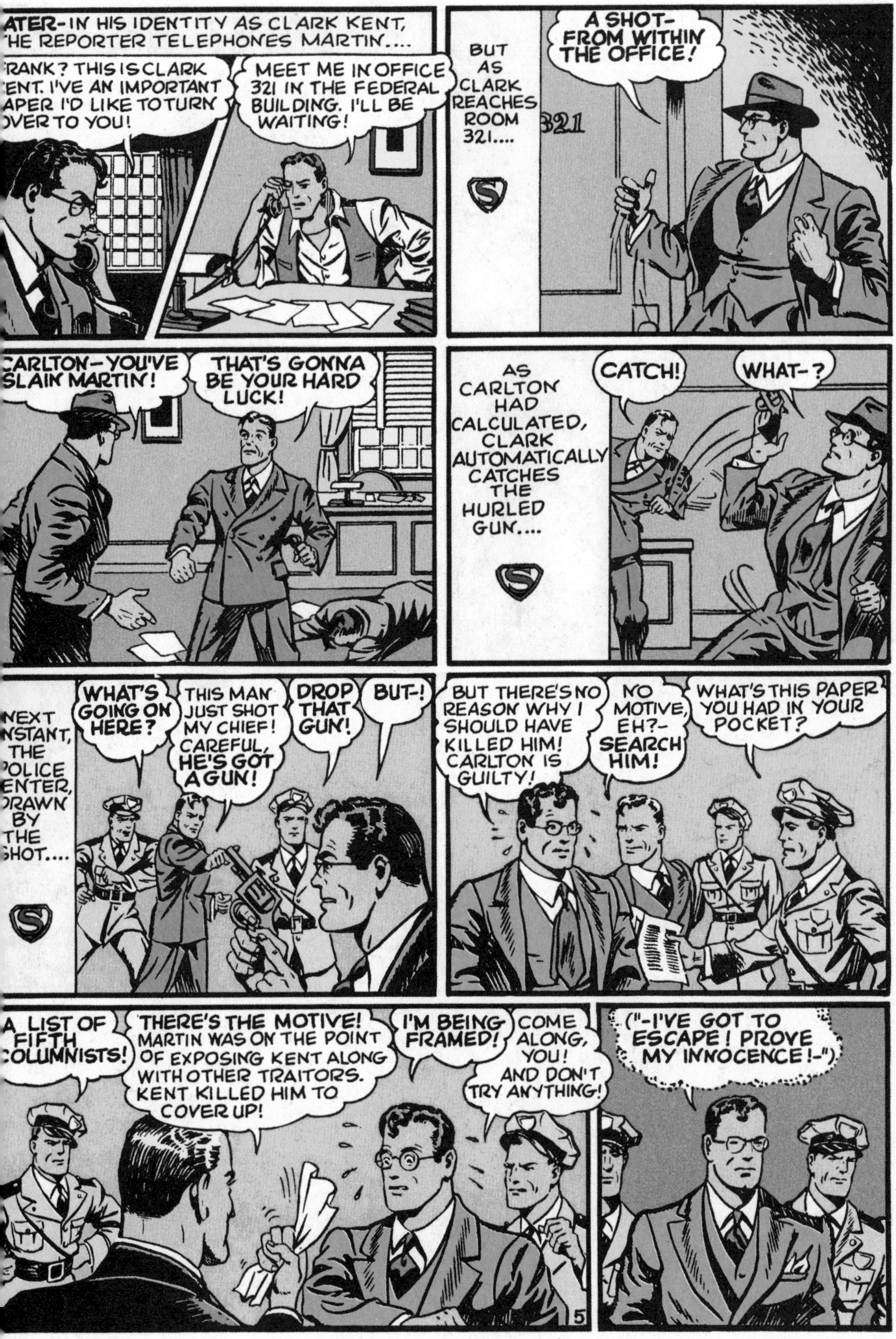
ATER- IN HIS IDENTITY AS CLARK KENT, HE REPORTER TELEPHONES MARTIN....
RANK? THIS IS CLARK ENT. I'VE AN IMPORTANT APER I'D LIKE TO TURN OVER TO YOU!
MEET ME IN OFFICE 321 IN THE FEDERAL BUILDING. I'LL BE WAITING!
BUT AS CLARK REACHES ROOM 321....
A SHOT- FROM WITHIN THE OFFICE!
321
CARLTON- YOU'VE SLAIN MARTIN!
THAT'S GONNA BE YOUR HARD LUCK!
AS CARLTON HAD CALCULATED, CLARK AUTOMATICALLY CATCHES THE HURLED GUN....
CATCH!
WHAT-?
NEXT INSTANT, THE POLICE ENTER, DRAWN BY THE SHOT....
WHAT'S GOING ON HERE?
THIS MAN JUST SHOT MY CHIEF! CAREFUL, HE'S GOT A GUN!
DROP THAT GUN!
BUT-!
BUT THERE'S NO REASON WHY I SHOULD HAVE KILLED HIM! CARLTON IS GUILTY!
NO MOTIVE, EH?- SEARCH HIM!
WHAT'S THIS PAPER YOU HAD IN YOUR POCKET?
A LIST OF FIFTH COLUMNISTS!
THERE'S THE MOTIVE! MARTIN WAS ON THE POINT OF EXPOSING KENT ALONG WITH OTHER TRAITORS. KENT KILLED HIM TO COVER UP!
I'M BEING FRAMED!
COME ALONG, YOU! AND DON'T TRY ANYTHING!
5
("-I'VE GOT TO ESCAPE! PROVE MY INNOCENCE!-")

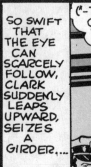

SO SWIFT THAT THE EYE CAN SCARCELY FOLLOW, CLARK SUDDENLY LEAPS UPWARD, SEIZES A GIRDER,...

("—THIS HAS GOT TO WORK!—")

...THEN SWINGS HIMSELF ATOP IT!

HUH!? WHERE IS HE?

NOW IF ONLY THEY DON'T LOOK UP!

HE WAS HERE A MOMENT AGO BUT NOW— HE'S GONE DISAPPEARED!

A GREAT LEAP CARRIES CLARK ATOP THE FEDERAL BUILDING...

MADE IT, UNNOTICED!

FIRST I'VE GOT TO GET RID OF THESE PUNY HANDCUFFS...!

...THEN I TRANSFORM MYSELF TO SUPERMAN!

SUPERMAN MAKES USE OF HIS X-RAY VISION TO NOTE....

CARLTON IS NO LONGER IN THE BUILDING!—I'LL HOP OVER TO THAT BUILDING WHERE THE SUBVERSIVE GROUP MET!

REIBEL— DEPARTING!

6.

I'LL KEEP HIM COMPANY!

36

THE AUTO DRIVES TO THE METROPOLIS AIRPORT. FROM HIS VANTAGE POINT, SUPERMAN OBSERVES REIBEL ENTER A HUGE PRIVATE PLANE ALONG WITH OTHER PROMINENT FIFTH COLUMNISTS....

("-LOOKS LIKE A MASS FLIGHT!-")

AS THE PLANE TAKES OFF, A CLOAKED FIGURE TACKLES THE UNDERCARRIAGE

LET'S SEE WHAT THEY'RE UP TO!

BUT I DON'T WANT TO GO! MY FAMILY... MY BUSINESS...

YOU'VE GOT TO FLEE WITH US! THE MOMENT THAT LIST BECOMES PUBLIC, WE'RE ALL MARKED MEN!

AS THE PLANE SWOOPS DOWNWARD TOWARD A VALLEY, SUPERMAN LOOSES HIS HOLD...

THEY'RE GOING TO LAND!

ALIGHTING ATOP A MOUNTAIN RANGE, THE MAN OF STEEL IS AMAZED AT THE SIGHT THAT GREETS HIS EYES....

WHAT-!!

IN THE VALLEY BELOW, A SCENE THAT MIGHT WELL BE LAID IN EUROPE...!

FROM THIS SECRET BASE - A SUBVERSIVE ARMY THAT CAN STRIKE TERROR AND DESTRUCTION FROM THE REAR WHEN THE MILITARY FORCES OF THE U.S. ARE ATTEMPTING TO DEFEND THE COAST AGAINST FOREIGN INVASION!

KEEPING TO THE SHADOWS, SUPERMAN TRAILS REIBEL....

HE'S ABOUT TO ENTER THAT LARGE TENT—OBVIOUSLY HEADQUARTERS!

REPORT!

WE WERE MAKING SPLENDID PROGRESS, SAGDORF, UNTIL WE WERE CONFRONTED BY A MAN POSSESSING SUPERHUMAN STRENGTH. HE WAS A VERITABLE ONE MAN ARMY. WE WERE NO MATCH FOR HIM!

WHAT LIES ARE YOU TELLING? IF YOU FAILED BE-CAUSE OF YOUR CLUMSINESS—ADMIT IT!

BUT WHETHER YOU BELIEVE ME OR NOT—I INSIST WE WERE ATTACKED BY A SUPER-STRONG MAN!

WE'LL DROP THE SUBJECT!—YOUR ORDERS ARE AS FOLLOWS. ADOPT ANOTHER NAME—RETURN TO METROPOLIS AND REPORT TO JEFF CARLTON, ONE OF OUR AGENTS WHO HAS SECURED A POST IN THE U.S. ANTI-ESPIONAGE SERVICE!

THEY'VE GONE!—THIS IS MY CHANCE TO GET A LOOK AT SAGDORF'S FILES!

HEADQUARTERS

BUT A SENTRY OBSERVES **SUPERMAN** ENTER THE TENT....

A SPY!

8.

SO VITAL INFORMATION IS STORED IN THE SAFE! I'LL TRY TO MAKE THIS AS QUIET AS POSSIBLE!

("—AS I THOUGHT! A SPY! ONE SWIFT THRUST.....AND HE'S DONE FOR!—")

AS THE SENTRY ATTEMPTS TO BAYONET SUPERMAN....

HUH?

OH-HH! SO I'M NO LONGER ALONE!

GIVE ME THAT! I'LL TEACH YOU A TRICK WITH IT THAT YOU NEVER DREAMED POSSIBLE!

HELP! —SPY!!!

SUPERMAN BENDS THE RIFLE SO THAT THE BAYONET IS BURIED IN THE BUTT...

THAT OUGHT TO HOLD YOU!

CRIES FOR HELP— FROM THAT TENT!

A SPY! BE MERCILESS!

BUT AS THE TROOPERS ATTEMPT TO RUSH INTO THE TENT, A HUMAN THUNDERBOLT SENDS THEM FLYING BACK....

LET ME THRU! CAN'T YOU SEE I'M IN A HURRY?

9.

SIGHTING A LONG LINE OF MILITARY PLANES, SUPERMAN RACES THRU THEM IN A WAVE OF DESTRUCTION....

THESE PLANES WILL NEVER BOMB AMERICAN CITIES!!

LEAPING AT THE SIDE OF A HANGAR, **SUPERMAN** SHOVES AT THE WALL.....

DOWN YOU GO!

SO THAT IT COLLAPSES UPON AND DESTROYS THE PLANES WITHIN IT!

ROUSED BY **SUPERMAN'S** ACTIVITIES, THE SOLDIERS MERCILESSLY BOMBARD HIM....

YOU'RE WASTING YOUR AMMUNITION!

I CAN USE YOU—!

USING THE FIELD GUN AS A BATTERING RAM, **SUPERMAN** SMASHES THE OTHER WEAPONS INTO CRUSHED MASSES....

NOT ONE MUST REMAIN UNDESTROYED!

INTO THE ELECTRIC-PLANT STREAKS THE **MAN OF STEEL**....

WITH A SURGE OF GIANT MUSCLES HE RIPS A GREAT DYNAMO FROM ITS RESTING PLACE—

UP—!

AND I DO MEAN UP!

NOW FOR THE MUNITIONS PLANT!

A TICKLISH SITUATION! IF I ATTACK THE MUNITIONS WORKS I'M SURE EVERYONE IN THE NEIGHBORHOOD WILL BE KILLED. BUT I CAN'T ALLOW THAT MENACE TO THE U.S. TO EXIST!!

SAGDORF SOLVES SUPERMAN'S PROBLEM....

FIRE!

BUT IF YOU SHOULD HIT THE PLANT...!

NEATLY, SUPERMAN DODGES THE SCREECHING SHELL....

MISSED ME!

BUT AS THE SHELL STRIKES THE FACTORY, THERE IS A TERRIFIC DETONATION..... THE WORLD SEEMS TO FLY APART....

COMPLETELY DESTROYED— INCLUDING THE PLOTTERS RESPONSIBLE —NOT A SOUL LEFT ALIVE—EXCEPT MYSELF!

THERE'S STILL THE MATTER OF CLEARING MY NAME TO BE ATTENDED TO! IT'S BACK TO METROPOLIS FOR ME!

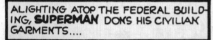

ALIGHTING ATOP THE FEDERAL BUILDING, **SUPERMAN** DONS HIS CIVILIAN GARMENTS....

NO MORE SUPER-STRENGTH TODAY! FROM NOW ON, I'VE GOT TO RELY ON MY **WITS**!

CLARK DESCENDS TO ROOM 321...

SOMEONE IS IN THE ROOM!

OPENING THE DOOR SLIGHTLY, CLARK SIGHTS....

IT'S POSSIBLE I MAY HAVE MISSED SOMETHING IMPORTANT!

STEPPING CAUTIOUSLY IN, KENT REMOVES A REVOLVER FROM A DESK DRAWER....

TURN!

WHAT--?

IT'S KENT!

YES. AND I'M HERE TO SEE THAT YOU CONFESS TO YOUR CRIME!

I KNOW THAT YOU'RE NOT RESPONSIBLE-- BUT TRY AND GET ME TO REPEAT IT IN PUBLIC!

THAT'S JUST WHAT I'M GOING TO DO! -- GET MOVING!

IN A TAXI BOUND FOR THE DAILY PLANET BUILDING

YOU CAN'T GET AWAY WITH THIS!

THAT REMAINS TO BE SEEN!

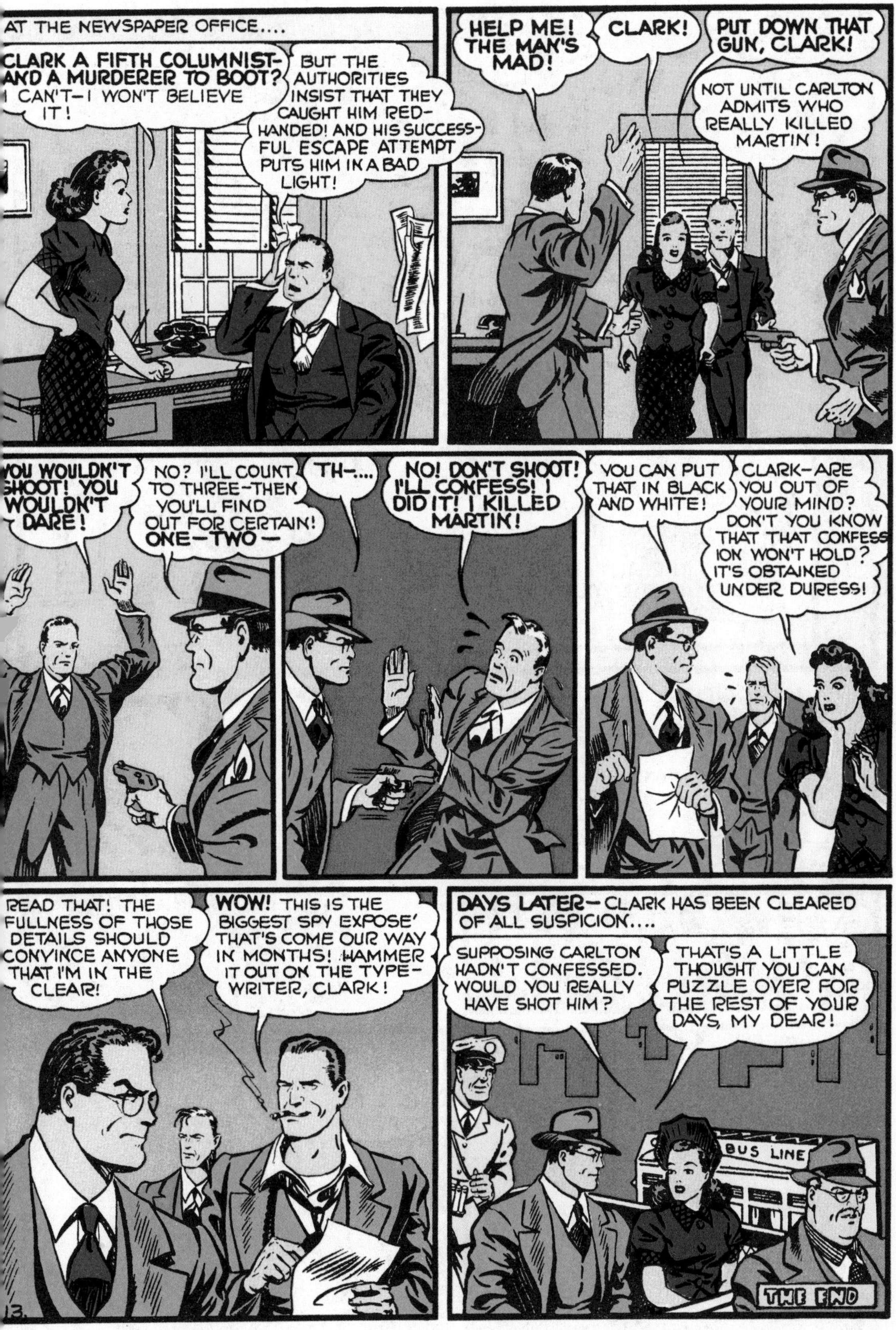
AT THE NEWSPAPER OFFICE....
CLARK A FIFTH COLUMNIST-AND A MURDERER TO BOOT? I CAN'T-I WON'T BELIEVE IT!
BUT THE AUTHORITIES INSIST THAT THEY CAUGHT HIM RED-HANDED! AND HIS SUCCESSFUL ESCAPE ATTEMPT PUTS HIM IN A BAD LIGHT!
HELP ME! THE MAN'S MAD!
CLARK!
PUT DOWN THAT GUN, CLARK!
NOT UNTIL CARLTON ADMITS WHO REALLY KILLED MARTIN!
YOU WOULDN'T SHOOT! YOU WOULDN'T DARE!
NO? I'LL COUNT TO THREE-THEN YOU'LL FIND OUT FOR CERTAIN! ONE-TWO-
TH-....
NO! DON'T SHOOT! I'LL CONFESS! I DID IT! I KILLED MARTIN!
YOU CAN PUT THAT IN BLACK AND WHITE!
CLARK-ARE YOU OUT OF YOUR MIND? DON'T YOU KNOW THAT THAT CONFESSION WON'T HOLD? IT'S OBTAINED UNDER DURESS!
READ THAT! THE FULLNESS OF THOSE DETAILS SHOULD CONVINCE ANYONE THAT I'M IN THE CLEAR!
WOW! THIS IS THE BIGGEST SPY EXPOSE' THAT'S COME OUR WAY IN MONTHS! HAMMER IT OUT ON THE TYPEWRITER, CLARK!
13.
DAYS LATER-CLARK HAS BEEN CLEARED OF ALL SUSPICION....
SUPPOSING CARLTON HADN'T CONFESSED. WOULD YOU REALLY HAVE SHOT HIM?
THAT'S A LITTLE THOUGHT YOU CAN PUZZLE OVER FOR THE REST OF YOUR DAYS, MY DEAR!
BUS LINE
THE END

SUPERMAN

by JERRY SIEGEL and JOE SHUSTER

CARNIVAL CROOKS, SCENTING AN EASY VICTIM IN CLARK KENT, TAKE THE MEEK REPORTER'S POCKETBOOK FOR A RIDE BUT IN SO DOING, THEY CHART THEIR OWN DOOM--FOR THE TIMID DAILY PLANET SCRIBE IS IN REALITY NONE OTHER THAN SUPERMAN, THE COURAGEOUS, CRUSADING MAN OF STEEL!

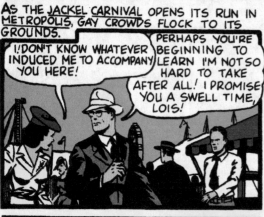

AS THE JACKEL CARNIVAL OPENS ITS RUN IN METROPOLIS, GAY CROWDS FLOCK TO ITS GROUNDS.

I! DON'T KNOW WHATEVER INDUCED ME TO ACCOMPANY YOU HERE!

PERHAPS YOU'RE BEGINNING TO LEARN I'M NOT SO HARD TO TAKE AFTER ALL! I PROMISE YOU A SWELL TIME, LOIS!

IT BEGINS TO APPEAR THAT CLARK IS CORRECT...

HAVING FUN?

LOTS!!

SEE THAT GUY, CHICK? I'LL BET WE COULD TAKE HIM FOR PLENTY!

LET ME HANDLE THIS, AL!

TOSS A BALL THRU THE OPENING AN' WIN A BEAUTIFUL PRIZE FOR THE LI'L LADY!

BUT-BUT I DON'T CARE TO PLAY!

LET'S TOSS JUST A FEW!

PLUNKING DOWN A QUARTER, CLARK TRIES TOSSING BALLS...

("-I'LL DELIBERATELY MISS!-") NO LUCK!

I MADE ONE!

KEEP SHOOTING! YOU'LL WIN A BETTER PRIZE!

I'D BETTER STOP! I'M AFRAID I'M NOT SO GOOD AT THIS!

GO AHEAD! **THROW THIS!**

AS FAST AS THEY THROW BALLS, THE PROPRIETORS OF THE "TOSS IT THRU" CONCESSION KEEP FORCING MORE UPON THEM.

BUT--!

YOU'RE DOING FINE! KEEP PLAYING!

THAT'S ENOUGH!

SEE THOSE LARGER AWARDS? GET ONE MORE BALL THRU, AND YOU CAN HAVE ONE OF THEM!

WHEN CLARK MAKES ANOTHER GOOD SHOT..

THAT'S ALL! HOW MUCH DO I OWE YOU?

I'LL TAKE ANOTHER!

AND ANOTHER!

-AND ANOTHER, ANOTHER, AND ANOTHER!

HEY, WAIT! JUST HOW MUCH DO I OWE YOU?

YOU OWE FOR THIRTY MORE SETS!

"SETS"? THIRTY MORE! BUT WE'VE BEEN PLAYING ONLY A FEW MINUTES! CLARK, DON'T PAY THEM ANY MORE UNTIL THEY TELL YOU HOW MUCH YOU OWE!

HOW MUCH DO I OWE?

ANOTHER TWO DOLLARS WILL COVER IT!

WILL YOU LEND ME A DOLLAR, LOIS? I'M ONE SHORT!

EIGHT DOLLARS FOR THIS CHEAP "AWARD" THAT COST YOU ONLY A FEW CENTS? IT'S THIEVERY!

TUT, TUT, LADY--THEM'S HARSH WORDS!

YOU'RE NOT GOING TO LET THESE CHEAP CROOKS GET AWAY WITH THIS, ARE YOU, CLARK?

ER--I DEMAND..

GET GOIN'!

WAIT, LOIS--!

I DON'T WANT A THING TO DO WITH YOU, YOU--YOU--NUMBSKULL!

OFFICE OF THE GROUNDS →

WASTE HERE PLEASE

LATER--AT THE DAILY PLANET..

WHAT'S EATING YOU?

PLENTY! CLARK WAS JUST TAKEN IN BY SOME CARNIVAL THIEVES! THEY DESERVE TO BE EXPOSED! THIS IS WHAT HAPPENED....

ANYONE WHO WOULD FALL FOR SUCH A SHODDY SKIN-GAME ALMOST DESERVES TO BE TRIMMED. HOWEVER, IF YOU CAN DIG UP ACTUAL PROOF OF WRONGDOING, I'LL BE GLAD TO GIVE IT SPACE IN THE PAPER.

GOOD NEWS, CLARK! YOU'VE A SPLENDID OPPORTUNITY TO GET EVEN WITH THOSE CROOKS!

EVEN? --ER-- HOW?

WHITE JUST INFORMED ME THAT IF WE CAN GET EVIDENCE OF THEIR CROOKEDNESS, HE'D PRINT THE EXPOSÉ!

NOW, WAIT! ACTUALLY, WE'RE NOT POSITIVE I WAS CHEATED!

THAT WEAK-KNEED PANTYWAIST MAKES ME SICK! IF HE'S AFRAID TO GO ALONG, I'LL JUST HAVE TO COVER THE ASSIGNMENT MYSELF!

EDITORIAL ROOMS

STEPPING INTO THE PRIVACY OF A STOREROOM, CLARK SWIFTLY CHANGES INTO HIS SUPERMA[N] OUTFIT....

I'M AFRAID THAT ONCE AGAIN LOIS IS GOING TO STEP RIGHT INTO A PECK OF TROUBLE!

SUPERMAN TRAILS THE PLANET SOB-SISTER, HIGH IN THE SKY...

JUST AS I THOUGHT! SHE'S HEADING STRAIGHT FOR JACKEL'S CARNIVAL --AND WITH A CAMERA UNDER HER ARM!

LOIS TAKES UP HER STATION A SHORT DISTANCE FROM THE "TOSS IT THRU" STAND....

NOW TO SNAP PICTURES OF VICTIMS BEING TRIMMED AND PAYING IN PROTEST!

FIVE DOLLARS FOR TOSSING A FEW BALLS! IT'S HIGHWAY ROBBERY!

WELL, PAY UP! NO ONE FORCED YOU TO PLAY!

SA-A-AY! IT'S THAT GIRL --AND SHE'S BEEN SNAPPING PICTURES!

UM-MM! THESE SNAPSHOTS OUGHT TO BE BEAUTIES!

LOIS IS ABOUT TO LEAVE, BUT THE CROOKED CONCESSION MEN HAVE NOTICED HER. HERE'S WHERE THE FUN BEGINS!

AS LOIS WALKS PAST THE STAND, AL DELIBERATELY TRIPS HER...

OOPS! MY ERROR!

WHA--??

PURPOSELY, CHICK STEPS ON LOIS' CAMERA, DESTROYING IT....

TCH! TCH! NOW AIN'T THAT *TOO BAD?*

SUPERMAN TRAILS CHICK AND AL...

AND THAT'S **THAT!** I CAN HARDLY WAIT TO TELL CLARK HOW **I** HANDLED THIS!

THERE SHE GOES!

AFTER LOIS DEPARTS, CHICK AND AL RETURN TO THE PAY-WAGON...

HOW'D I DO?

NICE ACT!

YOU ALMOST HAD ME BELIEVING YOU!

IT WAS AN OLD STALL, PRETENDING TO FIRE YOU. BUT IT ALWAYS WORKS!

AND THERE'S ALWAYS ANOTHER CHUMP BORN EVERY MINUTE!

LOIS WOULDN'T BE SO SELF-SATISFIED IF SHE COULD GET AN EARFUL OF **THIS!**

SEND IN THE "RIGHT" MEN. IT'S TIME TO COLLECT!

SHORTLY AFTER... A NUMBER OF INDIVIDUALS FILE INTO JACKEL'S PRESENCE.

NOT A BAD TAKE, "FINGERS." HERE'S YOUR CUT!

FUNNY! I PICK POCKETS IN CROWDS ... THEN **YOU** PICK **MINE!**

YOU'D BE SURPRISED HOW MUCH I PICKED UP SHORT-CHANGING THE CUSTOMERS!

YEAH? WELL, IT'S CHICKEN FEED COMPARED TO WHAT MY CROOKED GAMBLING DEVICES BRING IN!

AFTER THE OTHERS LEAVE, JACKEL GLOATS OVER HIS ILLEGAL HARVEST...

A LITTLE MORE OF THIS, AND I'LL BE ABLE TO RETIRE! NOT BAD! NOT BAD AT ALL!

AS **SUPERMAN** IS ABOUT TO ATTEND TO JACKEL, HE PAUSES AS HE HEARS A DISTURBANCE....

WHAT'S **THAT?**

INFURIATED, **SUPERMAN** TAKES A GREAT LEAP THAT CARRIES HIM TO THE REAR OF THE STAND....

SUDDENLY—**SUPERMAN'S** FISTS SMASH THR[OUGH] THE WALL... SEIZE THE COLLARS OF THE TWO THIEVES....

A TERRIFIC YANK--AND...

SNATCHING AWAY THE POCKET KNIFE, **SUPERMAN** PLACES [IT] IN HIS MOUTH, THEN...

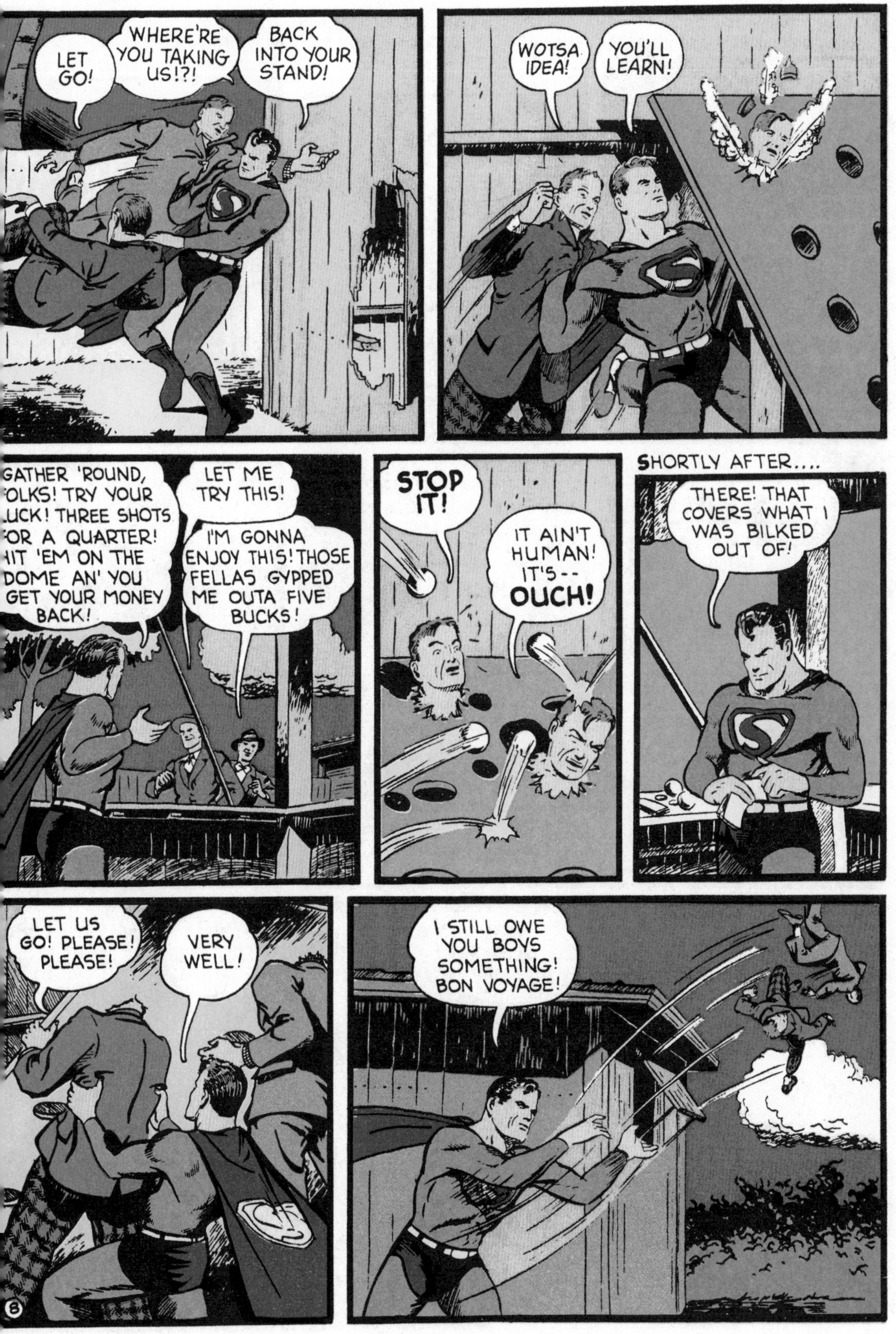
LET GO!
WHERE'RE YOU TAKING US!?!
BACK INTO YOUR STAND!
WOTSA IDEA!
YOU'LL LEARN!
GATHER 'ROUND, FOLKS! TRY YOUR LUCK! THREE SHOTS FOR A QUARTER! HIT 'EM ON THE DOME AN' YOU GET YOUR MONEY BACK!
LET ME TRY THIS!
I'M GONNA ENJOY THIS! THOSE FELLAS GYPPED ME OUTA FIVE BUCKS!
STOP IT!
IT AIN'T HUMAN! IT'S -- OUCH!
SHORTLY AFTER....
THERE! THAT COVERS WHAT I WAS BILKED OUT OF!
LET US GO! PLEASE! PLEASE!
VERY WELL!
I STILL OWE YOU BOYS SOMETHING! BON VOYAGE!
8

AS THE TWO TERRIFIED SHARPERS DROP EARTHWARD...

EE-EE-EE!

YI-II-II!

SUPERMAN DEMOLISHES THE CROOKED CONCESSION STAND WITH ONE WELL DELIVERED BLOW!

THERE'LL BE NO MORE THIEVERY HERE!

--THEN CATCHES THE FALLING MEN BEFORE THEY STRIKE EARTH!

WHY I'M BOTHERING TO CATCH YOU, I COULDN'T SAY!

HEY, RUBE

IN RESPONSE TO CHICK'S CRY FOR HELP, CARNIVAL TOUGHS CONVERGE ON SUPERMAN!

TALK ABOUT YOUR WARM RECEPTIONS!

BEFORE THE ATTACKERS' AMAZED EYES, SUPERMAN LEAPS AT THE GROUND BEFORE THEM AND BURROWS BENEATH ITS SURFACE....

HUH?

HE WAS HERE A MINUTE AGO!

WH-WHERE IS HE?

YOO-HOO! RIGHT BEHIND YOU!

AS THEY CHARGE AGAIN, SUPERMAN EASILY ESCAPES BY LEAPING FROM SHOULDER TO SHOULDER...

I'VE GOT HIM!

YOU MEAN YOU ALMOST HAD ME!

WHAT CAN WE DO? HE'S FAST AS LIGHTNING AND SLIPPERY AS GREASE

TELL YOU WHAT -- I PROMISE NOT TO MOVE THIS TIME!

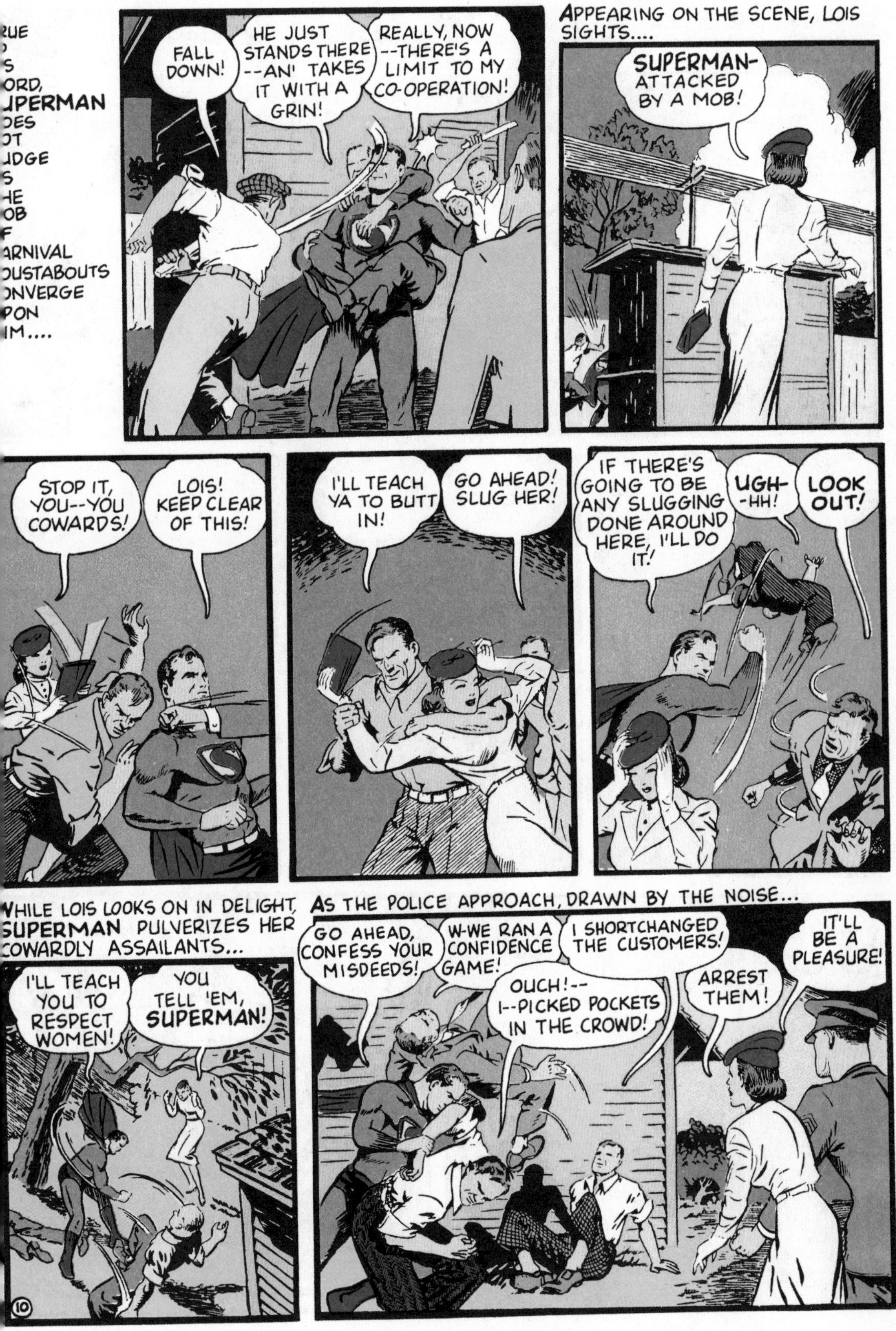
RUE
S
ORD,
UPERMAN
OES
OT
UDGE
S
HE
OB
F
ARNIVAL
OUSTABOUTS
ONVERGE
PON
IM....
FALL DOWN!
HE JUST STANDS THERE --AN' TAKES IT WITH A GRIN!
REALLY, NOW --THERE'S A LIMIT TO MY CO-OPERATION!
APPEARING ON THE SCENE, LOIS SIGHTS....
SUPERMAN- ATTACKED BY A MOB!
STOP IT, YOU--YOU COWARDS!
LOIS! KEEP CLEAR OF THIS!
I'LL TEACH YA TO BUTT IN!
GO AHEAD! SLUG HER!
IF THERE'S GOING TO BE ANY SLUGGING DONE AROUND HERE, I'LL DO IT!
UGH--HH!
LOOK OUT!
WHILE LOIS LOOKS ON IN DELIGHT, SUPERMAN PULVERIZES HER COWARDLY ASSAILANTS...
I'LL TEACH YOU TO RESPECT WOMEN!
YOU TELL 'EM, SUPERMAN!
10
AS THE POLICE APPROACH, DRAWN BY THE NOISE...
GO AHEAD, CONFESS YOUR MISDEEDS!
W-WE RAN A CONFIDENCE GAME!
I SHORTCHANGED THE CUSTOMERS!
OUCH!-- I--PICKED POCKETS IN THE CROWD!
ARREST THEM!
IT'LL BE A PLEASURE!

PREVIOUSLY, ONE OF THE CARNIVAL TOUGHS HAD SLIPPED AWAY...

I'VE GOT TO WARN JACKEL!

WHAT IS IT?

SUPERMAN --CLEANIN' UP ON THE MEN!

THE MAN OF STEEL--HERE? THAT'S MY CUE TO EXIT.

OFF SPEEDS JACKEL IN HIS PRIVATE CAR!

MY MEN CAPTURED BY COPS! I GOT TO GET OUTA HERE!

STOP! STOP THAT CAR!

LIKE BLAZES I WILL!

SIGHTING THE CARNIVAL OWNER'S RUTHLESS ACTION, SUPERMAN LEAPS IN PURSUIT...

HE WON'T GET AWAY WITH THAT!

YOUR ONE AND FINAL ORDER! STOP!!

GET AWAY--!

THIS IS ONLY THE BEGINNING! NOW WILL YOU STOP?

JACKEL'S ANSWER IS TO SWERVE SO **SUPERMAN** IS SENT FLYING OFF THE RUNNING BOARD!

SO YOU WANT TO GET ROUGH, EH?

...EAPING ...ORWARD, **...UPERMAN** ...ATCHES ...HE ...AR'S ...EAR ...UMPER ...ND ...ALTS ...TS ...ORWARD ...LUNGE....

THIS IS AS FAR AS YOU GO!

PEEK-A-BOO! I SEE YOU!

I'LL--!

...HE CARNIVAL OWNER ATTEMPTS TO DASH ...WAY, BUT--

COME ON ALONG!

LET GO, YOU--!

HERE'S YOUR MAN!

YOU CAN'T ARREST ME! I'M INNOCENT OF ALL WRONG-DOING!

HE'S RIGHT! WE CAN'T HOLD HIM!

IF YOU'LL EXAMINE THE CONTENTS OF HIS BAG, YOU'LL FIND IT CONTAINS VALUABLE ARTICLES THAT WERE STOLEN FROM VISITORS TO THE CARNIVAL BY PICKPOCKETS!

ER-...

TRY TO TALK YOUR WAY OUT OF **THAT**!

MEANWHILE--LOIS IS HAVING DIFFICULTY TELEPHONING IN HER STORY....

DOGGONE IT! THE LINE'S BUSY!

HERE'S WHERE I DO LOIS A GOOD TURN!

HAVING TROUBLE? I'LL BE GLAD TO DROP YOU OFF AT THE DAILY PLANET SOONER THAN YOU CAN PUT THAT CALL THRU!

THAT WOULD BE **SWELL**!

WHO ARE YOU? HOW DO YOU MANAGE TO SHOW UP EXACTLY WHEN I NEED YOU?

BE PATIENT, LOIS! SOME DAY I MAY BE ABLE TO GIVE YOU THE ANSWER!

MY EVERLASTING THANKS!

BETTER RUSH THAT STORY INTO PRINT BEFORE IT'S TOO OLD!

LATER-- **SUPERMAN** RETURNS TO THE DAILY PLANET, BUT IN HIS IDENTITY AS CLARK KENT....

LOIS--I'VE BEEN THINKING IT OVER! YOU'RE RIGHT! SOMETHING OUGHT TO BE DONE ABOUT THAT CROOKED CARNIVAL, AFTER ALL!

YOU'RE BEHIND THE TIMES CLARK. READ THIS! THANKS TO **SUPERMAN**, THE SCOUNDRELS RESPONSIBLE HAVE BEEN ARRESTED!

BE WARY OF UNSCRUPULOUS OPERATORS OF GAMBLING GAMES ---THEY ARE ALWAYS ON THE LOOKOUT FOR UNSUSPECTING VICTIMS!

THE END

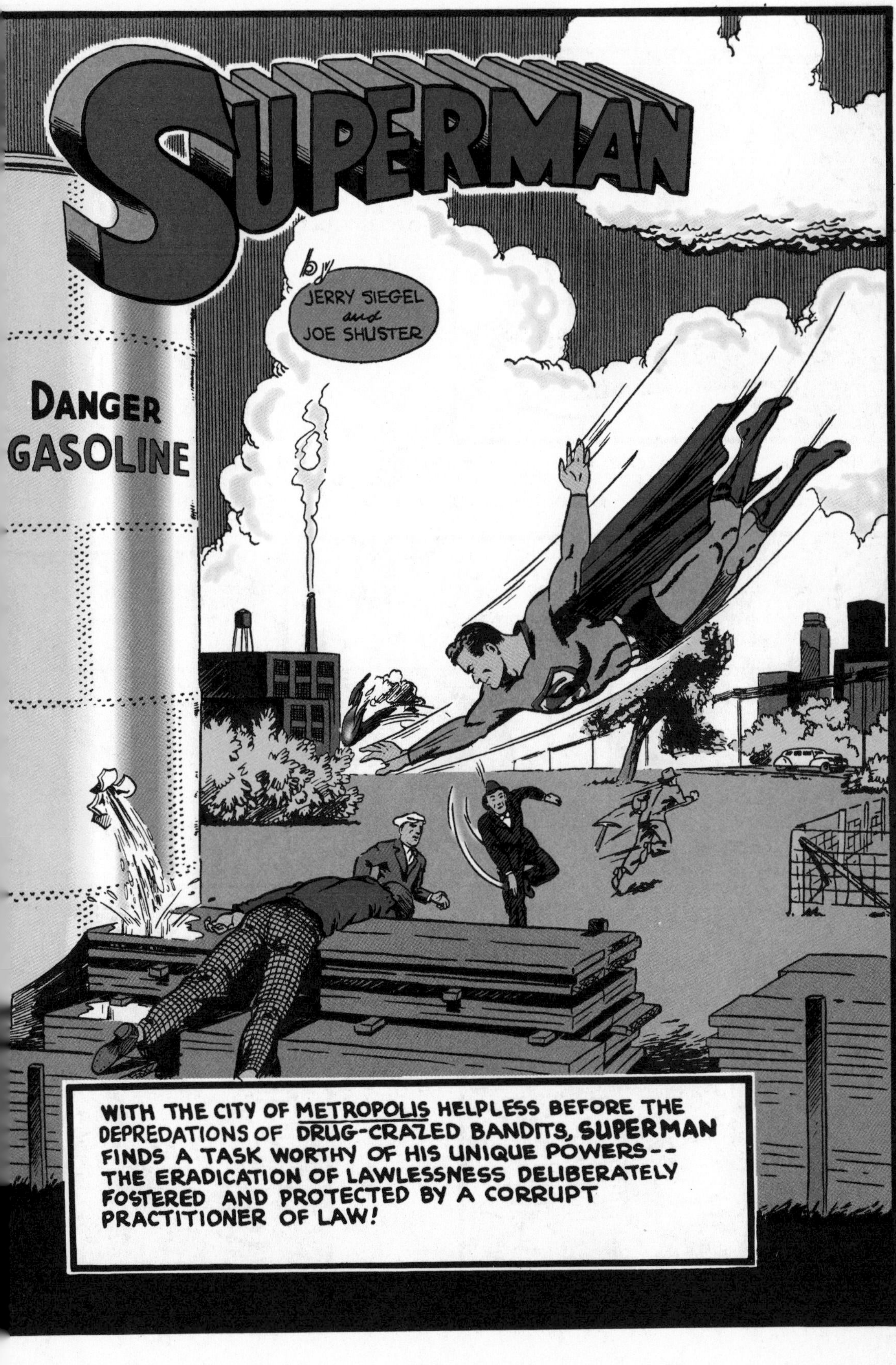
SUPERMAN
by
JERRY SIEGEL
and
JOE SHUSTER
DANGER
GASOLINE
WITH THE CITY OF METROPOLIS HELPLESS BEFORE THE DEPREDATIONS OF DRUG-CRAZED BANDITS, SUPERMAN FINDS A TASK WORTHY OF HIS UNIQUE POWERS-- THE ERADICATION OF LAWLESSNESS DELIBERATELY FOSTERED AND PROTECTED BY A CORRUPT PRACTITIONER OF LAW!

METROPOLIS IS THE SCENE OF A FLOOD OF BRUTAL DARING ROBBERIES....!

BUT THO CONFUSION GRIPS THOSE WHO ENFORCE LAW AND ORDER IN THE CITY, A LONE CLOAKED FIGURE PREPARES TO LAUNCH HIS BATTLE AGAINST THE EVIL FORCES THAT HARASS THE TOWN....

SUPERMAN!

SOMEONE HAS GOT TO STOP THESE RUTHLESS CRIMINALS -- AND I NOMINATE MYSELF FOR THAT JOB!

IN THE STREETS BELOW–A CAR FULL OF GANGSTERS DESPERATELY SEEKS TO ELUDE THE PURSUING POLICE....

ONE OF THE STRAY BULLETS NARROWLY MISSES LOIS LANE, SOB-SISTER ON THE DAILY PLANET...

WHEW! I'D BETTER DUCK FOR COVER!

RUTHLESSLY, THE SPEEDING CAR CRASHES A GREEN LIGHT AND SENDS A HELPLESS CRIPPLE CAREENING FROM HIS WHEEL CHAIR....

SCHOOL CHILDREN NARROWLY MISS BEING RUN DOWN...!

THE MAN OF STEEL PLUMMETS DOWN BEFORE THE GANGSTERS' AUTO...!

DON'T CARE WHO YOU RUN DOWN, EH? WHY NOT PICK ON ME?

AS THE MACHINE STRIKES HIM, THE MAN OF TOMORROW DOES NOT YIELD, BUT SENDS IT SOMERSAULTING BACK THRU THE AIR...!

YOU PICKED ON THE WRONG FELLA **THIS** TIME!

WAIT!

YOU'D BETTER DEVOTE ALL YOUR ATTENTION TO THOSE THUGS BEFORE THEY ESCAPE!

THE BANDITS ARE ALL NABBED... WITH ONE EXCEPTION...

GOT TO GET AWAY--!

HERE'S A NEWS STORY FOR YOU, LOIS! THESE CROOKS ARE ALL DOPE ADDICTS!

THEIR GANG CHIEF MUST DELIBERATELY DOPE HIS MEN BEFORE SENDING THEM OUT! HE'S GOT TO BE APPREHENDED AT ALL COSTS!

AFTER THE POLICE DEPART WITH THEIR PRISONERS, A SENTINEL REMAINS ON GUARD HIGH ABOVE THE STREET....

IT LOOKS AS THO' THE POLICE OVERLOOKED SOMEONE!

WHAT **SUPERMAN'S** TELESCOPIC X-RAY VISION REVEALS TO HIM...

CE ASHES INSIDE

THE FUGITIVE CRAWLS FORTH AND HURRIES OFF, UNAWARE THAT HE IS BEING TRAILED...

JOHN --I'LL GO TO GOOD OLD JOHN-- HE'LL TELL ME WHAT TO DO!

LATER...

HE'S LED ME DIRECTLY TO THE METROPOLIS TOWER BUILDING!

MOMENTS LATER...IN THE OFFICE OF "JOHN PARRONE, INVESTMENTS"...

NATE! DIDN'T I ALWAYS TELL YOU, GRANT, NEVER TO COME HERE?

YEAH--BUT I GOTTA HAVE ANOTHER SHOT OF DOPE! I JUST GOTTA!

I TELL YA, A CAPED FIGURE JUMPED DOWN BEFORE OUR CAR...FLIPPED IT OVER LIKE IT WAS A KIDDIE-CAR!

TRYING TO MAKE ME BELIEVE THAT SUPERMAN FAIRY-TALE, EH? MORE THAN LIKELY IT WAS THE DOPE THAT MADE YOU SEE THINGS!

TH' DOPE.. YOU'LL GIVE IT TO ME, WON'T YA?

HERE! CAN'T GIVE YOU MORE. THIS IS ALL I'VE GOT AND THE STUFF IS HARD TO GET!

FLIPPING A KEY ON HIS COMMUNICATION BOX, JOHN WHISPERS BRIEFLY INTO IT...

...AN' THAT'S HOW IT IS! OKAY, I'LL TELL NATE TO LIE LOW!

WONDER WHO PARRONE WAS TALKING TO? BROKENSHIRE'S BELIEVED TO BE A SHADY LAWYER. HM-MM! THERE MIGHT BE SOME CONNECTION!

I'VE A WILD PLAN -- WHETHER IT'LL SUCCEED IN TRAPPING THE REMAINDER OF PARRONE'S GANG IS PROBLEMATICAL --BUT WORTH TRYING!

SHORTLY AFTER, THE MAN OF STEEL SWINGS IN THRU THE WINDOW OF AN EXPRESS COMPANY

THE ROOM'S DESERTED! GOOD! I'LL HELP MYSELF!

SECURING AN EXPRESS COMPANY BLANK, **SUPERMAN** SWIFTLY SCRIBBLES A FEW BRIEF WORDS UPON IT...

THIS OUGHT TO DO THE TRICK!

LATER...DROPPED FROM THE MAN OF TOMORROW'S HANDS, A SHEET OF PAPER WAFTS DOWN TO NATE'S FEET...

HUH? WHAT'S **THIS**?

ONE GLANCE AT THE SCRAP OF PAPER, AND GRANT HURRIES BACK TO HIS EMPLOYER'S OFFICE.

WAIT'LL JOHN SEES THIS!

YOU BACK AGAIN? AND AFTER WHAT I JUST TOLD YOU?

THIS IS **IMPORTANT**! JUST LOOK AT THIS!

AN EXPRESS RECEIPT FOR THE DELIVERY OF $500,000 WORTH OF MORPHINE TO THE LAKE DRUG COMPANY!-SAY! YOU **HAVE** GOT SOMETHING HERE!

YOU'LL HELP ME STEAL THAT HAUL? YOU'LL LET ME HAVE SOME FOR TIPPING YOU OFF?

NO, NATE. YOU GO INTO HIDING. I'LL STEAL THAT STUFF MYSELF! I'LL GO ALONG WITH THE BOYS TO SEE THAT THIS JOB ISN'T BUNGLED!

AND I'LL BE THERE TOO PARRONE-- WAITING _FOR_ _YOU_!

LATER..AT THE DAILY PLANET...

TELL YOU WHAT, CLARK! I'M IN A BENEVOLENT MOOD. I'LL BREAK DOWN AND LET YOU TAKE ME TO A MOVIE TONIGHT.

ER--THAT'S--THAT'S FINE, JUST FINE! ("-BUT IS IT? I'VE GOT A CERTAIN PRESSING APPOINTMENT TONIGHT!-")

AND...THAT EVENING...

LET'S GO, LOIS! AT ONCE!

BUT WE HAVEN'T EVEN SEEN THE COMPLETE FEATURE!

WHAT SAY WE GO FOR A JOYRIDE!

JOYRIDE?-ER-I THINK I'LL DRIVE YOU STRAIGHT HOME!

I DON'T GET THIS! YOU'VE PESTERED ME FOR A DATE FOR DAYS. AND NOW THAT I'VE ACCEPTED, YOU ACT LIKE YOU'RE ANXIOUS TO GET RID OF ME!

YOU'LL HAVE TO EXCUSE ME, LOIS. I'M NOT USED TO THIS HECTIC NIGHT-LIFE. TO TELL YOU THE TRUTH, I'M SLEEPY!

TO MAKE CERTAIN HE HAS NOT MISSED AN IMPORTANT DEVELOPMENT, CLARK DRIVES PAST THE LAKE DRUG COMPANY'S WAREHOUSE BUT AS HE DOES...

DID YOU NOTICE HOW THAT CAR FULL OF TOUGH-LOOKING MEN PAUSED BEFORE THE WAREHOUSE, GAVE IT THE ONCE-OVER, THEN CONTINUED ON?

I DIDN'T NOTICE ANYTHING OUT OF THE ORDINARY. ("-PARRONE AND HIS MEN!-")

LAKE DRUG WAREHOUSE
OFFICE   OFFICE

LATER- AS CLARK DROPS LOIS OFF BEFORE HER APARTMENT...

YOU NEEDN'T TROUBLE TO ACCOMPANY ME TO THE DOOR. -HM..M-I STILL THINK THERE WAS SOMETHING SUSPICIOUS ABOUT THAT CAR'S ACTIONS!

FORGET IT! YOU'VE BEEN READING TOO MANY DETECTIVE STORIES!

HER REPORTORIAL INSTINCTS AROUSED, LOIS NO SOONER ENTERS HER APARTMENT THAN SHE TELEPHONES...

SERGEANT CASEY? LOIS SPEAKING! HOW QUICKLY CAN YOU GET HERE? IT'S IMPORTANT!

A SHORT DISTANCE FROM THE WAREHOUSE, THE PLANET REPORTER REMOVES HIS OUTER GARMENTS, TRANSFORMING HIMSELF INTO SUPERMAN....

I HAVEN'T A SECOND TO SPARE! JOHN PARRONE WILL STRIKE AT ANY MOMENT!

ARRONE'S MOBSTERS OVERCOME A LONE GUARD, UNAWARE OF **SUPERMAN'S** SURVEILLANCE...

UH-HH-HH!

THIS'LL ROCK YA TO SLEEP!

NICE WORK, DIRK!- INTO THE WAREHOUSE, MEN!

A LITHE, NOISELESS LEAP CARRIES **SUPERMAN** ATOP SOME PACKING CASES...

("-I WON'T GO INTO ACTION UNTIL THEY'VE THOROUGHLY INCRIMINATED THEMSELVES!-")

WHAT IS IT, LOIS?

DRIVE STRAIGHT TO THE LAKE DRUG COMPANY'S WAREHOUSE! I'LL TELL YOU ON THE WAY!

SHORTLY AFTER.. AS THEY APPROACH THE WAREHOUSE..

I STILL THINK YOU'RE LEADING ME ON A WILD-GOOSE CHASE!

YOU DO, EH? THEN EXPLAIN HOW THE WATCHMAN CAME TO BE BOUND AND GAGGED!

AS CASEY FREES THE GUARD..

YOU'D BETTER GO FOR HELP!

NOTHING DOING! I TIPPED YOU OFF TO THIS, AND I WANT TO WRITE UP AN EYE-WITNESS ACCOUNT. --THE WATCHMAN CAN DO THE ERRAND RUNNING!

("-LOIS... AND SERGEANT CASEY! I MIGHT HAVE KNOWN SHE'D PULL SOMETHING LIKE THIS!-")

MUST SAY THIS IS THE SLICKEST JOB OF SAFE-CRACKIN' I'VE PULLED IN A LONG TIME!

$500,000 WORTH OF MORPHINE FOR THE TAKING! WHAT A HAUL!

IN HER EXCITEMENT, LOIS FAILS TO NOTICE A SMALL BOX AT HER FEET, AND TRIPS...!

OOPS!

TH' COPS!

GET 'EM!

⑦

I'VE GOT TO ATTRACT THEIR FIRE...OR LOIS AND THE SERGEANT ARE GONERS!

THE MAN OF STEEL'S RUSE WORKS!

TH' BULLETS-BOUNCIN' RIGHT OFF HIM!

KEEP RIGHT ON SHOOTING! I DON'T MIND A BIT!

SUPERMA

IN YOU GO-!

DEFTLY, SUPERMAN OVERTURNS THE HUGE PACKING BOX SO THAT THE BURGLARS ARE IMPRISONED WITHIN IT....!

HOW'S THAT?

YOU'VE TRAPPED THEM NEATLY!

BUT YOU'VE ALSO SUCCEEDED IN TRAPPING YOURSELF, SUPERMAN! RAISE YOUR HANDS!

OKAY?

I TOLD YOU TO RAISE YOUR HANDS ...BUT NOT THAT HIGH!

PUT DOWN THAT GUN! DON'T YOU REALIZE HE SAVED OUR LIVES!?

WHEN MORE POLICE ARRIVE, THEY RAISE THE CRATE SO THAT THE IMPRISONED GANGSTER CAN CRAWL FREE...

KEEP THOSE HANDS RAISED!

YOU'RE UNDER ARREST, PARRONE!

WHAT A STORY! AND TO THINK I ALMOST LET CLARK TALK ME OUT OF IT!

⑧

—TER-AT THE POLICE STATION-

BROKENSHIRE, THIS IS JOHN. I'M IN QUITE A SPOT! YOU'D BETTER HURRY DOWN TO THE JAIL AT ONCE!

WHEN BROKENSHIRE ARRIVES, HE HAS HIS CLIENTS RELEASED ON BAIL...

IF YOU ASK ME, BROKENSHIRE IS THE WORST OF THE LOT!

WE NO SOONER ARREST THEM THAN HE GETS 'EM OUT!

FROM WHAT YOU TOLD ME, IT APPEARS THAT NATE MUST HAVE TIPPED OFF THE POLICE. YOU'LL BE WISE TO SEE TO IT HE DOESN'T TESTIFY FOR THE STATE!

DON'T WORRY ABOUT NATE, I'LL TAKE CARE OF HIM!

—N THE DAY OF THE TRIAL, —ITOR WHITE OF THE DAILY —ANET DICTATES AN EDITORIAL...

...IT'S A SHAME THAT JOHN —ARRONE, WHO HAS BROKEN —LMOST EVERY EXISTING —LAW, SHOULD ALWAYS HAVE —ESCAPED PUNISHMENT IN THE PAST THRU THE ADVICE —OF LAWYERS. HOWEVER, IT LOOKS LIKE HE WON'T BE ABLE TO DODGE THIS RAP...!"

—AND WITHIN THE COURT-ROOM.

NOW, MISS LANE, TELL THE JURY EXACTLY WHAT YOU SAW!

WELL, WHEN SERGEANT CASEY AND I ENTERED THE STOREROOM, WE SAW PARRONE AND HIS MEN WORKING AT THE SAFE...

—NEXT WITNESS...

WE CAUGHT THEM RED-HANDED, RIFLING THE CONTENTS OF THE SAFE!

WHY DON'T YOU DO SOME-THING? WHY DON'T YOU CROSS-EXAMINE THOSE WITNESSES? YOU'VE DONE NOTHING THRUOUT THIS TRIAL EXCEPT SIT THERE AND GRIN LIKE A CHESHIRE CAT!

COOL DOWN, JOHN! YOU'LL LEARN WHY SOON ENOUGH!

GENTLEMEN OF THE JURY, I HAVE PROVEN TO YOU THAT BEYOND THE SLIGHTEST DOUBT PARRONE AND HIS MEN ARE GUILTY OF ROBBING A STOREROOM! **THE STATE RESTS ITS CASE!**

YOUR HONOR, I CALL UPON YOU TO INSTRUCT THE JURY TO BRING IN A VERDICT OF NOT GUILTY. TRUE, THE PROSECUTOR HAS PROVEN MY CLIENTS GUILTY OF ROBBING A STOREROOM...

BUT HE HAS BROUGHT IN NO EVIDENCE TO INDICATE THEIR GUILT OF THE ROBBERY OF A STOREHOUSE, WHICH IS THE CHARGE IN THE INDICTMENT.

WH-WHAT-?

YOU WILL PLEASE BRING IN A VERDICT OF NOT GUILTY!

AFTER PARRONE IS PRONOUNCED NOT GUILTY...

HO! HO! HO! - BROKENSHIRE, YOU'RE A WONDER!

SH-HH! SAVE YOUR LAUGHT UNTIL LATER LET'S GET OUT OF HERE!

CLARK ACCOMPANIES AN INDIGNANT LOIS TO THE OFFICE OF THE CHAIRMAN OF THE GRIEVANCE COMMITTEE OF THE BAR ASSOCIATION.

IT'S A CRIME THAT LAWYERS SHOULD BE ABLE TO TWIST LEGALITIES SO THAT PROVEN CROOKS CAN GO FREE!

THERE IS NO REGULATION AGAINST A LAWYER PROVING HIS CLIENT IS NOT GUILTY OF THE CHARGE ON WHICH HE HAS BEEN INDICTED!

HOWEVER, SPEAKING AS AN INDIVIDUAL, I'M CERTAIN BROKENSHIRE ADVISES CRIMINALS HOW TO GET AWAY WITH THEIR DEPREDATIONS AND ENCOURAGES THEM IN THE COMMISSION OF CRIMES. I HOPE THAT SOMEDAY SOMEONE WILL PROVE THESE SUSPICIONS OF MINE.

AS LOIS AND CLARK DEPART..

WELL, WELL! IF IT ISN'T THE GIRL-REPORTER WHO TRIED TO SEND ME TO THE PENETENTIARY! I'M GIVING A VICTORY CELEBRATION AT THE GRAY GOOSE TONIGHT. WHY NOT COME?

WE WOULDN'T THINK OF IT!

OH, YES WE WOULD! SEE YOU THERE, PARRONE!

BUT PARRONE OWNS THE GRAY GOOSE ROADHOUSE! IF WE GO THERE, IT'LL BE LIKE PUTTING OUR HEADS INTO A TRAP!

NEVERTHELESS, WE'RE GOING! PARRONE MIGHT SAY SOMETHING THAT WILL BETRAY HIM, AND IF HE DOES, I WANT TO BE THERE TO WRITE IT DOWN ON MY LITTLE PAD!

THAT EVENING -- AS THEY ENTER THE ROADHOUSE WHICH IS ON THE OUTSKIRT OF METROPOLIS...

THEY'RE ALL IN EVENING CLOTHES!

SO THEY ARE! WE'RE LOOKING AT AN EXHIBITION OF WHAT THE WELL-DRESSED GANGSTER WILL WEA

⑩

S THE EVENING GROWS OLDER, THE JUBILATION F PARRONE'S PALS BECOMES EVEN WILDER..

A TOAST--A TOAST TO PARRONE AND BROKENSHIRE...WHO CAN MAKE THE LAW JUMP THRU A HOOP AT WILL!

THANKS LIL!

CAREFUL!.- REMEMBER --THE REPORTERS!

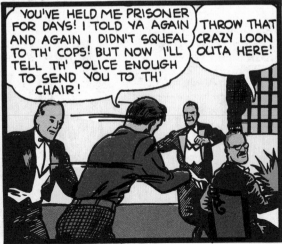

A SUDDEN COMMOTION IN THE KITCHEN, AND NATE DASHES INTO THE ROOM...

YOU'VE HELD ME PRISONER FOR DAYS! I TOLD YA AGAIN AND AGAIN I DIDN'T SQUEAL TO TH' COPS! BUT NOW I'LL TELL TH' POLICE ENOUGH TO SEND YOU TO TH' CHAIR!

THROW THAT CRAZY LOON OUTA HERE!

DON'T MIND THAT LUNATIC, FOLKS! CONTINUE WITH YOUR FUN!

JUST THE BREAK WE WANT, CLARK! C'MON!

CAREFUL, LOIS!

SORRY, SISTER-- NO ONE LEAVES ...YET!

ARE YOU GOING TO LET HIM KEEP US PRISONER?

ER--THERE DOESN'T SEEM MUCH WE CAN DO ABOUT IT!

LOIS WALKS OFF, PEEVED.. RETIRING BEHIND SOME DRAPES, THE MEEK REPORTER GOES INTO ACTION...

SOMETHING BIG IS ABOUT TO POP... I'M **CERTAIN** OF IT!

TWISTING THE FANCY GRILL-WORK OUT OF SHAPE WITH HIS BARE HANDS, **SUPERMAN** SLIPS THRU IT...

THAT SOUNDED LIKE **GUN SHOTS!**

YOU SHOULDN'T HAVE KILLED NATE!

YOU'VE FIXED OTHER MURDERS --YOU CAN FIX THIS ONE TOO!

THE PEOPLE DOWNSTAIRS WITNESSED YOU HAD A MOTIVE FOR KILLING NATE! ALL YOU CAN DO NOW IS DISPOSE OF THE BODY SO THAT IT CANNOT BE IDENTIFIED. WITHOUT A BODY, A PROSECUTOR CANNOT EVEN SECURE AN INDICTMENT!

PETE-GET OUT THE TRUCK, AND PLACE THE STIFF IN THE BACK!

THERE THEY GO TO EXECUTE THEIR FIENDISH PLAN!

SUPERMAN LEAPS NOISELESSLY ATOP THE SPEEDING TRUCK...

--AND HERE'S WHERE I THROW A MONKEY WRENCH INTO THEIR WELL LAID PLANS!

SHORTLY AFTER...

YOUR PLAN?

ONCE THIS GASOLINE IS LIGHTED, THEY'LL NEVER BE ABLE TO IDENTIFY THE BODY!

RETIRING A SHORT DISTANCE, PARRONE HURLS A BLAZING TORCH TOWARD THE GASOLINE ...BUT AS HE DOES...

WH--??

THIS TIME, PARRONE YOU **ARE** GOING TO PAY FOR YOUR CRIME!

SEIZING THE SQUEALING PARRONE, **SUPERMAN** HURLS HIM INTO THE TRUCK WITH THE OTHERS...

REJOIN YOUR PALS!

THE **MAN** OF TOMORROW TEARS OFF THE TRUCK'S WHEELS, AND TWISTS ITS METAL BODY TOGETHER SO THAT THE GANGSTERS ARE HOPELESSLY IMPRISONED WITHIN IT...

TRY BREAKING OUT OF **THERE**!

⑫

LEAPING BACK ACROSS THE COUNTRYSIDE **SUPERMAN** RETURNS TO THE GRAY GOOSE AND TWISTS THE GRILL-WORK BACK INTO PLACE...!

-- AND NOW TO RETURN TO MY IDENTITY AS CLARK KENT!

CLARK TELEPHONES THE POLICE STATION AND SPEAKS IN A DISGUISED VOICE...

THERE'S TROUBLE AT THE GASOLINE STORAGE TANK ON ROUTE 41 NEAR GATES ROAD!

A MINUTE LATER, HE TELEPHONES AGAIN, BUT SPEAKS AS KENT!

SERGEANT CASEY? COME OUT TO THE GRAY GOOSE AT ONCE! LOIS AND I ARE BEING HELD HERE AGAINST OUR WILL!

WHEN THE SERGEANT ARRIVES, HE SWIFTLY CONVINCES THE GUARD AT THE DOOR TO LET LOIS AND CLARK PASS...

I'D LIKE TO TELL PARRONE WHAT I THINK OF THE WAY HE ENTERTAINS GUESTS!

I SUPPOSE YOU'RE PESTERED A LOT BY ASSIGNMENTS LIKE THIS?

IF YOU WANT TO SEE THE KIND OF INCONSEQUENTIAL STUFF THE POLICE ARE CONTINUALLY BOTHERED WITH, ACCOMPANY ME TO A NEARBY GASOLINE STORAGE TANK!

BUT WHEN THEY REACH THE TANK...

WHAT HAPPENED HERE?

NATE GRANT-- MURDERED!

SOUNDS LIKE PARRONE, BROKENSHIRE, AND SOME OF THEIR THUGS ARE IM-PRISONED IN HERE!

AFTER THE TRUCK IS TOWED TO POLICE HEADQUARTERS...

WHAT IS IT, CASEY?

I THINK YOU'RE GOING TO ENJOY THIS, PROSECUTOR!

WHEN THE DOORS ARE FINALLY OPENED...

PARRONE AND BROKENSHIRE! LET'S SEE YOU CRAWL OUT OF **THIS** TECHNICALITY!

IT'S OBVIOUS THAT BROKENSHIRE AIDED PARRONE IN THE ATTEMPT TO DISPOSE OF NATE'S BODY! THAT MAKES HIM EQUALLY GUILTY OF THE CRIME!

ONLY ONE MAN COULD HAVE TRAPPED THEM IN THE TRUCK LIKE THAT! **SUPERMAN!**

BAH! YOU ALWAYS GIVE **SUPERMAN** CREDIT FOR EVERYTHING!

THE END

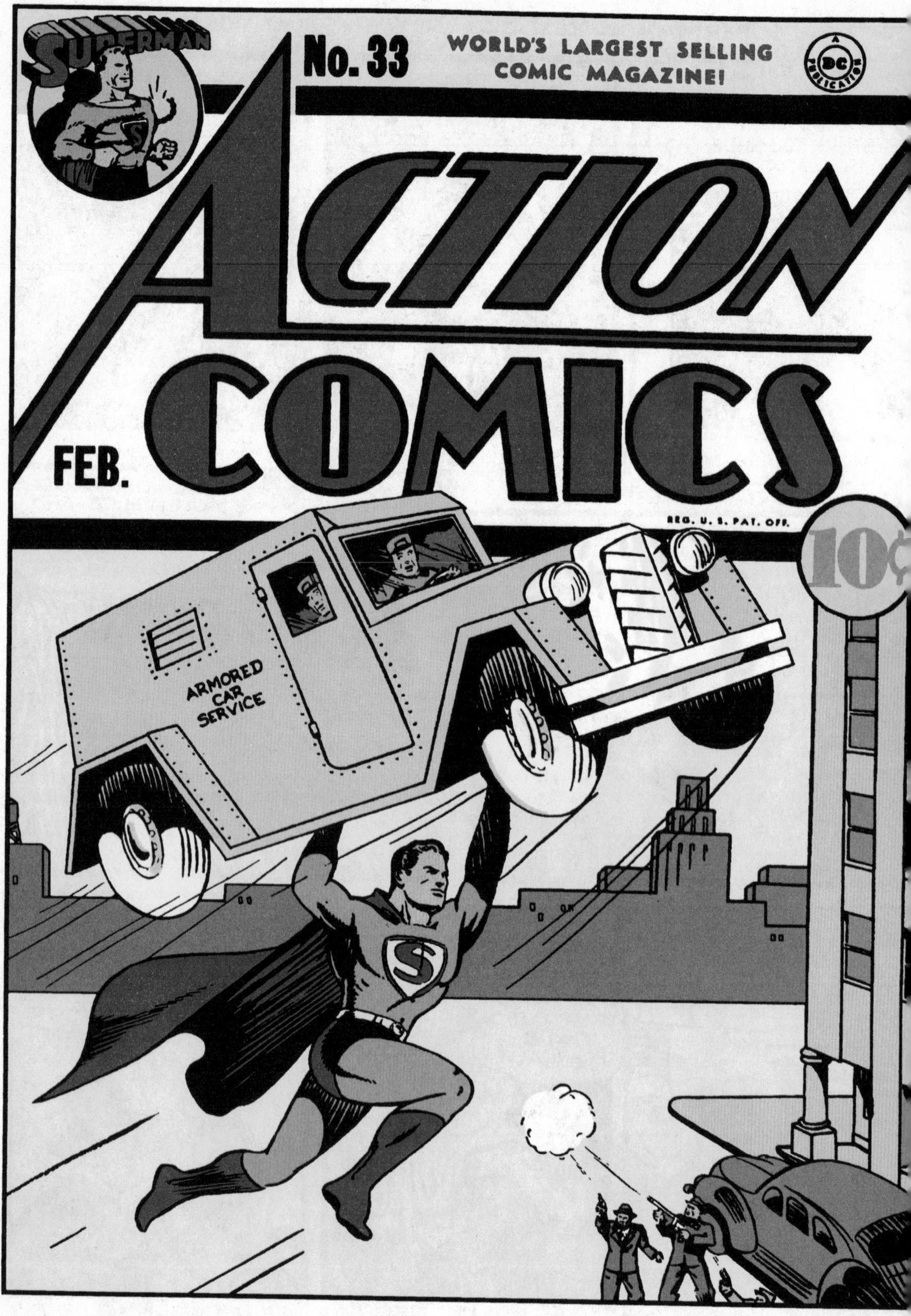
SUPERMAN
No. 33
WORLD'S LARGEST SELLING
COMIC MAGAZINE!
A DC PUBLICATION
ACTION
COMICS
FEB.
REG. U. S. PAT. OFF.
10¢
ARMORED
CAR
SERVICE

SUPERMAN

by Jerry Siegel and Joe Shuster

A LUMBER CAMP, DEEP IN THE WILDS OF THE NORTH WOODS-- FORMER FAT PROFITS DISAPPEARING--HUNDREDS OF UNDERPRIVILEGED CHILDREN SUFFERING AS A RESULT! CLARK KENT, DISPATCHED BY HIS NEWSPAPER TO INVESTIGATE, NOTES SOMETHING AMISS AT THE LUMBER CAMP-- BUT LATER, AS SUPERMAN, HE DOES SOMETHING ABOUT IT!

OFFICE OF KEN HALL, OWNER OF THE HUGE HALL LUMBER INTERESTS--ONE OF THE MOST PROFITABLE ENTERPRISES IN THE NORTH WOODS--

BUT THIS PLAN--THAT UPON YOUR DEATH, ALL PROCEEDS FROM YOUR LUMBER CAMPS AND MILLS ARE TO GO TOWARDS FOUNDING A FREE SUMMER CAMP FOR UNDERPRIVILEGED YOUTHS-- WHATEVER GAVE YOU SUCH AN IDEA?

I WAS A KID IN THE SLUMS, MYSELF, AND I HAVEN'T FORGOTTEN HOW I ROASTED IN THE CITY IN THE HOT SUMMER-- DRAW UP THOSE PAPERS!

--AT THE *DAILY PLANET* OFFICE--

THIS FELLOW HALL IS ALL RIGHT! I DIDN'T KNOW MILLIONAIRES WERE BUILT THAT WAY!

A MAN CAN HAVE A MILLION AND STILL HAVE A HEART!

ONE EVENING, HALL SAUNTERS ACROSS HIS VAST PROPERTY ON A LONE INSPECTION-- HIS FIGURE IS ENGULFED BY THE LONG DARK SHADOWS-- SUDDENLY--- A PIERCING SCREAM--

YAA-AAAaaa!

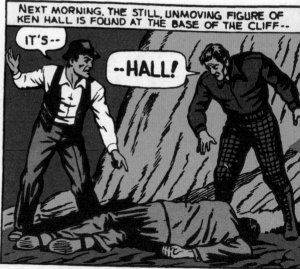

NEXT MORNING, THE STILL, UNMOVING FIGURE OF KEN HALL IS FOUND AT THE BASE OF THE CLIFF--

IT'S--

--HALL!

DAILY PLANET — EXTRA

LUMBER KING DIES IN FALL!

WILL BENEFITS UNDERPRIVILEGED!

WHITE OF THE DAILY PLANET? THIS IS BRETT HALL SPEAKING-- BROTHER OF KEN HALL-- YOU CAN INFORM YOUR READERS THAT I WILL FIGHT KEN'S RIDICULOUS WILL TO THE LIMIT!

THE NATION'S EYES FOCUS ON THE HALL CASE, WHICH IS FOUGHT IN THE HIGHEST COURTS

IT IS MY CONTENTION THAT MY BROTHER WAS OUT OF HIS MIND WHEN HE DREW UP THAT WILL!

GOOD NEWS! LOST HIS CASE! THE UNDERPRIVILEGED KIDS WILL GET THE REVENUE!

FINE! THAT RATES PLENTY OF SPACE!

BUT-- SEVERAL MONTHS LATER, CLARK AND LOIS ARE SUMMONED BY THE EDITOR--

YOU WANTED TO SEE US, CHIEF?

IT'S ABOUT THE HALL LUMBER INTERESTS! YOU'LL RECALL THAT THE UNFORTUNATE CITY YOUTHS' ORGANIZATIONS WON THE HALL CASE!

WITH THE REVENUE FROM THE LUMBER COMPANY THEY WERE TO OPERATE A FREE SUMMER CAMP FOR THE BOYS HOWEVER-- NOT ONE CENT OF REVENUE HAS BEEN FORTH- COMING!

THE MANAGEMENT CLAIMS THEY'VE BEEN HAMPERED BY SABOTAGE-- WORKERS KILLED IN A WAVE OF ACCIDENTS--EXPLOSIONS IN THE NIGHT--FALLING TREES--"

IT LOOKS LIKE SOMEONE IS DELIBERATELY CAUSING THESE ACCIDENTS--BUT FOR WHAT PURPOSE?

THAT'S WHAT I WANT **YOU** TO DISCOVER-- GET TO WORK ON IT AT ONCE!

LATER--CLARK AND LOIS TAKE A PLANE TOWARD THE HALL LUMBER CAMPS IN THE NORTH WOODS!

LANDING AT *BRONSTON*, THE REPORTERS LEAVE THE PLANE, AND WAIT UPON A WHARF FOR A BOAT TO TAKE THEM ACROSS THE RIVER TO THE CAMP!

IF WE GET IN ON THE INSIDE WE CAN INVESTIGATE QUIETLY-- SUPPOSE YOU TRY FOR A JOB AS COOK, WHILE I APPLY FOR A POSITION AS LUMBERJACK!

I MAY QUALIFY AS COOK, BUT I CAN'T VISUALIZE **YOU** AS A LUMBER- JACK!

WILL YOU TAKE US OVER TO THE ISLAND? WE'VE HEARD THERE ARE JOBS OPEN THERE!

ALL RIGHT-- **GIT IN!**

GOOD SOLID BOAT YOU'VE GOT HERE, SKIPPER-- IT HAS TO BE, TO BUCK **THIS** CURRENT!

IT **DOES** LOOK LIKE A TOUGH BODY OF WATER-- AND COLD AS ICE, TOO!

IF YOU THINK IT **AINT**, JUST TRY FALLIN' OVERBOARD! YOU WOULDN'T LIVE A MINUTE, SURE AS MY NAME IS CLIFF!

-- FROM THE OPPOSITE SHORE, A PAIR OF CRUEL, BEADY EYES SURVEYS THE TWO NEWCOMERS!

3.

WHO'S THAT MAN ON THE WHARF?

THAT'S FRANCOIS BERNIER, BOSS OF THE CAMP, TOUGHEST MAN IN THESE PARTS! I'VE SEEN HIM TAKE A MAN IN HIS TWO HANDS AND BREAK HIM OVER HIS KNEE JUST BECAUSE HE DIDN'T LIKE SOMETHING THE FELLA SAID!

ER--I WON'T SAY MUCH!

LANDING ON THE WHARF, THEY APPROACH BERNIER!

YOU WANT JOBS, HEY? WHAT YOU DO? YOU AIN'T LUMBERJACK!

--NO, I'M NOT-- BUT I'M WILLING TO LEARN!

--AND YOU'LL RAVE ABOUT MY COOKING!

LET'S SEE YOUR HANDS--H-MM-- ALL SOFT! BUT I SEE YOU GET WORK--WORK TO BREAK BACK MEBBE, AND PUT GOOD BLISTER ON DOSE SOFT HANDS! NOW YOU BOTH GO TO BUNKHOUSE-- ARRANGE FOR QUARTERS! GIRL, YOU COME BACK!

THEN WE'RE HIRED? GEE, THAT'S SWELL!

AS CLARK SURVEYS THE BUNKHOUSE--

NOT VERY COMFORTABLE QUARTERS!

ALWAYS COMPLAINING, THAT'S YOU! WHAT DID YOU EXPECT? A PARK AVENUE PENT-HOUSE?

--BACK AT THE WHARF, BERNIER CALLS CLIFF, THE GUIDE--

CLIFF, I DON' LAK DE LOOK OF DEM. I TINK SOMEBODY SEND DEM UP HERE TO SPY ON ME AND DE CAMP. DE ONE COMIN' BACK TO DE WHARF, WE FINISH NOW! CLIFF YOU GET RID OF HER LAK YOU DO DAT OTHER SPY LAST MONTH!

NO, MR. BERNIER-- PLEASE DON'T MAKE ME DO THAT AGAIN! I AIN'T BEEN ABLE TO SLEEP GOOD SINCE I KNOCKED THAT MAN INTO THE RIVER-- I-I--AIN'T GONNA DO IT!

DO LIKE I SAY--OR I BREAK BOTH ARMS!

LEGGO! I'LL DO IT! I'LL DO IT!

LISTEN WHAT I SAY! I SEND DAT GIRL IN BOAT WITH YOU--GETTIN' DARK-- NO ONE SEE FROM MAIN-SHORE--YOU GET BOAT BY BIG WHIRLPOOL, YOU HIT HER OVER HEAD, AND PUSH HER OVERBOARD--UNDERSTAND?

I-I UNDERSTAND-- HERE SHE COMES NOW!

GET IN DIS BOAT WITH CLIFF--GO TO MAINSHORE TO SEE SIGHTS--CLIFF GOOD GUIDE!

THAT'S MIGHTY NICE OF YOU!

YOU'RE GONNA ENJOY THIS SIGHTSEEING TRIP!

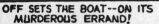

OFF SETS THE BOAT--ON ITS MURDEROUS ERRAND!

I SHOW HER WHAT FRANCOIS BERNIER DO TO SPIES!

SAY--THIS CURRENT IS TERRIFIC!

YES--WE'RE NEAR THE WHIRLPOOL--NOW YOU CAN SEE IT FROM A SAFE DISTANCE!

MEANWHILE--BERNIER PUTS CLARK TO WORK--

YOU--TAKE DIS AXE-- SPLIT DAT WOOD!

I-I'LL TRY!

FASTER, YOU SOFTIE, FASTER!

I'M DOING THE BEST I CAN! (--I COULD DO THIS JOB IN ONE SECOND FLAT, BUT THE THING TO DO RIGHT NOW IS PRE-TEND GREAT EFFORT!)

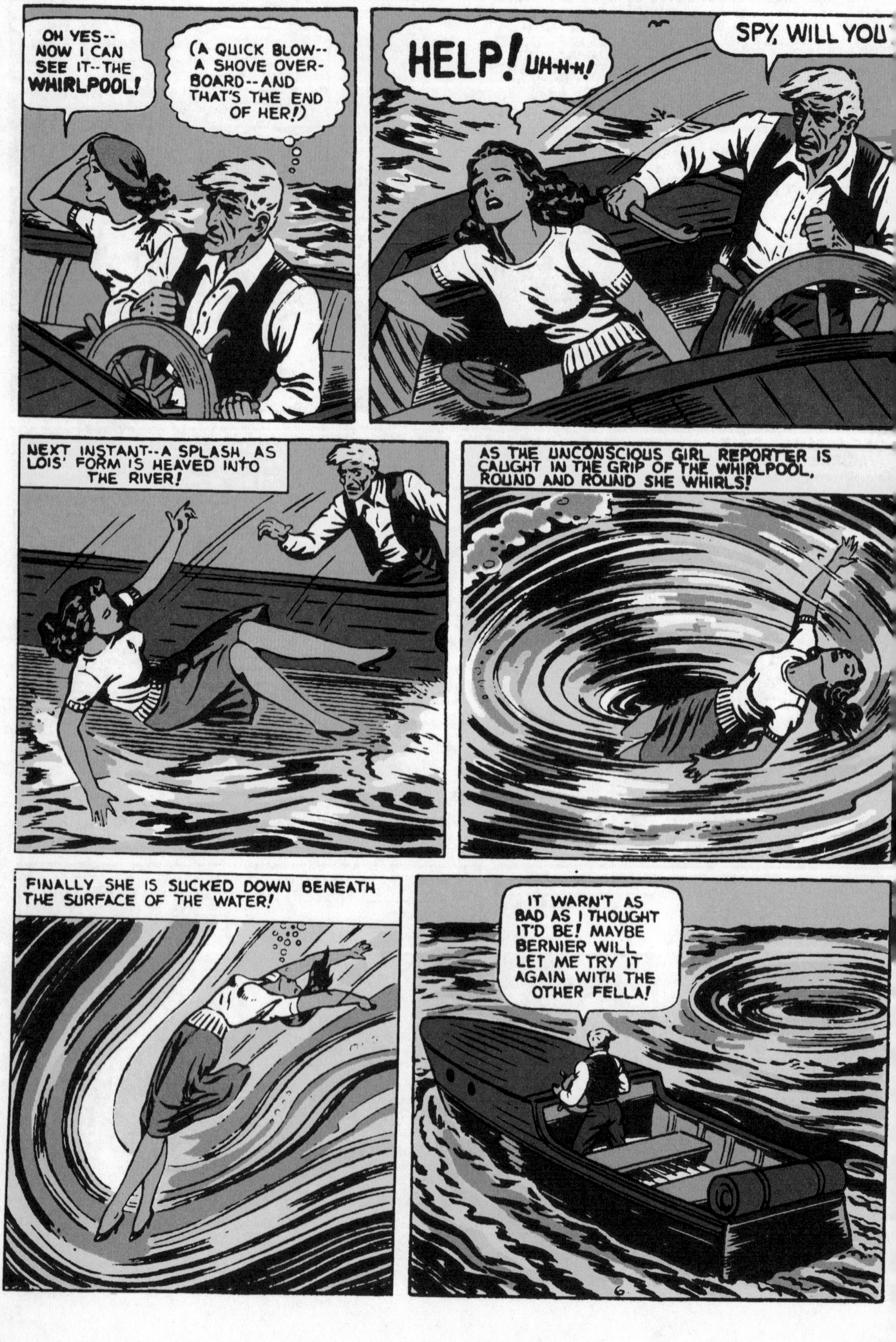
OH YES--
NOW I CAN
SEE IT--THE
WHIRLPOOL!
(A QUICK BLOW--
A SHOVE OVER-
BOARD--AND
THAT'S THE END
OF HER!)
HELP! UH-H-H!
SPY, WILL YOU
NEXT INSTANT--A SPLASH AS LOIS' FORM IS HEAVED INTO THE RIVER!
AS THE UNCONSCIOUS GIRL REPORTER IS CAUGHT IN THE GRIP OF THE WHIRLPOOL, ROUND AND ROUND SHE WHIRLS!
FINALLY SHE IS SUCKED DOWN BENEATH THE SURFACE OF THE WATER!
IT WARN'T AS
BAD AS I THOUGHT
IT'D BE! MAYBE
BERNIER WILL
LET ME TRY IT
AGAIN WITH THE
OTHER FELLA!
6.

WHAT'S THE MATTER WITH **YOU**?

--I THOUGHT I HEARD A SCREAM FOR HELP FROM THE RIVER-- SOUNDED LIKE LOIS!

NEVER MIND WHAT YOU THINK IT SOUND LIKE--GET BACK TO WORK!

SOMETHING'S HAPPENED TO LOIS OUT THERE, AND I'M GOING TO FIND OUT WHAT IT IS!

CLARK QUICKLY OUTDISTANCES THE LUMBERING BERNIER--

COME BACK HERE! YOU COME BACK, OR I BREAK YOUR NECK FOR YOU! COME BACK!

RUNNING SWIFTLY TOWARD THE RIVER, KENT PAUSES FOR A MOMENT IN THE UNDERBRUSH--

LOIS--IN TROUBLE-- IT'S TIME FOR ME TO CHANGE TO **SUPERMAN**!

UP--UP--AND AWAY!

LOIS-- IN THE GRIP OF THE **WHIRLPOOL**!

AS THE MAN OF STEEL SOARS OVER THE SWIRLING, TREACHEROUS RIVER, HE GLANCES DOWN---

DOWN PLUMMETS **SUPERMAN**, INTO THE VERY VORTEX OF THE WHIRLPOOL, AND DISAPPEARS FROM VIEW!

DOWN--DOWN--SWIMS THE *MAN OF STEEL* AT EXPRESS TRAIN VELOCITY, TRYING TO OVERTAKE LOIS' FIGURE--

A MATTER OF **SECONDS** NOW--BUT THAT'S ALL I NEED!

GOT HER!

TO TOP IT ALL--I CAN ONLY USE **ONE HAND!**

SUPERMAN BATTLES THE WAY UP THRU THE VORTEX AGAINST THE TERRIFIC FORCE OF THE CURRENT A FEAT ONLY HE COULD ATTEMPT!

UP THRU THE SURFACE OF THE WATER SHOOTS THE *MAN OF TOMORROW*

FREE! FREE OF THE WHIRLPOOL'S GRIP!

ALIGHTING BACK ON THE ISLAND, **SUPERMAN** LOWERS LOIS GENTLY TO THE GROUND--

IF SHE'S INJURED I'LL NEVER STOP BLAMING MYSELF FOR NOT KEEPING A CLOSER WATCH OVER HER!

THE MAN OF STEEL QUICKLY DONS HIS OUTER GARMENTS, RETURNING TO HIS IDENTITY AS CLARK KENT--

SHE'S BREATHING REGULARLY AGAIN--OUGHT TO REGAIN CONSCIOUSNESS ANY MINUTE!

WH-WHAT HAPPENED?

THAT'S WHAT I'D LIKE TO KNOW!

OH YES--CLIFF STRUCK ME FROM BEHIND--THAT'S ALL I RECALL! I MUST HAVE BEEN WASHED ASHORE!

IF WE ARE TO CARRY ON OUR INVESTIGATION, YOU MUST FORGET CLIFF'S ATTACK UPON YOU--SH-HH! HERE COMES BERNIER!

HEY!--WHAT'S DE MATTER HERE?

LOIS FELL OUT OF THE BOAT AND NEARLY DROWNED! SHE--SHE SWAM TO SHORE AND I PULLED HER IN!

IT'S A MIRACLE I DIDN'T DROWN!

THE GIRL ALIVE! BUT--

SHE SWAM TO DE SHORE WHEN SHE FELL FROM BOAT! I TALK TO YOU LATER! COME-I TAKE GIRL WHERE SHE CAN GET DRY!

GO IN SHACK--BOTH OF YOU! BUNKHOUSE, HE'S TOO BIG--TOO MUCH DRAFT!

BUT--AS CLARK AND LOIS ENTER THE SHACK, BERNIER SWIFTLY SLAMS THE DOOR SHUT--BOLTS IT--

NOW I FIX DEM SPIES--BUT GOOD!

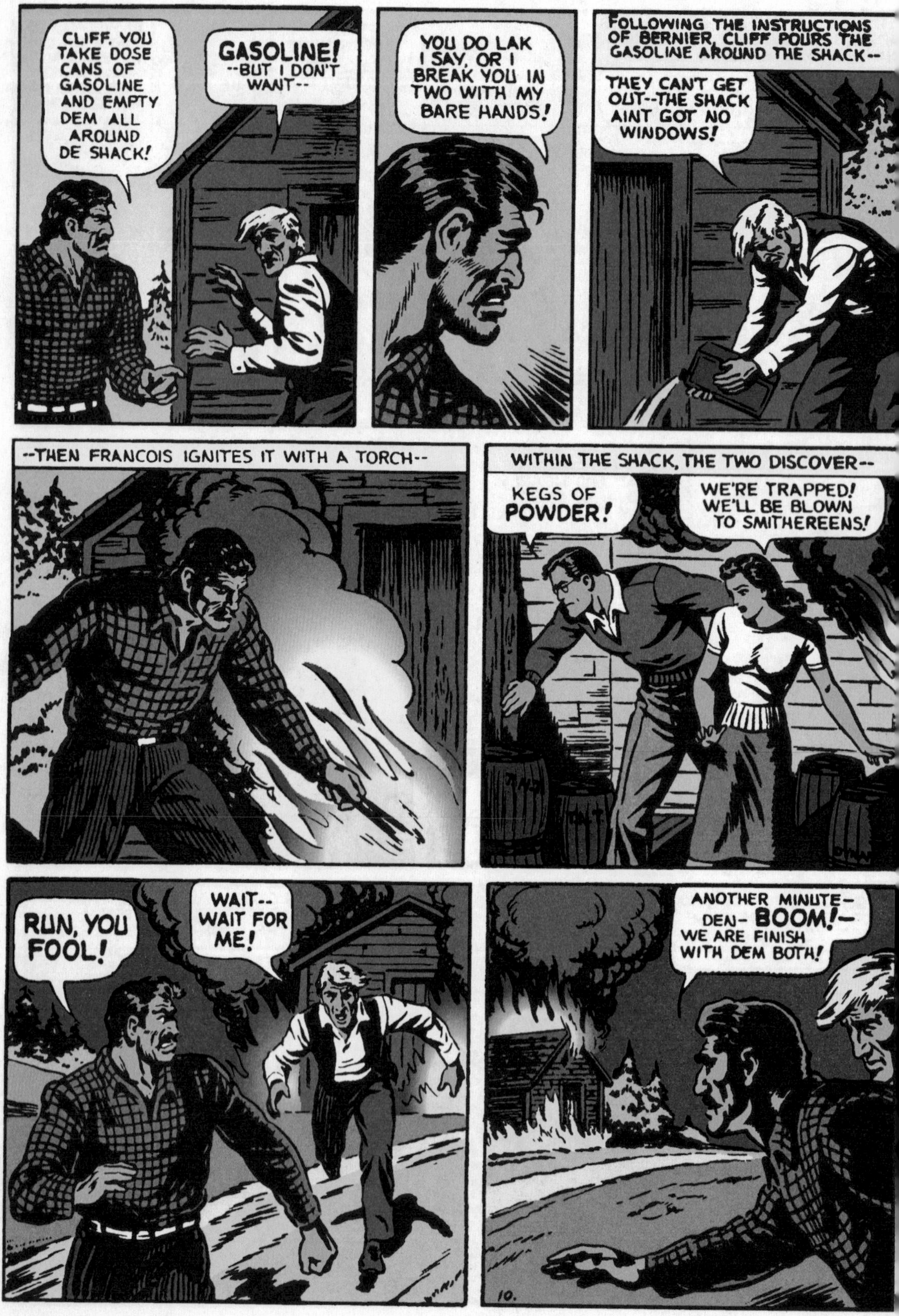

CLIFF, YOU TAKE DOSE CANS OF GASOLINE AND EMPTY DEM ALL AROUND DE SHACK!
GASOLINE! --BUT I DON'T WANT--
YOU DO LAK I SAY, OR I BREAK YOU IN TWO WITH MY BARE HANDS!
FOLLOWING THE INSTRUCTIONS OF BERNIER, CLIFF POURS THE GASOLINE AROUND THE SHACK--
THEY CAN'T GET OUT--THE SHACK AINT GOT NO WINDOWS!
--THEN FRANCOIS IGNITES IT WITH A TORCH--
WITHIN THE SHACK, THE TWO DISCOVER--
KEGS OF POWDER!
WE'RE TRAPPED! WE'LL BE BLOWN TO SMITHEREENS!
RUN, YOU FOOL!
WAIT-- WAIT FOR ME!
ANOTHER MINUTE-- DEN-- BOOM!-- WE ARE FINISH WITH DEM BOTH!
10.

THEN-- A TERRIFIC EXPLOSION!!

TH-THAT **FINISHES** THEM!

THAT IS HOW I HANDLE SPIES! MAYBE THEY SEND THEM NO MORE NOW!

FLASHBACK! WITHIN THE SHACK, JUST BEFORE THE EXPLOSION--

(NO TIME TO WASTE--I'LL HAVE TO RESORT TO HYPNOSIS--) YOUR MEMORY--BECOMING A BLANK!--YOU WILL NOT REMEMBER WHAT ENSUES!

I--WILL-- --NOT-- --REMEMBER--

A MOMENT BEFORE THE EXPLOSION, CLARK LEAPS UP THRU THE SHACK'S ROOF WITH LOIS!

BARELY IN TIME!

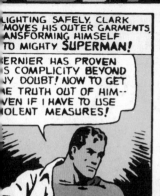

LIGHTING SAFELY, CLARK REMOVES HIS OUTER GARMENTS, TRANSFORMING HIMSELF INTO MIGHTY **SUPERMAN!**

BERNIER HAS PROVEN HIS COMPLICITY BEYOND ANY DOUBT! NOW TO GET THE TRUTH OUT OF HIM-- EVEN IF I HAVE TO USE VIOLENT MEASURES!

YOU ARE RELEASED FROM YOUR TRANCE!

I-I CAN'T RE- MEMBER A THING THAT HAPPENED AFTER WE WERE TRAPPED IN THAT SHACK!-- WHERE'S CLARK?

THERE'S BERNIER APPROACHING THE MAIN OFFICE OF THE LUMBER CAMP--

BERNIER TURNS TO SEE IF HE IS BEING TRAILE

(YOU'RE LOOKING IN THE WRONG DIRECTION, PAL!)

MAIN OFF

AS BERNIER ENTERS THE OFFICE--

I JUST POLISHED OFF THEM TWO SPIES--KENT AND LANE!

SPLENDID, BERNIER! YOU HAVE MORE BRAINS THAN I GAVE YOU CREDIT FOR!

FROM HIS PERCH ATOP THE CABIN, SUPERMAN SEES--

WHY-- IT'S LOIS APPROACHING!

LOIS EAVESDROPS AT THE WINDOW OF THE CABIN

(IF I COULD ONLY LEARN THAT MASKED MAN'S IDENTITY

BUT SHE IS SEIZED BY CLIFF, WHO HAS STEALTHILY APPROACHED BEHIND HER!

SNOOPIN', EH? I DON'T KNOW HOW YOU ESCAPED THAT EXPLOSION, BUT YOU WON'T GET AWAY THIS TIME!

CLIFF FORCES THE CAPTIVE LOIS INTO THE OFFICE--

LOOK WHO I CAUGHT SPYIN' AT THE WINDOW!

THE GIRL!--BUT I THOUGHT--

--THAT I WAS DEAD? GUESS AGAIN!

SO YOU KILLED BOTH SPIES, EH?

12.

82

ANYWAY, I SABOTAGE PRODUCTION LAK YOU SAY I SHOULD -- WHERE IS MY REWARD?

YOU'VE FAILED TO KEEP YOUR END OF THE BARGAIN -- SO--

AGH-HHH!

--YOUR REWARD IS -- DEATH!

THE MASKED KILLER THEN TURNS HIS GUN ON CLIFF--

YAA-AA!

THE GIRL IS NEXT!

ATOP THE CABIN, SUPERMAN ACTS-- SMASHING IN A PART OF THE ROOF--

THAT FIEND IS ABOUT TO SHOOT LOIS!

--AND AS THE KILLER FIRES AT LOIS, THE BULLET REBOUNDS FROM THE FALLING BEAM AND CRASHES BACK INTO HIS SKULL!

DON'T SHOOT-- --OH!

DIE, YOU SPY-- UGH-HH

LOIS REMOVES THE MASK FROM THE DYING KILLER--

--IT'S BRETT HALL!

YES--I WANTED KEN'S MILLIONS--I MURDERED HIM--LATER, I GOT BERNIER TO SABOTAGE THE LUMBER INTERESTS --MY MOTIVE--TO THEN BUY THE INTERESTS FOR A SONG!

A FEW MINUTES LATER--CLARK ENTERS--

--AND THAT'S WHAT HE CONFESSED! THE UNDERPRIVILEGED BOYS WILL NOW BE ABLE TO GET THEIR SUMMER CAMP! AND THOUGH I NEVER ONCE SAW HIM, I'VE A HUNCH THAT SUPERMAN HELPED US GET A SWELL STORY!

I WISH YOU'D STOP MOONING ABOUT SUPERMAN AND THINK ABOUT ME FOR A WHILE!

THE END.

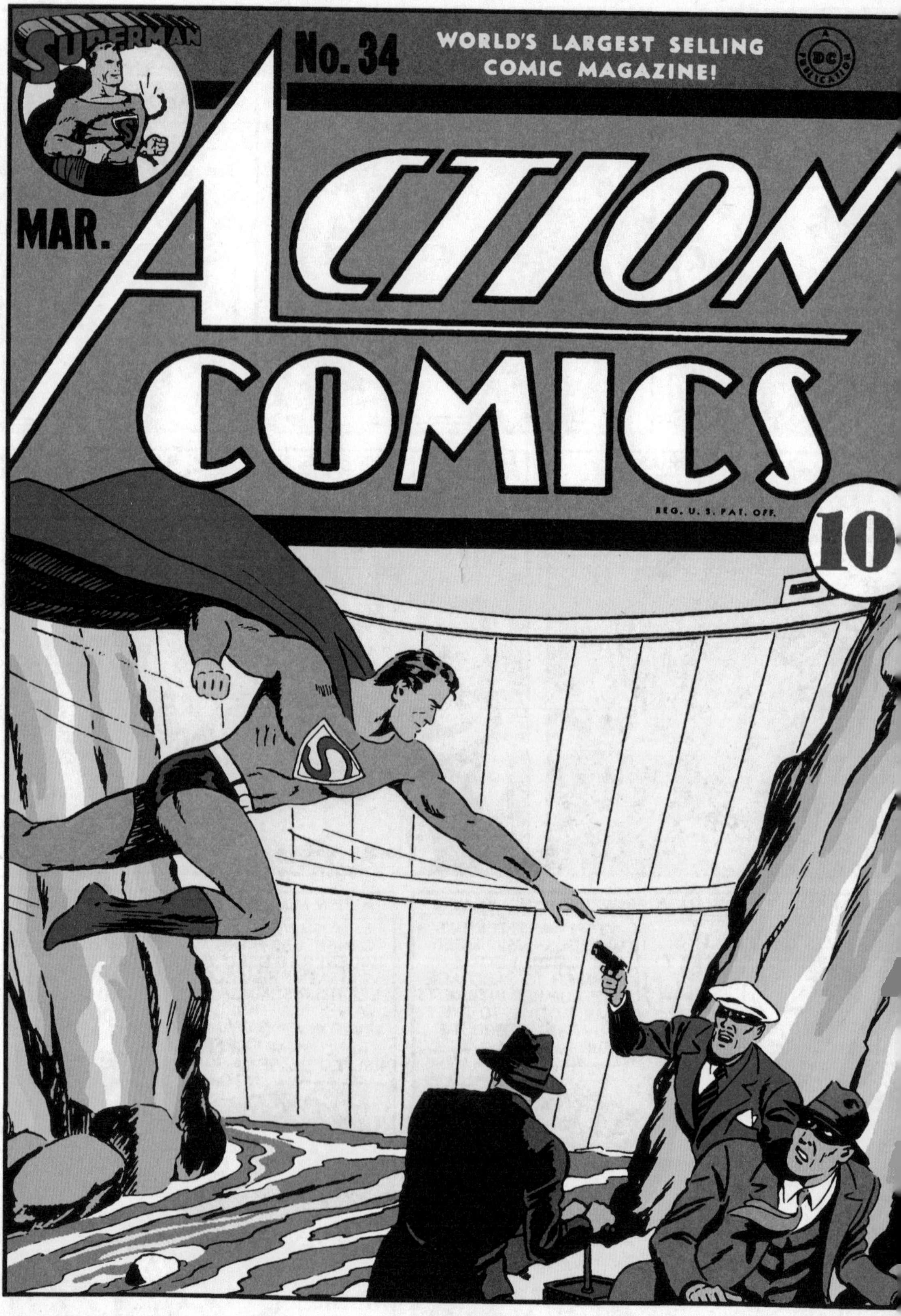
SUPERMAN
No. 34
WORLD'S LARGEST SELLING
COMIC MAGAZINE!
A DC PUBLICATION
MAR.
ACTION
COMICS
REG. U. S. PAT. OFF.
10

SUPERMAN

by JERRY SIEGEL AND JOE SHUSTER

A FABULOUSLY RICH COAL MINE IN THE HEART OF THE RUGGED ANTHRACITE COUNTRY, WHERE GRIMY MINERS BURROW FAR BELOW THE EARTH'S SURFACE SEEKING PRECIOUS FUEL--THIS IS THE SETTING FOR A THRILL-PACKED MYSTERY, IN WHICH **SUPERMAN** THWARTS A DIABOLICAL PLOT UPON THE LIFE OF A BEAUTIFUL YOUNG HEIRESS!

CLARK KENT IS CALLED INTO THE *PLANET* EDITOR'S OFFICE--

I'VE GOT AN ASSIGNMENT FOR YOU, CLARK-- DORIS LAUREY, DAUGHTER OF THE LATE WEALTHY COAL MAGNATE, AND NOW UNDER THE GUARDIANSHIP OF HER UNCLE, HAS JUST COME OF AGE AND INHERITED THE RICH LAUREY COAL MINES!

I DON'T SEE MUCH OF A YARN IN THAT!

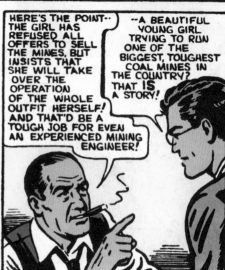

HERE'S THE POINT-- THE GIRL HAS REFUSED ALL OFFERS TO SELL THE MINES, BUT INSISTS THAT SHE WILL TAKE OVER THE OPERATION OF THE WHOLE OUTFIT HERSELF! AND THAT'D BE A TOUGH JOB FOR EVEN AN EXPERIENCED MINING ENGINEER!

--A BEAUTIFUL YOUNG GIRL TRYING TO RUN ONE OF THE BIGGEST, TOUGHEST COAL MINES IN THE COUNTRY? THAT **IS** A STORY!

CLARK AND LOIS LANE DRIVE OUT TO THE LAUREY MINES--

WHITE SAYS THE LAUREY GIRL SEEMS TO BE TRYING TO AVOID REPORTERS! THEY'RE NOT ALLOWED TO SEE HER--

THAT'S RIGHT--NO ONE HAS BEEN ABLE TO GET AN INTERVIEW WITH HER AS YET-- BUT I WILL!

YOU SEEM PRETTY SURE OF YOURSELF-- WHAT'S YOUR PLAN?

THE FIRST THING IS TO GAIN ADMITTANCE TO THE MINING GROUND, THEN, IT SHOULDN'T BE HARD TO LOCATE THE ELUSIVE MISS LAUREY

ARRIVING AT THE MINE, THE TWO REPORTERS GAIN ENTRANCE TO THE GUARDED GROUNDS BY MEANS OF A HASTILY COOKED-UP STORY!

WE'RE STUDENTS FROM STATE UNIVERSITY--I'M TAKING A COURSE IN MINING ENGINEERING-

--AND I'M STUDYING INDUSTRIAL ECONOMICS--DO YOU MIND IF WE LOOK AROUND A BIT?

STUDENTS, EH? THAT'S O.K.-- GO RIGHT AHEAD--

NOW--KEEP YOUR EYES PEELED FOR THE LAUREY GIRL-- SHE SHOULD BE AROUND HERE SOMEWHERE, IF SHE'S RUNNING THESE MINES!

THERE SHE IS, CLARK! I RECOGNIZE HER FROM HER PHOTOS! AND THAT MUST BE HER UNCLE WITH HER!

A PRETTY BLONDE GIRL EMERGES FROM A NEARBY MINE ENTRANCE, ACCOMPANIED BY A TALL ELDERLY HARD-FACED MAN--

SHAFT 3

EVERYTHING IS GOING FINE, UNCLE JIM!

SO THAT'S DORIS LAUREY-- WATCH ME GET AN INTERVIEW!

WAIT, CLARK! YOU CAN'T BARGE IN ON HER LIKE THAT!

--BEG PARDON, MISS LAUREY, BUT--

WHO ARE YOU?

JUST A MINUTE, DORIS--I'LL SPEAK TO THIS FELLOW AND FIND OUT WHAT HE WANTS-

I'M FROM THE DAILY PLANET, AND--

A REPORTER! I GAVE ORDERS THAT NO REPORTERS WERE TO BE ADMITTED! GUARD!

WHAT IS IT, MR. LAUREY?

THIS STRANGER IS ANNOYING MISS LAUREY--SEE THAT IT DOESN'T HAPPEN AGAIN!

--I ONLY WANTED TO ASK A FEW QUESTIONS!

SEE, SMARTIE? I TOLD YOU SO!

COME ON, YOU!

STOP! YOU CAN'T DO THIS TO ME!

OUTSIDE!

LAUREY MINES ENTRANCE

I CERTAINLY PUT MY FOOT INTO IT THAT TIME!

OUTSIDE THE WIRE FENCE WHICH SURROUNDS THE MINES, THE CHASTENED REPORTER STEPS BEHIND A BUSH AND REMOVES HIS OUTER GARMENTS--

DORIS' UNCLE JIM SEEMED GREATLY PERTURBED WHEN HE HEARD THAT I WAS FROM THE DAILY PLANET--

REVEALING HIMSELF AS **SUPERMAN**, HE LEAPS EASILY OVER THE HIGH BARBED FENCE--

I MUST LOOK INTO THIS FURTHER!

LAUREY MINES ENTRANCE

A POWERFUL LEAP CARRIES THE MAN OF STEEL TO THE ROOF OF A MINE BUILDING--

FROM HERE I'LL BE ABLE TO KEEP MY EYES ON MR. JIM LAUREY!

IF HE DISLIKES REPORTERS, IT MAY BE BECAUSE HE HAS SOMETHING TO HIDE

MEANWHILE--LAUREY LEAVES HIS NIECE LONG ENOUGH TO WHISPER TO A NEARBY PERSON--

--- COAL CAR INTO THE MINE WHEN I GIVE THE SIGNAL!

OKAY, JIM-- THAT'LL BE PERFECT.

ATOP THE NEARBY BUILDING, SUPERMAN HEARS PART OF THE WHISPERED MESSAGE--

JIM LAUREY MAY NOT BE UP TO MISCHIEF BUT I DON'T TRUST HIM! I WISH I COULD HAVE HEARD ALL OF THAT SENTENCE!

DORIS, I WANT YOU TO SEE THE NEW MINE SHAFT--IT'S ALMOST FINISHED!

SHAFT 5

THE PAIR DESCEND THE NARROW SHAFTWAY DEEP INTO THE NEW, DESERTED MINE. THEN--

YOU'RE SUCH A DEAR TO HELP ME OPERATE THE MINES, UNCLE JIM!

I WANT YOU TO LEARN THE MINING GAME FROM A TO Z, DORIS--NOW TAKE YOUR TIME INSPECTING THIS NEW SHAFT--I MUST GIVE AN IMPORTANT ORDER TO MANAGER CRAWFORD-- I'LL BE BACK IN A JIFFY!

LEAVING DORIS BELOW, JIM LAUREY HURRIES UP THE SHAFT-- PAUSING FOR A MOMENT, HE PRESSES A MYSTERIOUS SWITCH ATTACHED TO A BEAM IN THE WALL--

CRAWFORD IS READY--

--SMILING STRANGELY, HE LEAVES THE MINE--

NO ONE WILL EVER SUSPECT!

WHILE BACK IN THE MINE SHAFT--

WHAT CAN THAT STRANGE NOISE BE? IT SEEMS TO BE GETTING LOUDER!

HIGHER UP IN THE TUNNEL, A RUNAWAY COAL CAR ROARS AROUND A BEND-- FASTER, FASTER, IT GOES DOWN THE INCLINE!

THAT RUMBLING SOUND MUST BE A RUNAWAY COAL CAR COMING DOWN THE TRACK--I CAN'T ESCAPE IT IN THIS NARROW SHAFT--

HELP!

DORIS' CRIES ECHO UNHEARD IN THE EMPTY SHAFT-- BUT FAR ABOVE ON THE ROOF OF A MINE BUILDING, THE MAN OF STEEL HEARS HER CALL--

THAT CRY CAME FROM SHAFT FIVE!

SOMEONE CALLED FOR HELP IN THERE!

As HE TRIES TO ENTER THE MINE, **SUPERMAN** FINDS HIS WAY BLOCKED BY TWO BURLY MINERS WHO SUDDENLY STEP OUT OF THE SHADOWS!

SHAFT 5

YOU'RE HEARING THINGS, PAL--THIS MINE IS EMPTY--

WE GOT ORDERS TO KEEP EVERYONE OUT OF SHAFT 5-- BEAT IT!

5

SUPERMAN STREAKS PAST THE ASTONISHED GUARDS--

HEY! WHAT WAS THAT-- A STREAK OF LIGHTNING?

WHIZ

WHILE DEEP DOWN IN THE SHAFT THE CAR HURTLES TOWARD DORIS--

--AND THE MAN OF TOMORROW DASHES INTO THE MURKY TUNNEL AFTER THE RUNAWAY IN A RACE AGAINST DEATH!

THAT NOISE-- IT'S A RUNAWAY COAL CAR GOING AT TERRIFIC SPEED DOWN THE SHAFT-- IT WILL CRUSH WHOEVER IS IN ITS PATH-- IN THIS NARROW TUNNEL--

THE TERRIFIED DORIS HAS FLED TO THE VERY BOTTOM OF THE UNFINISHED MINE SHAFT--

THE CAR-- IT'S COMING CLOSER-- HELP!

--DORIS' VOICE-- COMING FROM THE END OF THE SHAFT I MUST CATCH THAT CAR IN TIME, BUT CAN I?

SUPERMAN LEAPS FOR THE SPEEDING COAL CAR AND EXERTING HIS SUPER-STRENGTH, HALTS ITS TREMENDOUS WEIGHT, INCHES AWAY FROM THE GIRL!

HELP! OHHH!

WITH A FLIP OF HIS HAND, THE MAN OF TOMORROW SENDS THE MASSIVE COAL CAR HURTLING BACK UP THE TRACK. THEN, HE TURNS TO ASSIST THE TERRIFIED DORIS, WHO IS NEAR COLLAPSE!

SAVED! I CAN HARDLY BELIEVE IT!

YOU CERTAINLY HAD A NARROW ESCAPE!

WE MUST GET OUT OF THIS MINE IMMEDIATELY-- I DON'T THINK THAT RUNAWAY COAL CAR BROKE AWAY BY ACCIDENT-- SOMEONE DELIBERATELY TRIED TO KILL YOU!

BUT AS THEY TURN TO LEAVE THE SHAFT, THERE IS A TERRIFIC EXPLOSION IN THE TUNNEL AHEAD-- ROCKS AND WOODEN STAVES HURTLE TOWARDS THEM!

IT'S A CAVE-IN!

STAND BACK! I'LL SHIELD YOU!

--AND THE ONLY EXIT HAS BEEN SEALED UP BY TONS OF FALLEN ROCK STRATA!

THIS CAVE-IN MIGHT HAVE BEEN CAUSED BY A GAS-POCKET-- BUT IT SOUNDED LIKE A BOMB EXPLOSION TO ME--

THIS IS HORRIBLE! WE'LL NEVER GET OUT OF HERE! WE'RE BURIED ALIVE!

BUT DORIS LAUREY SOON DISCOVERS THAT THE MAN OF STEEL IS EQUAL TO THE EMERGENCY. WITH A DYNAMIC CHARGE, HE QUICKLY BLASTS A PATHWAY THRU THE SOLID EARTH!

INCREDIBLE! HE'S PUSHING ASIDE TONS OF ROCKS AND EARTH WITH HIS BARE HANDS!

THESE BOULDERS ARE JUST PEBBLES TO ME!

WITH A SINGLE, TREMENDOUS LEAP, SUPERMAN CARRIES DORIS PAST THE CAVE-IN, OUT OF THE MINE, AND FAR UP INTO THE AIR!

WHAT AN AMAZING EXPERIENCE!

I MUST WARN YOU TO BE ON YOUR GUARD-- I THINK THOSE "ACCIDENTS" WERE DELIBERATE ATTEMPTS ON YOUR LIFE!

AS SUPERMAN SPRINGS AWAY--

THERE HE GOES-- UP--UP-- INTO THE SKY! --FASTER THAN AN AIRPLANE--

DORIS! I'M SO GLAD YOU'RE SAFE! I HEARD THERE WAS A CAVE-IN AT THE NEW SHAFT!

YES--AND I WAS ALMOST CRUSHED BY A RUNAWAY COAL CAR! SUPERMAN SAVED ME!

SUPERMAN? WHY, THERE'S NO SUCH PERSON, MY DEAR!

YOU'LL PROBABLY THINK THAT IT'S JUST MY HYSTERICAL IMAGINATION AFTER MY NARROW ESCAPE, BUT I TELL YOU HE CARRIED ME OUT OF THE MINE AND UP INTO THE SKY WITH THE SPEED OF A BULLET!

MEAN- WHILE, THE MAN OF STEEL RETURNS TO HIS IDENTITY AS CLARK KENT--

I'M CERTAIN THAT SOME SINISTER PERSON IS TRYING TO GET DORIS OUT OF THE WAY--BUT WHY?

REENTERING SHAFT 5, HE DESCENDS TO THE SCENE OF THE CAVE-IN AND FINDS--

THE REMAINS OF A TIME-BOMB! THAT WAS THE CAUSE OF THE CAVE-IN!

FARTHER UP THE SHAFT, KENT DISCOVERS THE SWITCH THAT JIM LAUREY HAD PULLED AFTER LEAVING DORIS--

--AND THIS SWITCH-- I'LL WAGER IT HAS SOMETHING TO DO WITH THE MYSTERY OF THE RUNAWAY COAL CAR!

SHAFT 5

THIS IS TURNING OUT TO BE A REALLY BIG STORY!

--BUT AS CLARK LEAVES THE MINE SHAFT--

OH, IT'S YOU AGAIN! I THOUGHT I THREW YOU OUT BEFORE!

OH-OH!

SNOOPING AROUND AGAIN, EH? I OUGHT TO KNOCK YOUR HEAD OFF--BUT FIRST, I'LL TAKE YOU TO THE MANAGER'S OFFICE--

TAKE YOUR HANDS OFF ME!

THE GUARD BRINGS KENT IN TO SEE MANAGER CRAWFORD IN THE MINE BUILDING--

I CAUGHT THIS REPORTER HANGING AROUND THE NEW SHAFT!

YOU CAN'T GET AWAY WITH THIS. I'VE FOUND OUT PLENTY!

YOU'D BETTER QUIT MEDDLING WITH MATTERS THAT DON'T CONCERN YOU, YOUNG MAN!

IS THAT SO? WELL, I'VE DISCOVERED EVIDENCE THAT SOMEONE DELIBERATELY TRIED TO INJURE MISS LAUREY-- WHAT DO YOU SAY TO THAT?

BOSH! I'VE HAD ENOUGH OF THIS! GUARD! THROW HIM OUT!

COME ON, YOU!

--BUT SURELY!-

I SAID, THROW HIM OUT!

THE GUARD TAKES CLARK TO THE EXIT GATE--THEN--

NOW GET THIS, CHUM--IF I CATCH YOU AROUND HERE AGAIN, IT'LL BE JUST TOO BAD!

I--I WON'T COME BACK!

NOW GET OUT-- AND STAY OUT!

BAM!

OUCH! (I MUST ACT AS IF HIS BLOW REALLY HURT ME!)

OUT OF VIEW, CLARK REMOVES HIS CIVILIAN CLOTHES ONCE AGAIN--

THOSE FELLOWS ARE UP TO NO GOOD! DORIS LAUREY'S LIFE MAY BE IN DANGER AT THIS VERY MOMENT!

SAY-- I DON'T KNOW WHO YOU ARE, BUT YOU CAN'T COME IN HERE!

THAT'S WHAT YOU THINK!

SUPERMAN TOSSES THE GUARD ATOP THE BARBED FENCE, SO THAT HE HANGS SUSPENDED!

HELP! LET ME DOWN!

TAKE IT EASY, PAL! YOU'VE HAD ENOUGH EXERCISE FOR TODAY!

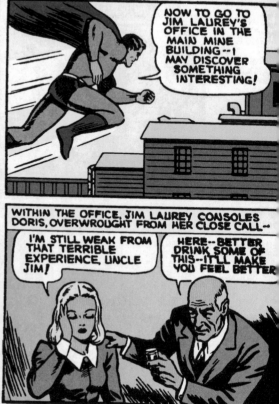

NOW TO GO TO JIM LAUREY'S OFFICE IN THE MAIN MINE BUILDING--I MAY DISCOVER SOMETHING INTERESTING!

WITHIN THE OFFICE, JIM LAUREY CONSOLES DORIS, OVERWROUGHT FROM HER CLOSE CALL--

I'M STILL WEAK FROM THAT TERRIBLE EXPERIENCE, UNCLE JIM!

HERE--BETTER DRINK SOME OF THIS--IT'LL MAKE YOU FEEL BETTER

HANGING OUTSIDE THE OFFICE WINDOW, **SUPERMAN's** X-RAY VISION ENABLES HIM TO SEE THAT LAUREY IS OFFERING HIS NIECE A **POISONED DRINK!**

DON'T DRINK THAT! IT'S DEADLY POISON!

WHY, IT'S SUPERMAN!

HUH?

I-I CAN'T BELIEVE THAT THIS DRINK IS POISONED!

YES, DORIS--YOUR "KIND" UNCLE WAS TRYING TO POISON YOU! GIVE ME THAT DRINK AND I'LL PROVE IT TO YOU!

PAY NO ATTENTION TO HIM, DORIS! HE'S LYING!

YOU CLAIM THIS IS A HARMLESS DRINK, EH? DRINK IT, THEN!

NO! DON'T MAKE ME DRINK IT! I DON'T WANT TO DIE!

UNCLE JIM! THEN, YOU DID PLAN TO KILL ME!

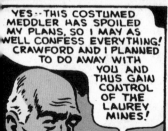

YES--THIS COSTUMED MEDDLER HAS SPOILED MY PLANS, SO I MAY AS WELL CONFESS EVERYTHING! CRAWFORD AND I PLANNED TO DO AWAY WITH YOU AND THUS GAIN CONTROL OF THE LAUREY MINES!

NOW, THERE'S NOTHING FOR ME TO DO BUT PAY THE PENALTY FOR MY CRIMES! THIS ELEVATOR WILL TAKE US TO THE GROUND--

THERE'S PLENTY OF EVIDENCE TO CONVICT YOU OF ATTEMPTED MURDER, LAUREY!

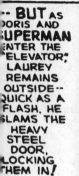

--BUT AS DORIS AND **SUPERMAN** ENTER THE "ELEVATOR," LAUREY REMAINS OUTSIDE-- QUICK AS A FLASH, HE SLAMS THE HEAVY STEEL DOOR, LOCKING THEM IN!

SAY! THIS IS NO ELEVATOR!

--OH! I SEE NOW--IT'S A DECOMPRESSION ROOM FOR THE MINERS! HE CAN ADJUST THE AIR PRESSURE AT WILL!

WHILE OUTSIDE, LAUREY TURNS THE CONTROL TO THE HIGHEST AIR PRESSURE--

NO HUMAN BEING CAN STAND THIS AIR PRESSURE--IT WILL BURST THEIR LUNGS AND I'LL BE RID OF THEM BOTH!

HIGH

MY OWN LUNGS CAN STAND ANY PRESSURE--BUT I MUST GET HER OUT OF HERE AT ONCE--OR IT WILL BE TOO LATE!

OHH--I CAN HARDLY BREATHE! (GASP)

WHAT!? THIS IS IMPOSSIBLE!

THAT WAS A MURDEROUS PLAN, LAUREY, BUT YOU FORGOT MY SUPER-STRENGTH!

THRU THE SOLID STEEL WALL OF THE DEADLY DECOMPRESSION CHAMBER CRASHES THE MAN OF TOMORROW, CARRYING DORIS WITH HIM!

RIPPING OFF SOME OF THE METAL PIPING ON THE WALLS, SUPERMAN TWISTS IT AROUND LAUREY FROM HEAD TO FOOT, HIS MIGHTY HANDS BENDING THE IRON PIPES LIKE STRANDS OF ROPE!

W-WHAT ARE YOU GOING TO DO TO ME?

I'VE HAD ENOUGH OF YOUR PLAYFUL LITTLE TRICKS--THIS IRON PIPING WILL HOLD YOU TILL THE POLICE GET HERE!

I STILL HAVE ONE MORE TRICK UP MY SLEEVE! IF I CAN'T HAVE THESE MINES, NO ONE ELSE WILL! A GIANT TIME BOMB PLANTED IN THE MAIN MINE SHAFT IS DUE TO EXPLODE IN EXACTLY TEN SECONDS!

--JUST AS YOU CRASHED THRU THE WALL, I PULLED THE SWITCH WHICH STARTED THE TIME FUSE IN THE MINE! THERE IS NOTHING YOU CAN DO TO STOP THE EXPLOSION! --SO I HAVE THE LAST LAUGH AFTER ALL!

A BLAST IN THE MAIN SHAFT WILL CAVE IN ALL THE MINE TUNNELS! HUNDREDS OF MINERS WILL BE CRUSHED AND ENTOMBED!

9 SECONDS TO GO

THERE'S THE MAIN SHAFT-- NOW, IF MY SUPER-HUMAN FACULTIES CAN LOCATE THE HIDDEN BOMB BEFORE--

MAIN SHAFT

SEIZING THE BOMB, HE LEAPS OUT OF THE MINE AND HIGH UP INTO THE AIR--NEXT MOMENT, THERE IS A TERRIFIC EXPLOSION!

I JUST MADE IT IN TIME!

WHAM!

STREAKING INTO THE MAIN SHAFT WITH BLINDING SPEED, SUPERMAN QUICKLY FINDS THE TIME BOMB BY MEANS OF HIS SUPER-HEARING!

THAT FAINT TICKING SOUND OF THE TIME BOMB LED ME TO IT!

DESCENDING. HE SEES CRAWFORD FLEEING--

NOT SO FAST, CRAWFORD! LAUREY'S CONFESSION SHOWED THAT YOU WERE HIS ACCOMPLICE!

SUPERMAN BINDS THE TWO CULPRITS WITH THE STRIPS OF IRON PIPING, THEN CALLS THE POLICE!

CRAWFORD SENT THE COAL CAR INTO THE SHAFT WHEN LAUREY GAVE HIM THE SIGNAL--THEY ARE BOTH GUILTY OF ATTEMPTED MURDER! THE POLICE WILL ARRIVE SHORTLY!

I OWE YOU MY LIFE-- AND YOU SAVED THE LIVES OF HUNDREDS OF MINERS BY REMOVING THAT BOMB!

MEANWHILE, LOIS DRIVES BACK TO METROPOLIS, DISAPPOINTED AT HER FAILURE TO INTERVIEW DORIS LAUREY--

OH WELL, I DON'T THINK THERE WAS MUCH OF A STORY IN THE LAUREY GIRL, AFTER ALL! I WONDER WHERE CLARK WENT AFTER THEY THREW HIM OUT?

AT THE PLANET OFFICE--

HELLO, LOIS! HAVE YOU HEARD THE NEWS? FOR ONCE, SUPERMAN HELPED ME TO GET A SCOOP!

WHAT !?

THIS IS TERRIFIC, CLARK! DORIS LAUREY IN NARROW ESCAPE FROM DEATH! HER UNCLE INVOLVED IN PLOT ON HER LIFE! WHAT A STORY!

THE END.

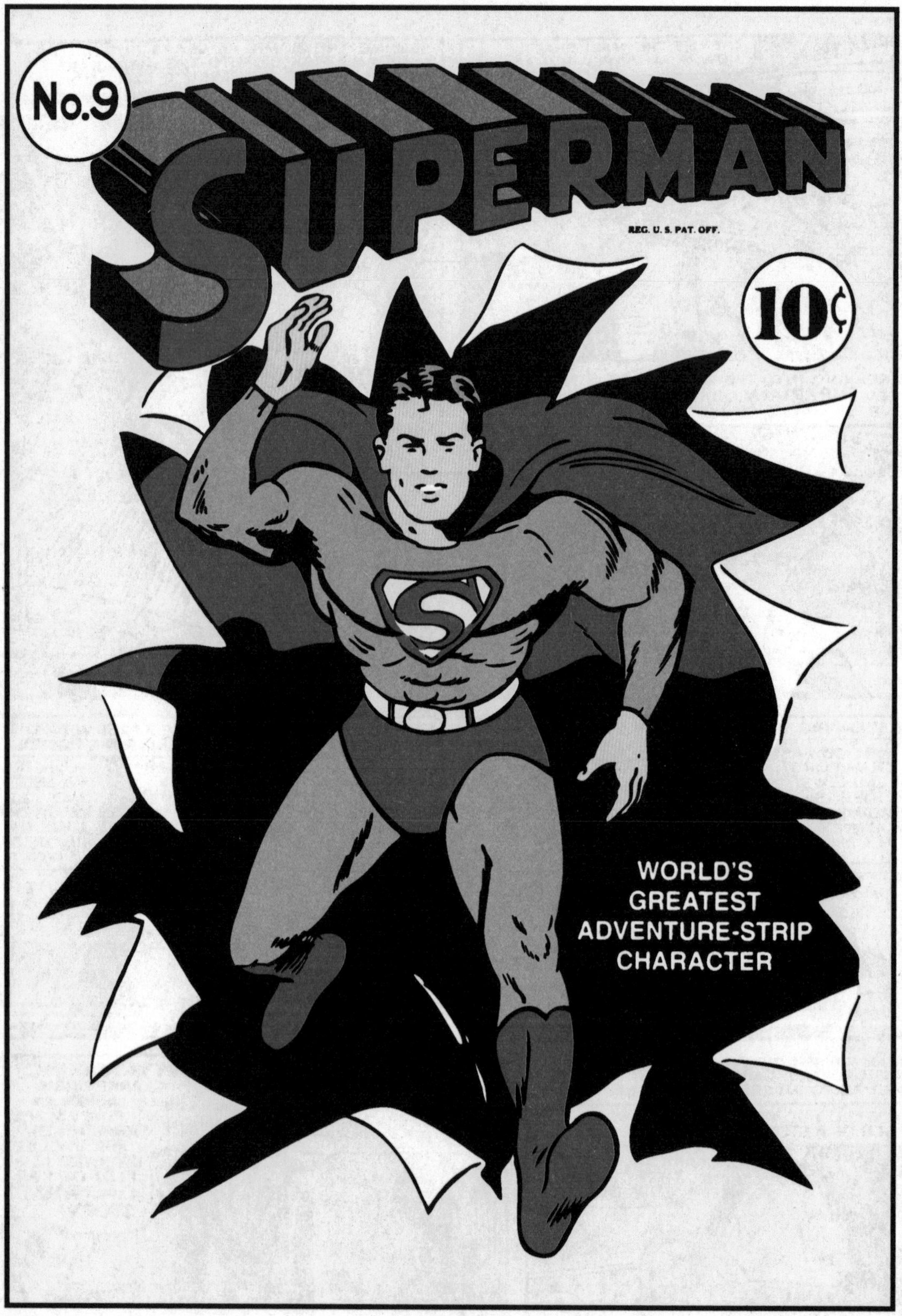
No.9
SUPERMAN
REG. U. S. PAT. OFF.
10¢
WORLD'S GREATEST ADVENTURE-STRIP CHARACTER

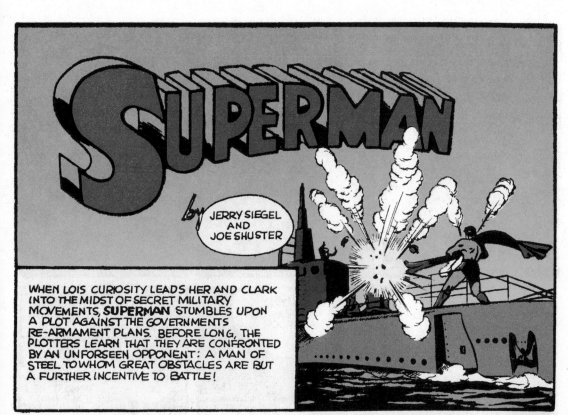

SUPERMAN

by JERRY SIEGEL AND JOE SHUSTER

WHEN LOIS CURIOSITY LEADS HER AND CLARK INTO THE MIDST OF SECRET MILITARY MOVEMENTS, **SUPERMAN** STUMBLES UPON A PLOT AGAINST THE GOVERNMENTS RE-ARMAMENT PLANS. BEFORE LONG, THE PLOTTERS LEARN THAT THEY ARE CONFRONTED BY AN UNFORSEEN OPPONENT: A MAN OF STEEL TO WHOM GREAT OBSTACLES ARE BUT A FURTHER INCENTIVE TO BATTLE!

ONE EVENING AS LOIS LANE AND CLARK KENT DRIVE HOMEWARD FROM A MOVIE. THEY SIGHT UNUSUAL ACTIVITY ON THE WATERFRONT...

LOOK -- HEAVY TRUCKS UNDER AN ESCORT OF MOTORCYCLE POLICE.... AND THERE'S SERGEANT CASEY! LET'S ASK HIM WHAT IT'S ALL ABOUT.

PLEASE, LOIS. CAN'T YOU EVER KEEP YOUR MIND OFF BUSINESS?

WHAT'S GOING ON HERE?

GET GOING! NO ONE IS ALLOWED ON THIS WHARF!

YOU HEARD HIM, LOIS. LET'S GO!

LATER.....

GOSH, I'M SLEEPY! GOOD NIGHT, CLARK. ("-FIRST I'VE GOT TO GET RID OF CLARK! THEN .....(-")

SORT OF SLEEPY MYSELF. SO LONG, LOIS!

BUT SHORTLY AFTER...IN A NEARBY DESERTED ALLEY, CLARK KENT REMOVES HIS OUTER CIVILIAN GARMENTS, TRANSFORMING HIMSELF INTO THE CHAMPION OF JUSTICE... **SUPERMAN!**

SO LOIS IS TIRED, EH? TWENTY TO ONE SHE ISN'T TIRED ENOUGH TO PREVENT HER FROM MAKING A BEE LINE BACK TO THAT WHARF!

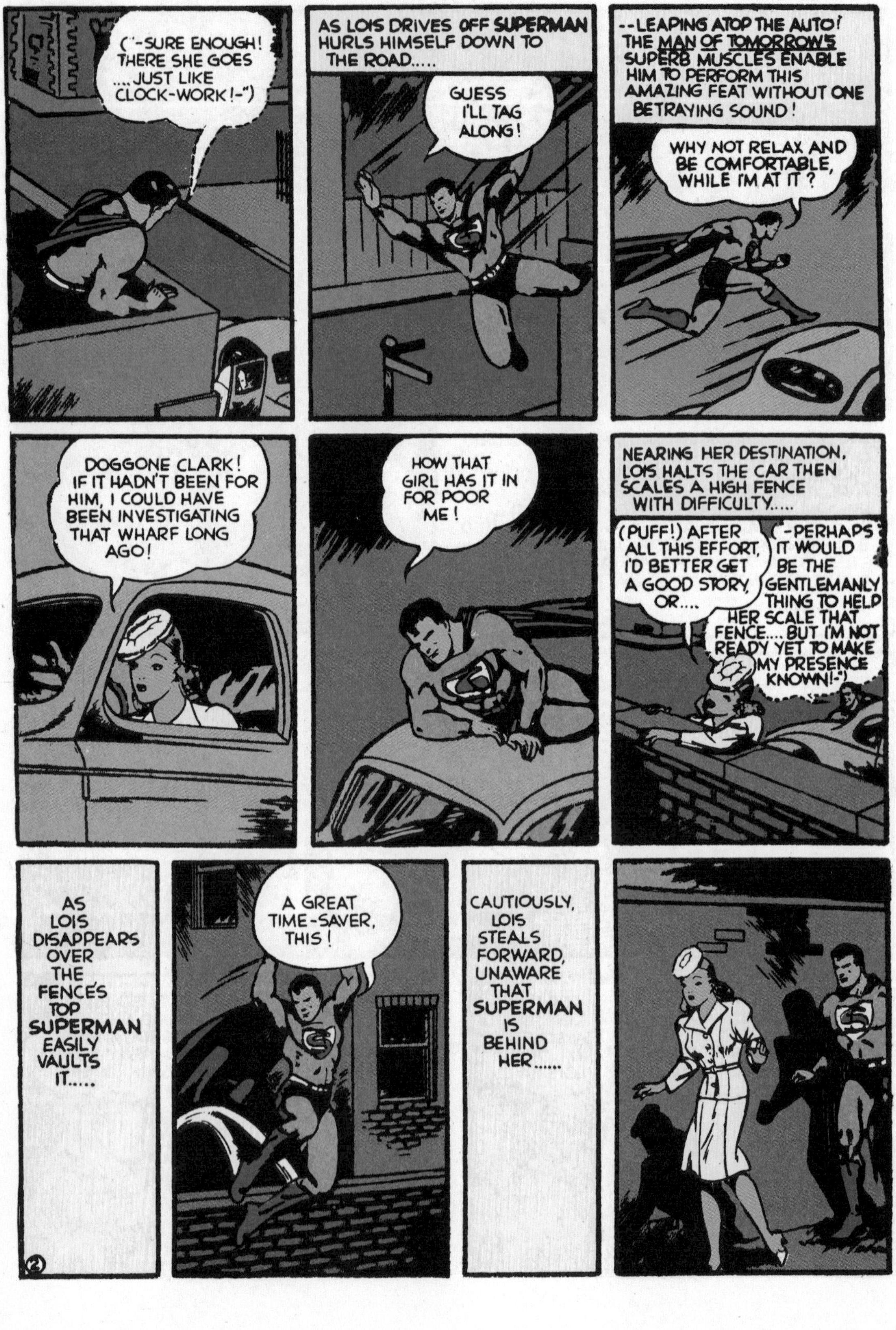
('-SURE ENOUGH! THERE SHE GOES ....JUST LIKE CLOCK-WORK!-")
AS LOIS DRIVES OFF SUPERMAN HURLS HIMSELF DOWN TO THE ROAD.....
GUESS I'LL TAG ALONG!
--LEAPING ATOP THE AUTO! THE MAN OF TOMORROW'S SUPERB MUSCLES ENABLE HIM TO PERFORM THIS AMAZING FEAT WITHOUT ONE BETRAYING SOUND!
WHY NOT RELAX AND BE COMFORTABLE, WHILE I'M AT IT?
DOGGONE CLARK! IF IT HADN'T BEEN FOR HIM, I COULD HAVE BEEN INVESTIGATING THAT WHARF LONG AGO!
HOW THAT GIRL HAS IT IN FOR POOR ME!
NEARING HER DESTINATION, LOIS HALTS THE CAR THEN SCALES A HIGH FENCE WITH DIFFICULTY.....
(PUFF!) AFTER ALL THIS EFFORT, I'D BETTER GET A GOOD STORY, OR....
('-PERHAPS IT WOULD BE THE GENTLEMANLY THING TO HELP HER SCALE THAT FENCE.... BUT I'M NOT READY YET TO MAKE MY PRESENCE KNOWN!-")
AS LOIS DISAPPEARS OVER THE FENCE'S TOP SUPERMAN EASILY VAULTS IT.....
2
A GREAT TIME-SAVER, THIS!
CAUTIOUSLY, LOIS STEALS FORWARD, UNAWARE THAT SUPERMAN IS BEHIND HER......

BUT A SUDDEN INSTINCT WARNS LOIS......

("-SOMEONE BEHIND ME!-")

SWIFTLY, LOIS WHIRLS, BUT AS SHE DOES, SUPERMAN JUST AS SWIFTLY SPRINGS LITHELY BEHIND HER BACK AGAIN!

NO ONE THERE!

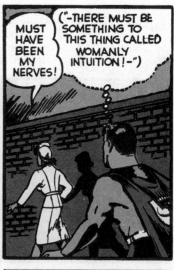

MUST HAVE BEEN MY NERVES!

("-THERE MUST BE SOMETHING TO THIS THING CALLED WOMANLY INTUITION!-")

A LIGHT FLASHING ON THAT FREIGHTER-- SOMEONE'S SIGNALLING!

HALT! WHO GOES THERE?

J-JUST ME! WHEW! YOU SHOULDN'T POP OUT AT PEOPLE LIKE THAT! YOU ALMOST FRIGHTENED ME SILLY!

SUMMONED BY THE SENTRY, MAJOR LESTER AND SERGEANT CASEY COME ON THE RUN......

IT'S THAT GIRL REPORTER!

LOIS--I WARNED YOU THAT IF YOU INTERFERED, YOU'D GO TO JAIL--AND THAT'S JUST WHAT YOU'RE GOING TO DO!

J-JAIL? I'M SURE YOU WON'T DO THAT WHEN I TELL YOU OF SOMETHING IMPORTANT!

I THREATENED JAIL, AND I'M A MAN OF MY WORD!

STOP BANDYING WORDS WITH HER, SERGEANT! TAKE HER AWAY!

WILL YOU LISTEN TO ME! I SAID I KNEW SOMETHING IMPORTANT!

SOMEONE FLASHED A SIGNAL FROM THE FREIGHTER!

A SIGNAL!?! ESPIONAGE!

WE'LL SOON SEE IF LOIS IS TELLING THE TRUTH. AND IF SHE ISN'T.....!

AT THAT MOMENT--! SUPERMAN'S TELESCOPIC VISION ENABLES HIM TO SIGHT A DECKHAND DROP OFF THE SIDE OF THE FREIGHTER WITH A FLASHLIGHT.....

WONDER WHAT HE'S UP TO?

WE'VE MADE A COMPLETE SEARCH OF THIS BOAT. NONE OF TH' DECKHANDS QUESTIONED COULD HAVE SIGNALLED.

BUT I TELL YOU! WITH MY OWN EYES, I SAW....

YOU'VE LIED ENOUGH, YOUNG LADY! GET INTO THAT CABIN!

THERE -THAT WILL HOLD HER UNTIL A PATROL WAGON COMES!

SHE'S VIOLATED A MILITARY LAW AND MAY BE CHARGED WITH ESPIONAGE!

MEANWHILE -- SUPERMAN, UNDERWATER, CLOSELY PURSUES THE DECKHAND....

("-I'M SURE HE'S UP TO NO GOOD!-")

HE'S SEATED ON LAND-AS THO WAITING FOR SOMEONE -OR SOMETHING. BUT FOR WHAT--??

NEXT INSTANT, THE MAN OF STEEL LEARNS THE ANSWER AS A DARK LOW SHAPE RAISES ABOVE THE WAVES...!

A SUBMARINE!

EMERGING QUICKLY ON DECK A GUN CREW FIRES TOWARD THE FREIGHTER....

....DESTROYING ONE OF THE FUNNELS, BUT CAUSING LITTLE DAMAGE

LOIS CONFINED ON THAT FREIGHTER -- I'VE GOT TO ACT FAST IF I'M TO SAVE HER LIFE !

AS A SECOND SHELL IS FIRED, SUPERMAN STREAKS UP TOWARD IT, RECEIVING IT FULL UPON HIS CHEST...

STOPPED THAT ONE !

AS THE CREW PREPARES TO FIRE AGAIN, DOWN SWOOPS SUPERMAN...!

NO YOU DON'T -- NOT THIS TIME !

I'M GOING TO TWIST THIS SHINY NEW CANNON OF YOURS... JUST TO TEACH YOU A LESSON !

FIRE !

AS THE SHELL IS FIRED, SUPERMAN BLOCKS THE CANNON WITH HIS BODY SO THAT IT EXPLODES !

SUPERMAN LEAPS FOR THE TURRET COVER, BUT BEFORE HE CAN REACH IT, IT SLAMS SHUT...

BASHFUL. EH?

NEXT INSTANT, THE SUB BEGINS TO SUBMERGE...

NOT THINKING OF RUNNING OUT ON A FIGHT, ARE YOU?

NEXT INSTANT, A TORPEDO IS LAUNCHED -- NOT TOWARD THE FREIGHTER, BUT TOWARD THE SHORE...

WAIT FOR ME!

BEFORE THE MAN OF TO-MORROW CAN REACH SHORE, THE TORPEDO STRIKES ITS DESTINATION....

THE END OF THE TRAITOROUS DECKHAND!

WHIRLING, SUPERMAN SWIMS AT TERRIFIC SPEED AFTER THE FLEEING SUB, RAPIDLY OVERTAKING IT...

THEY WERE AFRAID THE DECKHAND MIGHT TALK! WELL, LET'S SEE IF I CAN LOOSEN THEIR TONGUES!

SEIZING THE PROPELLER, SUPERMAN RIPS IT CLEAR OFF!

OFF YOU GO!

HE POUNDS A MORSE CODE MESSAGE ON THE VESSEL'S SIDE...

THIS IS TO WARN THEM TO OFFER NO OPPOSITION OR- I'M CRASHING IN!

THE SUB RISES TO THE SURFACE. BUT AS SUPERMAN GRASPS THE TURRET WITH THE INTENTION OF RIPPING IT OPEN -- THE GREAT SUBMARINE EXPLODES!

SHORTLY AFTER....

THEY CHOSE TO PERISH -- ALONG WITH THEIR SECRET! NOW TO HURRY BACK TO THE WHARF, AS CLARK KENT, AND SECURE LOIS' RELEASE!

LATER -- AT THE WHARF....

I'VE BEEN LOOKING ALL OVER FOR YOU, CASEY. I CAN'T FIND LOIS. PERHAPS YOU CAN HELP ME.

SHE'S ABOARD THAT FREIGHTER -- A MILITARY PRISONER! THERE HAVE BEEN MANY UNUSUAL OCCURRENCES TONIGHT, AND SHE MAY KNOW SOME OF THE ANSWERS.

LOIS UNDER ARREST? NOW, CASEY, YOU KNOW BETTER THAN TO SUSPECT LOIS OF ESPIONAGE. RELEASE HER OR THE DAILY PLANET WILL PUBLISH AN EXTRA THAT WILL...

ER-MAYBE WE'D BETTER LET HER GO AFTER ALL.

VERY WELL. BUT ON CONDITION THAT SHE OFFER ALL CO-OPERATION!

CLARK'S X-RAY VISION ACQUAINTS HIM WITH AN ASTONISHING DISCOVERY....

("-MERCURY!- THE U.S. MUST BE IMPORTING TREMENDOUS QUANTITIES TO BUILD UP A SUFFICIENT RESERVE SUPPLY FOR DEFENSE PURPOSES SHOULD THE SOURCE OF SUPPLY SUDDENLY BE CUT OFF!-")

YOU'RE FREE TO GO, NOW.

I KNEW YOU COULDN'T HOLD ME. AND IT'S A GOOD THING FOR YOU THAT YOU RELEASED ME BEFORE I... BEFORE I LOST MY TEMPER!

YOU CAN THANK THIS YOUNG MAN FOR YOUR RELEASE. IT WAS DUE ENTIRELY TO HIS EFFORTS!

A CHECKUP OF THE SHIP'S PERSONNEL HAS SHOWN A DECKHAND TO BE MISSING. A CHECK BY TELEPHOTO WITH WASHINGTON OF HIS FINGERPRINTS SHOWS THAT HE FORMERLY WORKED AT THE METROPOLIS RESERVE DEPOT WHERE WAR SUPPLIES ARE STORED. WOULD YOU CARE TO LOOK THE DEPOT OVER TOMORROW?

YOU--AWAKE! I THOUGHT BY THIS TIME YOU'D BE FAST ASLEEP!

DELIGHTED!

NEXT MORNING -LOIS AND CLARK ARE GREETED AT THE RESERVE DEPOT BY MAJOR LESTER....

⑦

STORED HERE ARE TIN, MERCURY, RUBBER, AND SILK-- ESSENTIAL WARTIME MATERIALS!

("-I DETECT THE SOUND OF TICKING... FROM BELOW!-") MY FEET PAIN ME. MIND IF I REST HERE UNTIL YOU RETURN?

HOW INTERESTING!

THE MOMENT THE OTHER TWO WALK OFF, CLARK MAKES USE OF HIS X-RAY VISION TO DISCOVER, IN A TUNNEL BELOW....

THERE! IT'S SET!

IT WILL GO OFF IN A FEW MINUTES -- DETONATING THE VAST STORE OF MUNITIONS ABOVE!

THEN, LET'S GET OUT OF HERE!

SWIFTLY, CLARK KENT STRIPS OFF HIS OUTER GARMENTS....

TIME FOR SUPERMAN TO MAKE HIS ENTRY!

DOWN AT THE GROUND DIVES SUPERMAN, BURROWING OUT OF VIEW....!

A MOMENT LATER HE DROPS DOWN TOWARDS THE CONSPIRATORS AMIDST A SHOWER OF EARTH..

LOOK! A MAN!

SHOOT HIM!

BEFORE THE SPIES HAVE TIME TO REALIZE WHAT IS HAPPENING SUPERMAN SNATCHES THEIR WEAPONS AWAY.....

I'LL TAKE THOSE!

THE KNIFE! USE THE KNIFE!

AS THE MEN ATTACK SUPERMAN WITH SHARP BLADES, THEIR LEADER DASHES AWAY ALONG THE TUNNEL....

DON'T!

GOT HIM!

BUT SECONDS LATER—TO THEIR ASTONISHMENT...

THE BLADE-- BROKEN!

SAME HERE!

YOU— YOU'RE NOT INJURED!

I WANTED YOUR LEADER TO THINK HE WAS GETTING AWAY!

WHY DID YOU PRETEND TO BE?

SNATCHING UP HIS FOUR OPPONENTS, SUPERMAN RACES ALONG THE TUNNEL....

HEY—!

LET GO OF US!

YOU'RE COMING WITH ME!

AS SUPERMAN EMERGES AT THE TUNNEL'S ENTRANCE, HE SIGHTS....

THAT PLANE! I WONDER IF....

AGAIN AVAILING HIMSELF OF HIS TELESCOPIC VISION, SUPERMAN SIGHTS THE ESCAPING SPY LEADER AT THE CONTROLS.....

GOT AWAY IN TIME! NOW TO ATTEND THAT MEETING, AS PRE-ARRANGED!

YIIIII!

WH-WHERE YOU TAKIN' US?

UP INTO THE AIR, OBVIOUSLY. WHY? DON'T YOU WANT TO ACCOMPANY ME?

NO! NO!!

VERY WELL. THEN MAKE YOURSELVES COMFORTABLE ...IF YOU CAN!

DON'T LEAVE US HERE!

HEIGHTS SCARE ME!!

NOW TO PUT ON A LITTLE STEAM AND OVERTAKE THAT PLANE!

GOT IT! I'LL JUST DRIFT ALONG UNTIL IT REACHES ITS DESTINATION!

WHEN THE PLANE NEARS THE WASHINGTON AIRPORT, SUPERMAN LEAPS ATOP A HANGAR.....

⑨

THE SPY LEADER IS TAKING A TAXI INTO THE CITY. I'LL KEEP IT IN SIGHT!

LATER -- OUTSIDE THE SENATE OFFICE BUILDING....

HE'S ENTERING SENATOR GALSWORTHY'S OFFICE! -THIS OUGHT TO PROVE INTERESTING!

THE SPY LEADER ENTERS A CROWDED OFFICE.....

THOUGHT YOU'D NEVER GET HERE, DER-WING! YOU'RE LATE.

I WAS UNAVOIDABLY DETAINED GATHERING LAST MINUTE MATERIAL, BUT I'LL HAVE **PLENTY** TO TELL YOU!

SENATOR GALSWORTHY HASN'T ARRIVED YET.

BEGIN YOUR ADDRESS ANYWAY!

AS YOU ALL KNOW, I AM CHAIRMAN OF THE **COMMITTEE AGAINST MILITARISM**. SENATOR GALSWORTHY HAS KINDLY PERMITTED US TO USE THIS OFFICE FOR OUR MEETING, BECAUSE HE SYMPATHIZES WITH OUR CAUSE.--OUR STAND: NO REARMAMENT IN THE U.S., AND NO AID TO WARRING DEMOCRACIES!

I'VE JUST RECEIVED WORD THAT SOME OF THE ARMY'S SUPPLIES STORED HERE IN METROP-OLIS ARE ABOUT TO BE EXPLODED-- JUST SO THAT THE GRAFTERS CAN SELL NEW MATERIALS.... AT THE TAXPAYER'S EXPENSE!

IT'S OUTRAGEOUS!

WE'LL PROTEST!

WHEN YOU LEAVE THIS OFFICE I WANT YOU TO BEGIN THE BATTLE IMMEDIATELY. ORGANIZE YOUR COMMUNITIES-- BE MILITANT IN YOUR FIGHT AGAINST RE-ARMAMENT!

BRAVO!

WITH YOU TO LEAD US WE CAN'T FAIL!

BUT AFTER MOST OF THE MEN DEPART, AND ONLY A FEW REMAIN......

NOW THAT THE GULLIBLE SAPS HAVE GONE, HOW ABOUT GETTING DOWN TO BRASS TACKS?

WHAT ARE **WE** GOING TO GET OUT OF THIS?

YOU'RE NOT OPPOSING RE-ARMAMENT JUST FOR THE LOVE OF IT. WHERE DO WE CASH IN?

YOU AREN'T WIDE-EYED PATRIOTS LIKE THE OTHERS. I'LL TAKE YOU INTO MY CONFIDENCE

I AM IN THE EMPLOY OF A WARRING TOTALITARIAN NATION. MY DUTY HERE IN AMERICA IS TO SEE THAT NO AID IS OFFERED TO THE DEMOCRACIES, AND THAT THE U.S. FAILS TO RE-ARM. LATER--WHEN THE COUNTRY I REPRESENT TAKES OVER AMERICA-- YOU AND I WILL PROFIT!

SPLENDID!

WE'LL ALL BE BIG-SHOTS WHEN THAT DAY ARRIVES!

SUPERMAN ACTS....

("-THIS CONVERSATION IS TOO INCRIMINATING TO GO UNRECORDED!-")

⑩

RACING SO SWIFTLY HE CAN-NOT BE SEEN, **SUPERMAN** FLIPS THE CONTROLS OF A DICTOGRAPH MACHINE ON THE DESK....

("-THAT'LL DO THE TRICK!-")

SWISH

AFTER **SUPERMAN** LEAVES THE ROOM....!

THAT STRONG WIND -- ALMOST LIKE A HURRICANE!

WHAT COULD HAVE CAUSED IT?

NEVER MIND. IT'S GONE!

ALREADY THE NATION I REPRESENT IS MAKING ACTIVE EFFORTS TO INTERFERE WITH THIS COUNTRY'S EFFORTS TO RE-ARM. ONLY YESTERDAY ONE OF OUR SUBMARINE'S ATTACKED A SUPPLY SHIP UNFORTUNATELY, IT WAS DESTROYED.

THE DICTAPHONE RECORD WHIRLS RAPIDLY, TAKING DOWN EVERY INCRIMINATING WORD.....

("-LET THEM PLOT! EVERY WORD THEY SPEAK SEALS THEIR DOOM!-")

("-SOMEONE EAVESDROPPING OUTSIDE MY OFFICE!-")

WHAT ARE YOU UP TO?

SENATOR GALSWORTHY!

UH-HH! WHA--!

SH-HH! LISTEN!

THE SENATOR'S EYES WIDEN AS HE OVERHEARS THE CONVERSATION WITHIN HIS OFFICE....

AS SUPERMAN RELEASES HIS CAPTIVE....

DERWING HAS BEEN IMPOSING UPON YOUR GOOD FAITH TO SABOTAGE THIS COUNTRY'S BEST INTERESTS, ARE YOU GOING TO LET HIM GET AWAY WITH IT?

JUST WATCH ME!

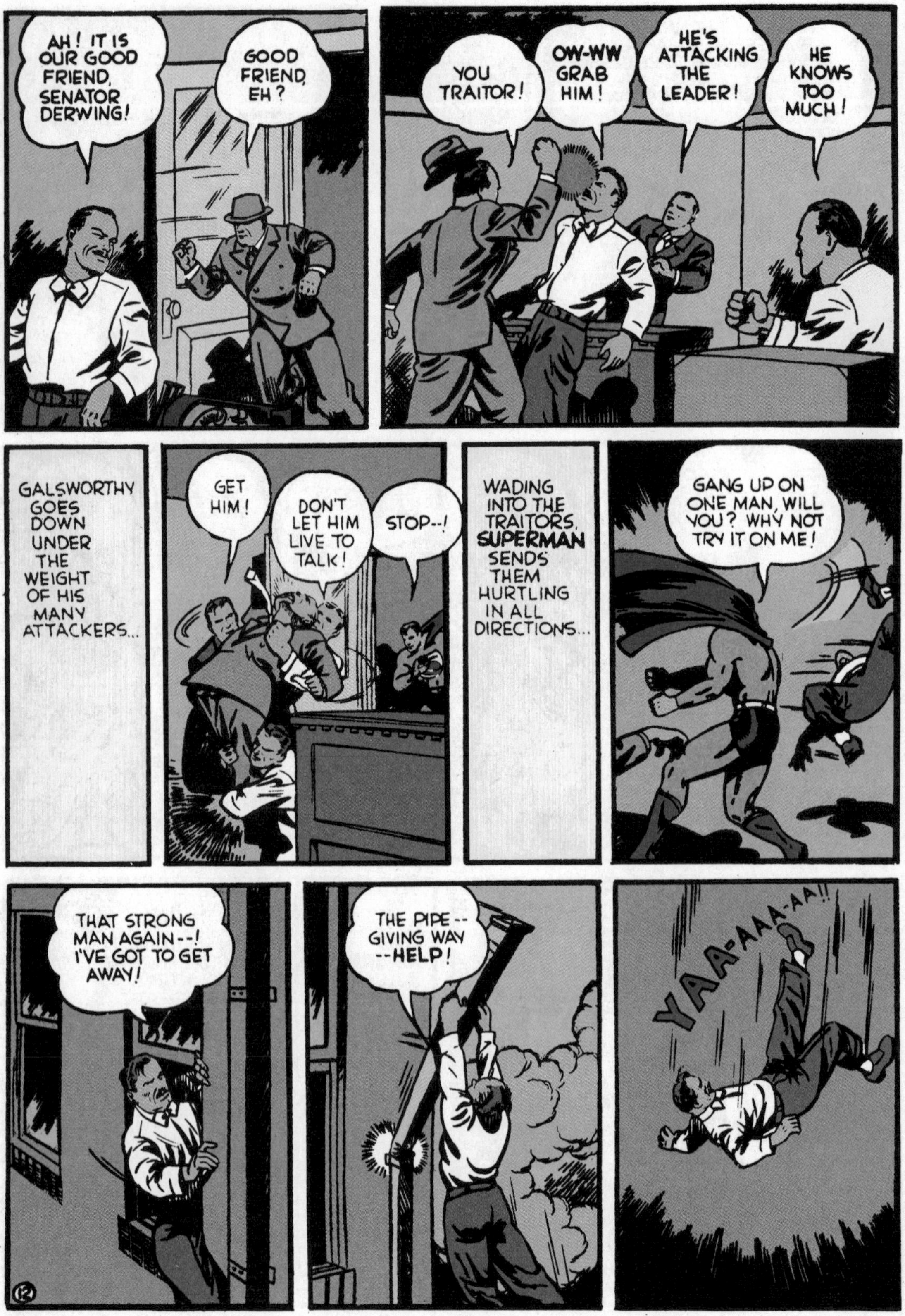
AH! IT IS OUR GOOD FRIEND, SENATOR DERWING!
GOOD FRIEND, EH?
YOU TRAITOR!
OW-WW GRAB HIM!
HE'S ATTACKING THE LEADER!
HE KNOWS TOO MUCH!
GALSWORTHY GOES DOWN UNDER THE WEIGHT OF HIS MANY ATTACKERS...
GET HIM!
DON'T LET HIM LIVE TO TALK!
STOP--!
WADING INTO THE TRAITORS, SUPERMAN SENDS THEM HURTLING IN ALL DIRECTIONS...
GANG UP ON ONE MAN, WILL YOU? WHY NOT TRY IT ON ME!
THAT STRONG MAN AGAIN--! I'VE GOT TO GET AWAY!
12
THE PIPE--GIVING WAY --HELP!
YAA-AAA-AA!!

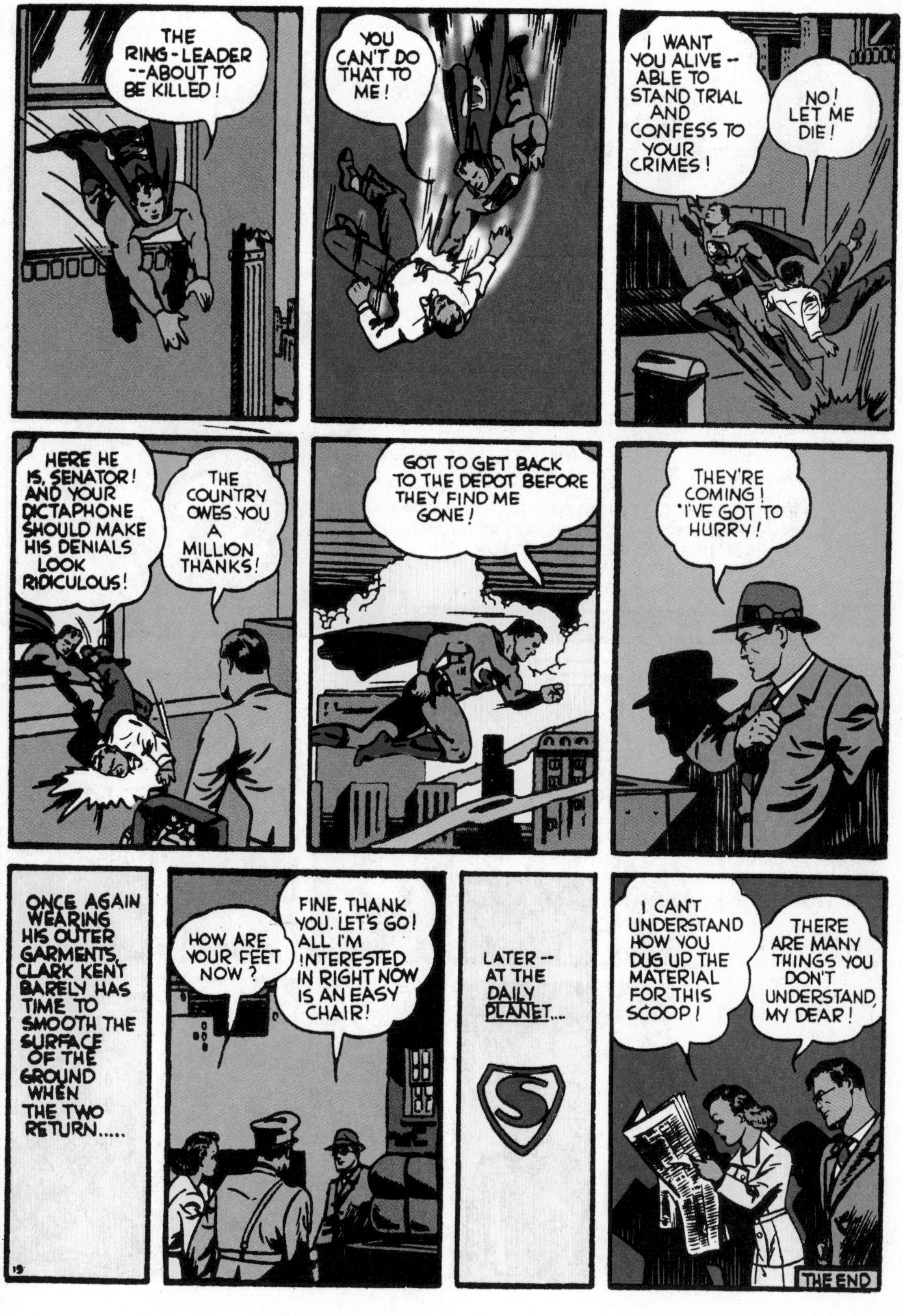
THE RING-LEADER --ABOUT TO BE KILLED!
YOU CAN'T DO THAT TO ME!
I WANT YOU ALIVE -- ABLE TO STAND TRIAL AND CONFESS TO YOUR CRIMES!
NO! LET ME DIE!
HERE HE IS, SENATOR! AND YOUR DICTAPHONE SHOULD MAKE HIS DENIALS LOOK RIDICULOUS!
THE COUNTRY OWES YOU A MILLION THANKS!
GOT TO GET BACK TO THE DEPOT BEFORE THEY FIND ME GONE!
THEY'RE COMING! I'VE GOT TO HURRY!
ONCE AGAIN WEARING HIS OUTER GARMENTS, CLARK KENT BARELY HAS TIME TO SMOOTH THE SURFACE OF THE GROUND WHEN THE TWO RETURN.....
19
HOW ARE YOUR FEET NOW?
FINE, THANK YOU. LET'S GO! ALL I'M INTERESTED IN RIGHT NOW IS AN EASY CHAIR!
LATER -- AT THE DAILY PLANET....
S
I CAN'T UNDERSTAND HOW YOU DUG UP THE MATERIAL FOR THIS SCOOP!
THERE ARE MANY THINGS YOU DON'T UNDERSTAND, MY DEAR!
THE END

SUPERMAN

by
JERRY SIEGEL and JOE SHUSTER

BULWARK OF MAN'S CIVILIZATION IS HIS COURT OF LAW WHERE WRONGS ARE RIGHTED AND CRIMINALS PUNISHED ACCORDING TO THEIR MERITS, BUT WHEN EVILDOERS SEEK TO INJECT THEIR VILLAINOUS METHODS DIRECTLY INTO THE COURTROOM, **SUPERMAN**, SUPER-STRONG CHAMPION OF JUSTICE, STEPS IN TO TEACH THE CRIMINAL HORDE RESPECT FOR LAW AND ORDER....

LOIS LANE AND CLARK KENT, REPORTERS ON THE CRUSADING DAILY PLANET, METROPOLIS LEADING NEWSPAPER, HURRY TOWARD CRIMINAL COURT....

HURRY, CLARK! THE TRIAL IS ABOUT TO BEGIN! AND YOU KNOW HOW MUCH OF A STICKLER FOR PUNCTUALITY JUDGE CRANE IS!

IF YOU HADN'T STOPPED TO POWDER YOUR NOSE HALF A DOZEN TIMES, WE'D HAVE BEEN IN THE COURTROOM LONG AGO!

LATER...

THAT'S ODD! IT'S WAY PAST STARTING TIME!

THAT PRACTICALLY RATES AN EXTRA!

CLARK NOTES THAT THE DEFENDANT, JOE GATSON FACING THE POSSIBILITY OF GOING TO JAIL FOR A MINOR RACKETEERING CHARGE, DOESN'T APPEAR PARTICULARLY WORRIED...

①

THE JUDGE FINALLY ENTERS THE COURTROOM --TWENTY MINUTES LATE....

THIS COURT WILL ADJOURN UNTIL TEN O'CLOCK TOMORROW!

THE COURT ALREADY ADJOURNED! THAT'S WHAT I CALL FAST WORK!

DID YOU NOTICE HOW PALE AND DRAWN JUDGE CRANE APPEARS?

WHAT CLARK'S SUPER-HEARING OVERHEARS...

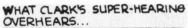

HE CAN'T DO THIS TO ME! I'LL...

CAREFUL, JOE! DON'T START ANYTHING... YET!

LOOK, CLARK! GATSON IS WALKING DIRECTLY TOWARD US!

D-DO YOU THINK HE'S READ ANY OF THOSE THINGS I WROTE ABOUT HIM? PARTICULARILY THE ONE IN WHICH I CALLED HIM A "BEETLE-BROWED MORON"?

SO YOU'RE CLARK KENT, EH? THE REPORTER WHO'S BEEN MAKIN' ALL THOSE SMART CRACKS ABOUT ME!

ER--I-- OF COURSE, I DIDN'T MEAN THEM!

WELL, YOU'D BETTER LOCK THAT TYPEWRITER OF YOURS, SEE! YOU'RE LIABLE TO INSULT ME JUST ONCE TOO OFTEN!

OUCH!

HIT HIM, CLARK!

WHY DID YOU STAND THERE, SHAKING LIKE A FOOL? YOU SHOULD HAVE PUNCHED THE HOODLUM!

I-I THOUGHT OF IT. BUT BEFORE I COULD MAKE UP MY MIND, HE WALKED OFF!

AND THAT'S JUST EXACTLY WHAT I'M DOING! I CAN STAND JUST SO MUCH OF YOUR COWARDICE, AND NO MORE!

BUT, LOIS--!

LOCATING A SECLUDED SPOT, CLARK REMOVES HIS OUTER GARMENTS TRANSFORMING HIMSELF INTO THE DYNAMIC SUPERMAN!

THE JUDGE SEEMED VERY WORRIED ABOUT SOMETHING. I'LL SEE IF HE NEEDS HELP!

STEPPING THRU THE WINDOW, **SUPERMAN** SWARMS UP THE SIDE OF THE COURTHOUSE LIKE A STARTLED ANTHROPOID...

...UNTIL HE IS SUSPENDED OUTSIDE THE JUDGE'S CHAMBER...

WHAT--?

WITHIN THE CHAMBER...

I CAN'T FACE THIS ANY LONGER!

JUDGE CRANE'S FINGER TIGHTENS ON THE GUN'S TRIGGER, PREPARATORY TO LAUNCHING A BULLET INTO HIS BRAIN....

BEFORE THE FATAL EXPLOSION CAN OCCUR **SUPERMAN** SPRINGS IN THRU THE WINDOW WITH DART-LIKE SPEED, AND GRASPS THE BULLET CYLINDER BEFORE IT CAN COMPLETE ITS ROTATION....

SUPERMAN!

I'M SURPRIZED, JUDGE! A MAN OF YOUR CALIBRE-- STOOPING TO SUICIDE!

CHAMBER

WHY DID YOU DO IT?

MY DAUGHTER, SYLVIA, KIDNAPPED! I'VE BEEN INSTRUCTED TO EITHER FREE GATSON, OR I'D NEVER SEE HER AGAIN!

I'VE BEEN SUFFERING A LIVING DEATH THESE LAST FEW DAYS WHAT A CHOICE! EITHER TO BETRAY MY OFFICE-- OR FORSAKE SYLVIA. IT'S TOO MUCH FOR ME --AND SO- I CHOSE THE EASY WAY OUT!

UNFORTUNATELY, YOUR DEATH WOULD SOLVE **NOTHING!** YOUR DAUGHTER WOULD STILL BE IN DANGER, AND GATSON WOULD BE FREE TO FLOUT THE LAW MORE THAN EVER.

THE TELEPHONE RINGING! --PERHAPS IT'S NEWS ABOUT MY DAUGHTER!

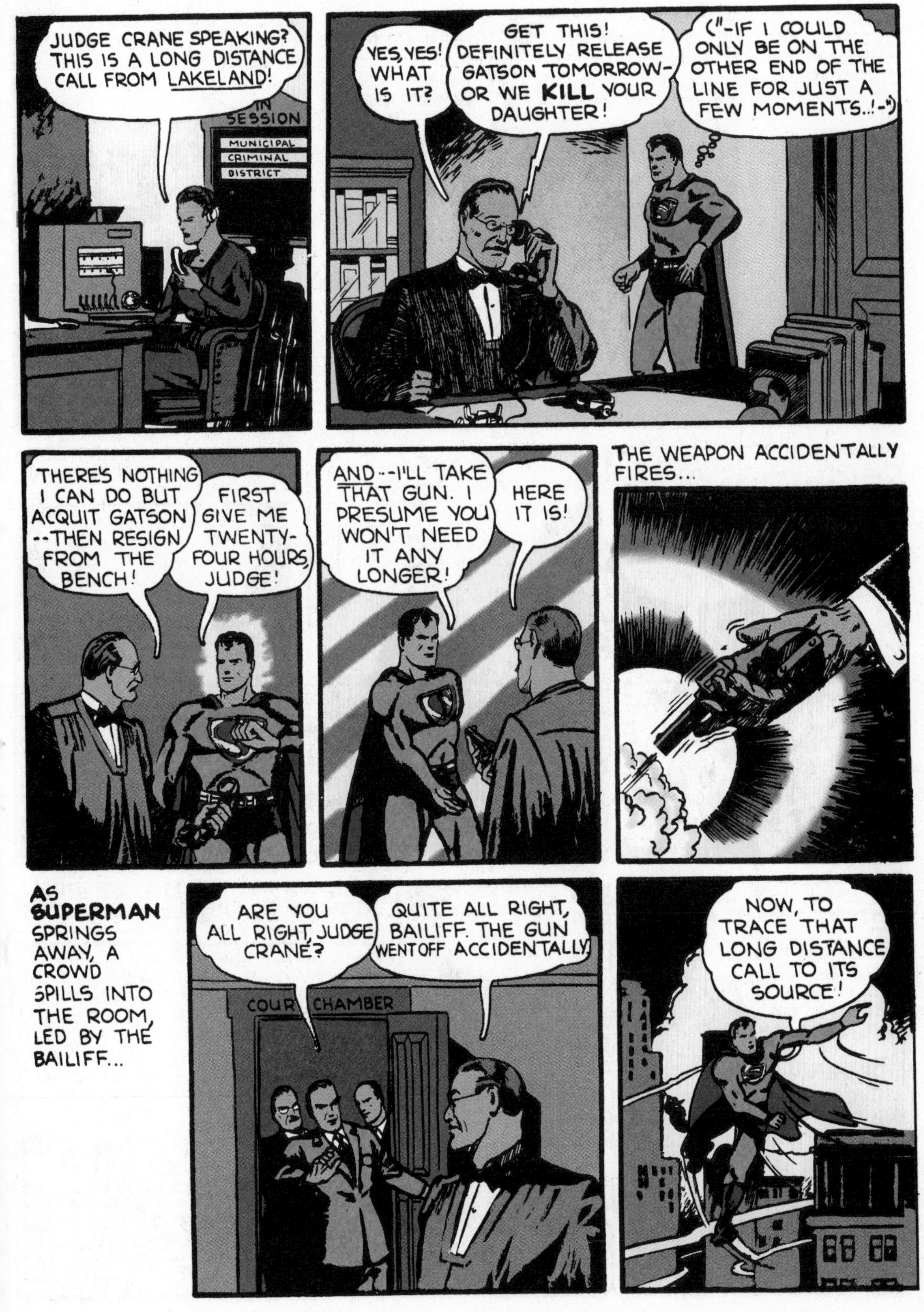
JUDGE CRANE SPEAKING? THIS IS A LONG DISTANCE CALL FROM LAKELAND!
IN SESSION
MUNICIPAL
CRIMINAL
DISTRICT
YES, YES! WHAT IS IT?
GET THIS! DEFINITELY RELEASE GATSON TOMORROW- OR WE KILL YOUR DAUGHTER!
("-IF I COULD ONLY BE ON THE OTHER END OF THE LINE FOR JUST A FEW MOMENTS..!-")
THERE'S NOTHING I CAN DO BUT ACQUIT GATSON --THEN RESIGN FROM THE BENCH!
FIRST GIVE ME TWENTY-FOUR HOURS, JUDGE!
AND--I'LL TAKE THAT GUN. I PRESUME YOU WON'T NEED IT ANY LONGER!
HERE IT IS!
THE WEAPON ACCIDENTALLY FIRES...
AS SUPERMAN SPRINGS AWAY, A CROWD SPILLS INTO THE ROOM, LED BY THE BAILIFF...
ARE YOU ALL RIGHT, JUDGE CRANE?
QUITE ALL RIGHT, BAILIFF. THE GUN WENT OFF ACCIDENTALLY!
COUR CHAMBER
NOW, TO TRACE THAT LONG DISTANCE CALL TO ITS SOURCE!

SHORTLY AFTER... SUPERMAN CLAMBERS UP THE SIDE OF THE TELEPHONE BUILDING...

THE OFFICE WINDOW OF THE CHIEF ENGINEER --DEAD AHEAD!

THE ENGINEER WHIRLS AS HE HEARS THE WINDOW-LOCK SNAP BEHIND HIM...

WHAT--?

DON'T BE ALARMED. I JUST WANT TO ASK YOU A FEW QUESTIONS!

I'LL DO NOTHING OF THE-- YE GODS! IT'S-- IT'S SUPERMAN!

NOW, WILL YOU TELL ME WHERE THE LONG DISTANCE CALL TO JUDGE CRANE CAME FROM?

YOU SAY THE CALL CAME FROM SAN COLUMBO?

BUT WHEN THE ENGINEER CONTACTS THE OPERATOR IN SAN COLUMBO....

WHAT'S THAT? YOU SAY YOU DID NOT PUT THROUGH ANY SUCH CALL?

I CAN'T UNDERSTAND IT! THE CALL CAME FROM SAN COLUMBO--AND YET IT DIDN'T! CAN YOU EXPLAIN THAT?

THAT'S ONE OF THE THINGS I CAN'T ANSWER--

...YET! BUT THE DAY IS YOUNG!

LATER. WHEN THE MAN OF STEEL RETURNS TO THE DAILY PLANET IN HIS IDENTITY AS CLARK KENT.

I'M CERTAIN THERE'S SOMETHING STRANGE AFOOT! SYLVIA CRANE WAS TO BE THE GUEST-OF-HONOR AT A LUNCHEON TODAY AND SHE DIDN'T EVEN SHOW UP!

I'LL GIVE YOU CREDIT FOR ONE THING, LOIS-- AN ACTIVE IMAGINATION! BUT THAT'S ALL YOU'RE DOING ..IMAGINING THINGS!

GLANCING THRU A WINDOW, CLARK NOTES A LINEMAN ATTACHING HIS HANDSET TO A TELEPHONE CIRCUIT ON A TELEPHONE POLE....

("-SAY! I WONDER IF THAT'S HOW THOSE MYSTERIOUS CALLS GOT ONTO A TELEPHONE CIRCUIT! -")

RETIRING TO A STORE-ROOM, CLARK CHANGES TO HIS SUPERMAN GARMENTS....

HERE'S WHERE I FIND OUT!

A GREAT LEAP LAUNCHES THE MAN OF TOMORROW HIGH THRU THE AIR OVER BUILDINGS, HOUSES, FIELDS, RIVERS....

MY TELESCOPIC X-RAY VISION ENABLES ME TO SEE THE LONG DISTANCE CABLE BENEATH THE GROUND, BUT IT SEEMS ALMOST IMPOSSIBLE THAT SOMEONE COULD CUT THRU THE LEAD SHEATH AND PICK OUT THE PROPER WIRES TO BREAK IN ON THE DIFFERENT LONG DISTANCE CIRCUITS!

LATER--AS SUPERMAN SOARS OVER A SWAMP...

A CABLE-BOX AND PLATFORM ATTACHED TO THAT POLE! I'LL INVESTIGATE!

LOCKED! BUT THAT'S NO OBSTACLE...!

BUT BEFORE SUPERMAN CAN MAKE A THOROUGH INVESTIGATION....

SOMEONE COMING!

FROM CONCEALMENT IN THE HIGH GRASS, THE MAN OF STEEL WATCHES TWO MEN APPROACH ONE OF THEM CLIMBS TO THE PLATFORM.

ODD ... I DON'T REMEMBER LEAVING THIS UNLOCKED!

JUDGE CRANE, THIS IS YOUR LAST WARNING! EITHER SET GATSON FREE TOMORROW MORN-ING, OR YOU GET YOUR DAUGHTER'S BODY IN THE AFTERNOON!

⑥

("—WHAT A LUCKY BREAK! MY HUNCH WAS CORRECT! AND THESE MEN ARE DIRECTLY INVOLVED IN THE KIDNAPPING!—")

AS THE TWO MEN CLIMB INTO A ROWBOAT AND SET OFF INTO THE SWAMP, **SUPERMAN** TRAILS THEM!

BUT SUDDENLY....

QUICKSAND!

BEFORE HE SCARCELY REALIZES WHAT HAS HAPPENED, THE MAN OF TOMORROW SINKS DOWN TO HIS WAIST!

I OUGHT TO GET FREE WITHOUT ANY DIFFICULTY...

—BUT NOT IF THIS FELLOW CAN HELP IT!

AS THE ALLIGATOR LEAPS UPON HIM, THE TWO GRIP IN STRUGGLE, ALL THE MORE DEADLY BECAUSE OF THE TREACHEROUS QUICKSAND'S MENACE...

A QUICK FLIP OF HIS WRISTS, AND THE HUGE CREATURE GOES SAILING ALOFT..

WE'LL WRESTLE SOME OTHER TIME ...NOT NOW!

TERRIFIC EFFORT ...THEN... **SUPERMAN** LEAPS FREE OF THE QUICKSAND'S GRIP!

NOW, TO CONTINUE THE CHASE!

IT TAKES BUT MOMENTS FOR **SUPERMAN** TO OVERTAKE THE MEN. HE KEEPS THEM IN SIGHT BY LEAPING NIMBLY FROM TREE TO TREE....

THAT SHACK OVER YONDER MUST BE THEIR DESTINATION!

AS THEY ENTER THE SHACK, HE APPROACHES THE WINDOW....

("-SYLVIA CRANE --A PRISONER IN THERE!-")

PLEASE LET ME GO!

HEAR THAT? HO! HO!

WE'LL FREE YOU WHEN YOUR DAD ACQUITS GATSON --MAYBE!

I WON'T FORGET THIS! I'LL REMEMBER YOUR FACES! I'LL--

YOU'LL DO **WHAT**?!

THAT'S MY CUE!

WHAT--?

KEEP AWAY FROM THAT GIRL!

GET HIM!

SHOOT HIM DOWN!

WHAT A SURPRIZE **YOU'RE** IN FOR!

AS THE KIDNAPPER PLUNGES THE KNIFE AGAINST THE MAN OF STEEL'S SIDE, IT BREAKS WITH A SHARP TINKLE...

SEIZING THE TWO **SUPERMAN** BINDS THEM TOGETHER, BACK-TO-BACK, WITH A CLOTHES RACK....

THERE! THAT OUGHT TO HOLD YOU SECURELY UNTIL I SEND SOMEONE TO TAKE YOU INTO CUSTODY!

MERCY!

DON'T LEAVE US HERE -- LIKE **THIS!**

WH-WHAT ARE YOU GOING TO DO TO ME?

DON'T BE AFRAID IN CASE IT HASN'T PENETRATED YET, I'M YOUR FRIEND!

DON'T! PUT ME DOWN! PUT ME DOWN!

QUIET! YOU WON'T BE HARMED. ("--I'LL GIVE LOIS CREDIT FOR ONE THING. THESE BREATH-TAKING LEAPS NEVER DROVE HER TO HYSTERICS!--")

SHE'S FAINTED! IT'S JUST AS WELL. THE POOR GIRL HAS BEEN UNDER A TERRIBLE STRAIN.

MEANWHILE -- WITHIN THE SHACK...

WE'VE GOT TO GET FREE AND WARN THE BOSS!

OUCH! CAREFUL!

THAT'S BETTER! NOW TO TELEPHONE THE CHIEF!

HEY! HELP ME OUTA THIS!

LISTEN BOSS! THE CRANE GIRL HAS ESCAPED -- RESCUED BY AN INCREDIBLY STRONG GUY...!

WITHIN GATSON'S APARTMENT.

YOU FUMBLING FOOLS! I'LL ATTEND TO YOU LATER. RIGHT NOW I'VE GOT TO ACT FAST!

121

SO THE CRANE GAL ESCAPED, EH?

WELL, IT WON'T DO HER ANY GOOD. HER DAD FREES ME, OR...!

MEANWHILE--AT JUDGE CRANE'S HOME....

THANK YOU FOR ACCOMPANYING ME HOME, BAILIFF! I'M ALL RIGHT NOW!

IF YOU WANT ME TO REMAIN UNTIL YOU FEEL BETTER.

SOMEONE AT THE DOOR!

HAVE YOUR GUN READY-- JUST IN CASE!

GATSON! JOE GATSON!

THAT'S RIGHT! I WANTA TALK TO YOU!

YOUR DAUGHTER'S BEEN RESCUED AND IS BEING BROUGHT HERE. WHEN SHE ARRIVES, THERE'LL BE A FEW THINGS I'LL HAVE TO SAY!

GET OUT OF HERE!

SORRY, ----I'M STAYING!

COVER HIM! DON'T LET HIM ESCAPE!

RAISE YOUR HANDS! FOR YOUR INFORMATION I'VE BEEN WORKING FOR GATSON FOR YEARS!

THE DOORBELL--!

I'LL ANSWER IT! KEEP THE OLD COOT COVERED!

LOIS HAS ARRIVED FOR AN INTERVIEW WITH THE JUDGE..

I'D LIKE TO SPEAK TO... OH-HHH! IT'S ....

JOE GATSON! DO STEP IN AND I DO MEAN DO!

YOU'RE HOLDING THE JUDGE CAPTIVE IN HIS OWN HOME?

AND I ASSURE YOU, HE'LL PAY FOR IT!

QUIET!

I'M GOING TO STEP INTO THE CLOSET UNTIL THE GIRL RETURNS. AND WHEN SHE DOES, IF ANY OF YOU LEAVE OUT A WARNING PEEP...!

MINUTES LATER- **SUPERMAN** SWINGS IN THRU THE WINDOW..

HELLO-- WHAT GOES ON HERE?

JUST THIS-- STEP BACK, OR I DRILL THE GIRL!

CAUTIOUSLY OPENING THE CLOSET DOOR, GATSON STEPS OUT AND RAMS HIS GUN INTO **SUPERMAN'S** BACK...

I'LL TEACH YOU TO INTERFERE WITH MY PLANS...! --BAILIFF-- **SHOOT THE GIRL!**

SMIRKING, THE BAILIFF OBEYS HIS EVIL EMPLOYER...

YOU'RE THE BOSS!

BUT ACTING SWIFTLY, **SUPERMAN** HAD REACHED BACK, AND SWUNG GATSON OVER HIS HEAD....

WHAT--?

YOU ASKED FOR IT!

SO THAT THE GANGSTER RECEIVES THE BULLET MEANT FOR SYLVIA CRANE...

VA-AA-AA!!

THE BAILIFF IS STRUCK UNCONSCIOUS BY GATSON'S HURTLING BODY...

HERE YOU ARE--TELEPHONE THE POLICE, BUT KEEP THE BAILIFF COVERED!

YES --BUT WAIT--!

NO TIME TO WAIT-- I HAVE OTHER PRESSING ENGAGEMENTS!

LATER-- CLARK ENTERS WITH THE POLICE...

CONGRATULATIONS, LOIS! WHAT A FEATHER IN YOUR CAP THIS WILL BE! WHERE'S A TELEPHONE?

DON'T BOTHER ABOUT THE YARN. I'VE ALREADY DONE SO THANKS TO SUPERMAN!

--AND REMEMBER, A BRAND-NEW **SUPERMAN** STORY APPEARS EVERY MONTH IN **ACTION COMICS** MAGAZINE! DON'T MISS AN ISSUE!

THE END

124

SUPERMAN

JERRY SIEGEL
AND
JOE SHUSTER

SAFE-KEEPING OF A SCIENTIFIC DISCOVERY OF TREMENDOUS IMPORT THREATENED BY UNKNOWN PERSONS OR FORCES! LOIS HUNDREDS OF MILES AWAY, IN DIRE PERIL! **SUPERMAN** HAS HIS HANDS MORE THAN FULL IN THIS MOST AMAZING OF HIS MANY ADVENTURES...WHEN HE COMES TO GRIPS WITH A MENACE SO FANTASTIC THAT EVEN THE DARING <u>MAN</u> <u>OF</u> <u>TOMORROW</u> IS HARD PUT FOR AN EXPLANATION!

IN FAR OFF <u>ROVERTOWN</u>, IN THE <u>LAMSON LABORATORIES</u>... A SCORE OF SCIENTISTS WORK BUSILY AT THEIR VARIOUS TASKS....

HAVE YOU HEARD? LAMSON HAS RECEIVED MYSTERIOUS THREATS! ALL SORTS OF THINGS ARE THREATENED IF HE DOESN'T REVEAL THE W-142 FORMULA!

THEY'LL SOON LEARN LAMSON ISN'T THE TYPE WHO FRIGHTENS EASILY!

NEXT INSTANT.... AN UNDETECTED KILLER SHOOTS DOWN ONE OF THE WORKERS...

YA-AAA-AA!

AND THAT EVENING, A PORTION OF THE PLANT BLOWS UP!

SO THEY TRIED TO GET THE FORMULA FROM THE SAFE, EH, LAMSON?

BUT THEY FAILED! ONLY A FEW OF MY MOST TRUSTED ASSISTANTS KNOW WHERE THE FORMULA ACTUALLY IS HIDDEN! ENEMIES ARE TRYING TO TERRORIZE ME INTO PLAYING BALL BUT—IT WON'T WORK!

AND MANY, MANY HUNDREDS OF MILES DISTANT..... ON THE BORDER OF THE SWASEY SWAMP....

DING BLAST IT! THE BLAMED THING WON'T WORK!

ALL WE'VE GOTTEN FROM IT FOR DAYS IS THAT EARSPLITTING STATIC!

EEEE (SQUEE!)

MAY I USE YOUR TELEPHONE, PLEASE ?

WON'T DO YOU ANY GOOD. NONE OF THE TELEPHONES HEREABOUTS HAVE BEEN IN ORDER FOR A WEEK!

FOOD AND DRY-GOODS

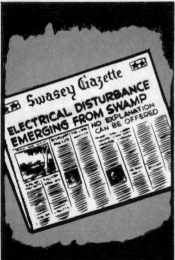

Swasey Gazette

ELECTRICAL DISTURBANCE EMERGING FROM SWAMP

NO EXPLANATION CAN BE OFFERED

EDITORIAL OFFICE OF THE METROPOLIS *DAILY PLANET*....

YOU KNOW, LOIS, LAST NIGHT I DREAMED THAT YOU AND I WERE ON THE BEST OF TERMS.

IT **MUST** HAVE BEEN A DREAM!

WHITE WANTS TO SEE BOTH OF YOU!

TWO INTERESTING STORIES HAVE BROKEN! I WANT YOU TO HANDLE THEM!

HOW ABOUT SOME DETAILS?

SOME UNKNOWN PERSON OR PERSONS ARE CAUSING A TERROR UP AT THE *LAMSON LABORATORIES* IN AN ATTEMPT TO FORCE THE W-142 FORMULA FROM LAMSON. CLARK, YOU'RE TO GET TO THE BOTTOM OF IT!

RIGHT!

YOU SAID SOMETHING ABOUT AN ASSIGNMENT FOR ME, TOO!

YOU'RE TO INVESTIGATE THE POWERFUL ELECTRICAL DISCHARGE EMANATING FROM *SWASEY SWAMP.*

LEAVE IT TO CLARK TO GET THE MORE INTERESTING ASSIGNMENT!

("-ROVERTOWN..... *SWASEY SWAMP!* HM-MM! THEY'RE HUNDREDS OF MILES APART! LOIS HAS A GENIUS FOR POKING HER NOSE INTO TROUBLE! THIS MAY BE ONE TIME I MIGHT NOT BE ON HAND TO HELP HER!-")

LATER—
CLARK
SEES
LOIS
OFF
AT
THE
RAILROAD
STATION.....

YOU'LL BE CAREFUL —TAKE GOOD CARE OF YOURSELF..?

STOP BEING SO SOLICITOUS, CLARK, OR YOU'LL SUCCEED IN MAKING ME NERVOUS. TO TELL YOU THE TRUTH I CONSIDER THIS LITTLE TRIP MORE OR LESS OF A VACATION JAUNT!

FOR ONCE I'VE GOT CLARK OUT OF MY HAIR WHEN I'M ON THE TRACK OF A YARN! THIS MAY BE MY BIG OPPORTUNITY TO SHOW THAT GENT JUST WHAT I CAN DO WHEN I'M ON MY OWN!

CLARK
BOARDS
A
BUS
FOR
ROVERTOWN...

SOMEHOW, I CAN'T HELP WORRYING ABOUT LOIS. I'VE AN ANNOYINGLY PERSISTENT HUNCH THAT THE GIRL IS HEADED INTO THE CENTER OF A BEAUTIFUL MESS!

LATER ..
LOIS
LEAVES
THE
TRAIN
AT
HER
DESTINATION..

WHAT A FORSAKEN SPOT THIS IS. NOT A SOUL IN SIGHT!

HELLO! ANYBODY AROUND?

SHE STARTS VIOLENTLY AT AN UNEXPECTED TOUCH UPON HER SHOULDER

WERE YOU CALLIN' ME MA'M?

WHO ARE YOU?

JUST THE STATION AGENT, MA'AM THAT'S ALL DIDN'T MEAN TO FRIGHTEN YOU

MAYBE YOU CAN TELL ME JUST WHAT IS ALL THIS TALK ABOUT AN ELECTRICAL DISTURBANCE EMERGING FROM AN UNINHABITED PORTION OF THE SWAMP?

WALL-LL... AIN'T MUCH I CAN TELL YOU, 'CEPT.... PERSONALLY, I THINK IT'S **SPOOKS**!

YOU WOULD! I CAN SEE YOU'RE GOING TO BE A LOT OF HELP!

CAN YOU AT LEAST TELL ME WHERE I CAN LOCATE A GUIDE TO TAKE ME INTO THE SWAMP, SO THAT I CAN INVESTIGATE THE SOURCE OF THE TROUBLE?

WHY NOT TRY JEFF GRADY'S GROCERY STORE? THERE'S ALWAYS A BUNCH OF TH' FELLAS HANGIN' AROUND HIS CRACKER BARREL!

UNAIDED, LOIS LABORIOUSLY CARRIES HER HEAVY SUIT-CASES TO THE DISTANT STORE...

ANY ONE OF YOU CARE TO GUIDE ME INTO THE SWAMP?

AS NO ONE REPLIES...

WHAT'S THE MATTER? ARE YOU ALL DEAF? I ASKED FOR A GUIDE!

NONE OF THEM CARE TO ACCEPT THE JOB, MISS. WE DON'T LIKE WHAT'S GOIN' ON IN TH' SWAMP-- NO-SIR...NOT AT ALL!

I'VE GOT A WIFE AN' KIDS...

I'LL TAKE THAT JOB!

THAT'S MORE LIKE IT!

WHO ARE YOU? NEVER SEEN YOU AROUND HERE BEFORE!

HOW CAN YOU-- A STRANGER-- GUIDE ANYONE INTO THE SWAMP AND GET OUT... ALIVE?

I'M TOM JEPSON. STILL WANT ME TO GUIDE YOU?

I CERTAINLY DO! IT'S A PLEASURE TO MEET SOMEONE WHO ACTUALLY ISN'T AFRAID THE BOOGEY-MAN IS LURKING IN THE SWAMP.

AS LOIS DEPARTS FROM THE STORE, SHE DOES NOT SEE THE TRIUMPHANT GLEAM IN JEPSON'S EYES....

④

SHORTLY AFTER ....THE TWO SET OFF INTO THE SWAMP IN A BOAT....

HOW LONG WILL IT TAKE US TO REACH THE CENTER OF THE SWAMP?

MAYBE A FEW HOURS ...MAYBE NEVER...!

LOIS TURNS ON A PORTABLE RADIO.....

LISTEN! NOTE HOW THE STATIC INCREASES IN VOLUME AS WE GO FURTHER AND FURTHER INTO THE SWAMP!

AN ALLIGATOR!

YOU NEEDN'T WORRY ABOUT HIM...AS LONG AS YOU'RE IN THE BOAT!

THE STATIC -- DEAFENING! WE MUST BE VERY CLOSE TO THE END OF OUR JOURNEY! I CAN HARDLY WAIT TO SEE THE CAUSE OF THE ELECTRICAL DISTURBANCE!

("PERHAPS YOUR EAGERNESS MAY CHANGE TO HORROR!·")

AS THEY ROUND A TURN IN THE SWAMP....

LOOK! A METEOR HAS FALLEN INTO THE SWAMP-- FORMED A SMALL ISLAND!

I'VE SEEN IT BEFORE!

WHEN THE BOAT STRIKES THE ISLAND....

NOW...!

KEEP BACK! HAVE YOU GONE MAD?

TERRORIZED, LOIS RACES ALONG METEOR ISLAND HEARING THE SOUND OF PURSUIT CLOSE BEHIND....

HE'S COMING CLOSER! CLOSER!

AS SHE ATTEMPTS TO ROUND A HUGE ROCK, A WEIRD FIGURE STEPS FORTH AND BLOCKS HER PATH....

WHAT--!?!

WHIRLING, SHE ATTEMPTS TO RUN IN ANOTHER DIRECTION, BUT FINDS....

MORE OF THE METAL CREATURES!

SWIFTLY, THE MONSTER-MEN CLOSE IN ON THE FEAR-STRICKEN GIRL...!

THEN CALMLY REGARD HER FALLEN FIGURE AS SHE FAINTS!

THE REPORTER-- LOIS LANE-- IS CAPTURED!

INDEED! THEN IT ONLY REMAINS FOR US TO REMOVE CLARK KENT!

MEANWHILE-- CLARK HAS ALREADY ARRIVED IN ROVERTOWN...

THE LAMSON LABORATORIES ARE SO CLOSE TO THE BUS TERMINAL, I MIGHT AS WELL WALK.

MESSAGE FOR CLARK KENT! MESSAGE FOR MR. KENT!

I'LL TAKE THAT MESSAGE, BOY!

THAT'S ODD! --THE SHEET'S BLANK!

ENIGMATIC EYES REGARD CLARK FROM AFAR. A PURPOSE HAS BEEN ACCOMPLISHED. CLARK HAS IDENTIFIED HIMSELF!

THERE IT IS -- STRAIGHT AHEAD

BUT IN THE SKY ABOVE....!

CLARK KENT!

THAT'S HIM!

DOWN PLUMMETS THE PLANE TOWARD THE SMALL FIGURE BELOW MACHINE GUNS SPITTING LEADEN FLAME...!

NOW, I BEGIN TO UNDERSTAND THE PURPOSE OF THAT MESSAGE!

BUT WHAT CAN I DO? IF I STAND HERE AND PERMIT THE BULLETS TO CAREEN OFF MY IDENTITY AS **SUPERMAN** WILL BE REVEALED. WHATEVER I DO, I'VE GOT TO MAKE UP MY MIND QUICK!

CLARK DIVES FOR A NEARBY BRICK WALL PRETENDING TERROR.

H-HELP!!

THERE HE CROUCHES AS THE PLANE SWEEPS PAST!!

IT WOULD HAVE BEEN MORE DIGNIFIED TO JUST STAND THERE IN THE ROAD AND LET THEM WASTE THEIR BULLETS, BUT THIS WAY THEY WILL BELIEVE THEY HAVE SIMPLY MISSED ME!

CONTINUING THE ROLE OF FEAR, KENT RACES THE REMAINING DISTANCE TO THE LABORATORY BUILDING....

("-THIS OUGHT TO LOOK MIGHTY CONVINCING...!-)

OPEN! PLEASE! OPEN THE DOOR!

IN ANSWER TO HIS REQUEST THE DOOR SLOWLY COMMEN-CES TO OPEN.....

NEXT INSTANT, CLARK IS LOOKING INTO THE MUZZLE OF AN AUTOMATIC!

?

BANG! - AS THE TRIGGER IS PULLED A BULLET CATAPULTS FORTH FROM THE MUZZLE-AND IS FLATTENED HARMLESSLY AGAINST CLARK'S CHEST!

("-WHAT A RECEPTION!-")

AS THE DOOR BANGS SHUT, CLARK CONTINUES HAMMERING AT IT......

LET ME IN!

ABRUPTLY, THE DOOR OPENS....

I HEARD A A SHOT! WERE YOU HARMED--?

LET ME IN! I'LL ANSWER QUESTIONS LATER!

EXACTLY WHAT HAPPENED?

THE DOOR OPENED AND SOMEONE FIRED AT ME. BUT FORTUNATELY HE MISSED. I'M CLARK KENT OF THE DAILY PLANET. I'VE COME TO INTERVIEW MR. LAMSON.

I'M KRAWL, LAMSON'S ASSISTANT. COME--I'LL LEAD YOU TO HIM!

THIS--THIS HAS BEEN A MOST EXCITING AFTERNOON!

LABS A-B-C

SO YOU'RE A REPORTER FROM METROPOLIS, EH? I'LL BE GLAD TO SUPPLY YOU WITH ANY INFORMATION YOU WANT.

THAT'S FINE -TELL ME, WHO DO YOU THINK IS BEHIND THESE ATTEMPTS TO TERRORIZE YOU?

FANATICS, INTERNATIONAL SPIES, OLD ENEMIES --WHO KNOWS? BUT WHOEVER THEY ARE, THEY'RE DETERMINED TO GET THE W-142 FORMULA!

AND JUST EXACTLY WHAT IS THE NATURE OF THIS MYSTERIOUS FORMULA?

IT'S A NEW SUBSTANCE CAPABLE OF YIELDING ENERGY EQUAL TO 5,000,000 POUNDS OF COAL IN A SINGLE POUND OF IT. IT WILL REVOLUTIONIZE INDUSTRY...!

ITS POTENTIALITIES ARE UNLIMITED! INCREDIBLY CHEAP POWER FOR MANUFACTURING ....TRANSPORTATION ....WAR...!

NO WONDER THEY'RE SO EAGER TO GET THEIR HANDS ON IT!

AS A SUDDEN SHADOW DARKENS THE WINDOWS.....

LOOK OUT!

JUMP FOR COVER!

I DON'T NEED ANY URGING!

OUT OF SIGHT OF THE OTHERS, CLARK REMOVES HIS OUTER GARMENTS, TRANSFORMING HIMSELF INTO **SUPERMAN, MAN OF STEEL**....

LOOKS LIKE I MAY HAVE SOME ACTION ON MY HANDS!

A LARGE PLANE LANDS OUTSIDE THE LABORATORY....

MEN WEARING METALLIC GARMENTS AND SCREENING GOGGLES, EMERGE.....

QUICK!

INTO THE LABORATORY!

WHAT DO YOU MEAN BY....

RAISE THOSE HANDS!

NOW.... WHAT IS THE W-142 FORMULA!

I REFUSE TO TELL YOU! AND IF YOU THINK YOU CAN DRAG THE INFORMATION OUT OF ME, YOU'RE WASTING YOUR TIME!

I BELIEVE HIM. LET'S GET TO WORK ON SOMEONE ELSE!

YOU--TELL ME WHERE I CAN FIND A COPY OF THE FORMULA OR I'LL BEAT IN YOUR SKULL!

THERE! --IN THAT CABINET DRAWER!

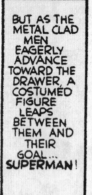

BUT AS THE METAL CLAD MEN EAGERLY ADVANCE TOWARD THE DRAWER, A COSTUMED FIGURE LEAPS BETWEEN THEM AND THEIR GOAL... **SUPERMAN!**

STOP! AND I DO MEAN YOU!

GET HIM!!

THE BANDITS RUSH THE MAN OF TOMORROW....ONLY TO DISCOVER THEY HAVE TANGLED WITH A ONE-MAN ARMY...

A DOZEN TO ONE....THAT'S THE WAY I LIKE MY ODDS!

BUT FLEEING TO THE PLANE, ONE OF THE INVADERS FLINGS A SWITCH....

THIS'LL ATTEND TO HIM!

INSTANTLY, EVERY METAL OBJECT IN THE ROOM STREAKS TOWARD SUPERMAN.....

WHAT--!?!

AS HE BATTLES THE DELUGE OF METAL, SUPERMAN GUESSES THE ANSWER.....

IT'S DONE BY DIRECTIONAL MAGNETIC ATTRACTION, THREE DIMENSIONAL WORKED BY A DEVICE IN THE PLANE WHICH ALLOWS THE OPERATOR TO ESTAB-LISH A MAGNETIC FIELD ANYWHERE IN SPACE!

SEIZING A HUGE METAL BENCH, SUPERMAN HURLS IT THRU THE LARGE WINDOWS AT THE PLANE, DESTROYING THE VESSEL. INSTANTLY THE RAIN OF METAL OBJECTS ENDS.....

I THOUGHT THAT WOULD DO IT!

AS THE MAN OF STEEL SPRINGS TOWARD THEM, THE TERRIFIED INVADERS LEAP TO DESTRUCTION..... !

NOW TO ATTEND TO YOU!

DON'T LET HIM TOUCH ME!

JUMP FOR IT!

SUDDENLY, KRAWL LEAPS FORWARD....SEEKS TO SHOVE SUPERMAN THRU THE WINDOW...

FOLLOW THEM, BLAST YOU!

AS I THOUGHT! YOU'RE A TRAITOR TO LAMSON!

AS KRAWL PLUMMETS DOWNWARD HE THRUSTS A VIAL INTO HIS MOUTH....

I HAVE FAILED!

135

SUPERMAN CATCHES THE FALLING ASSISTANT BEFORE HE STRIKES GROUND.....

GOT YOU!

TOO LATE! I'VE SWALLOWED POISON!

YOU HAVEN'T MUCH LONGER TO LIVE! TELL ME-- WHO IS YOUR REAL EMPLOYER?

A MAN OF-- GIGANTIC INTELLIGENCE. --YOU'LL NEVER OUTWIT HIM! AT THIS MOMENT HE HAS ---- IMPRISONED --LOIS LANE....

WITH A FINAL GASP, KRAWL DIES!

A MIGHTY LEAP LAUNCHES SUPERMAN UP INTO THE SKY! HE STREAKS THRU THE CLOUDS LIKE A SKYROCKET GONE WILD....!

LOIS--IN DANGER --IN THE SWASEY SWAMP!

THE CATAPULTING MAN OF STEEL SPANS FORESTS, HAMLETS.... COVERING HUNDREDS OF MILES IN MINUTES! THEN AS HE SIGHTS METALLIC-CLAD MEN BELOW, DOWN HE HURTLES..!

THEY KNOW WHERE LOIS IS! AND HERE'S WHERE I LEARN THE ANSWER!

THE ENEMY PUTS UP FEEBLE OPPOSITION BUT IS NO MATCH FOR THE STEELY, FLAILING FISTS OF THE MAN OF TOMORROW...

THIS IS TO KNOCK SOME OF THE CUSSEDNESS OUT OF YOU!

TELL ME WHERE LOIS LANE IS. OR.....

THERE! SHE'S IN THE SECRET CHAMBER BENEATH THAT BOULDER!

DOWN BURROWS SUPERMAN THRU THE SOLID ROCK.....

INTO A METAL-LINED ROOM...

BACK--OR I'LL DESTROY LOIS IN THE MAGNETIC FIELD!

TRY IT!

VERY WELL! WATCH HER DIE BEFORE YOUR VERY EYES!

AS THE SWITCH IS FLUNG, EVERY BIT OF METAL IN THE ROOM FLIES TOWARD LOIS! BUT **SUPERMAN** SMASHES IT BACK.. BACK...!

YOU CAN'T WIN! THE MAGNETIC FORCE IS TOO POWERFUL!

I'M SURPRISED YOU HAVEN'T MORE CONFIDENCE IN ME!

THE CRUSH OF THE METAL DESTROYS THE MAGNETIC DEVICE. SWIFTLY **SUPERMAN** BENDS BACK THE METAL....

THERE YOU ARE!

BUT--WHAT HAPPENED TO THE EVIL SCIENTIST?

HE'S SOMEWHERE BENEATH THERE!

DESTROYED BY HIS OWN FIENDISH MACHINE!

AS THEY STREAK UP INTO THE SKY, **SUPERMAN** BRINGS JEPSON ALONG AS CAPTIVE...

WHO WAS YOUR BOSS?

WILL **THIS** MAKE A FRONT PAGE YARN!

A FOREIGN AGENT, WHO WAS DETERMINED TO GET THE W-142 FORMULA AT ANY COST!

SUPERMAN ALIGHTS BEFORE THE METROPOLIS JAIL....

HERE YOU ARE, SERGEANT CASEY-- A PRISONER!

WHAT--?

HOLD ONTO HIM, CASEY! I'LL EXPLAIN EVERYTHING TO YOU LATER!

AFTER **SUPERMAN** SPRINGS OFF LOIS HURRIES TO THE DAILY PLANET NEWSPAPER OFFICE.....

HOLD THE FRONT PAGE OPEN CHIEF! I'VE A STORY ABOUT **SWASEY SWAMP** AND THE **LAMSON LABORATORIES** THAT WILL....

I GUESS YOU HAVEN'T YET READ THE FRONT PAGE OF THE LATEST EDITION.

M-MY STORY! UNDER THE BY-LINE OF **CLARK KENT!**

PAGING ME, LOIS?

THE END.

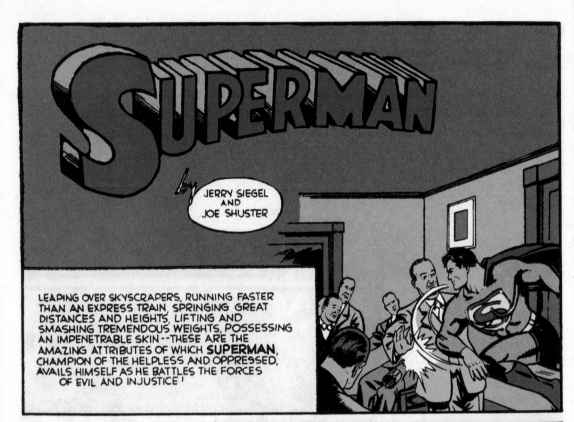

SUPERMAN

by
JERRY SIEGEL
AND
JOE SHUSTER

LEAPING OVER SKYSCRAPERS, RUNNING FASTER THAN AN EXPRESS TRAIN, SPRINGING GREAT DISTANCES AND HEIGHTS, LIFTING AND SMASHING TREMENDOUS WEIGHTS, POSSESSING AN IMPENETRABLE SKIN--THESE ARE THE AMAZING ATTRIBUTES OF WHICH **SUPERMAN**, CHAMPION OF THE HELPLESS AND OPPRESSED, AVAILS HIMSELF AS HE BATTLES THE FORCES OF EVIL AND INJUSTICE!

AS LOIS LANE AND CLARK KENT STROLL NEAR THE METROPOLIS TOWER, SHRIEKS ABOUT THEM CAUSE THE TWO TO LOOK UPWARD....

LOOK!

SOMEONE FALLING!

("-I CAN EASILY CATCH HIM AND SAVE HIS LIFE. NATURALLY, IT WILL GIVE AWAY MY TRUE IDENTITY AS **SUPERMAN**, BUT....-")

TOWER 1929 AD

BUT THEN CLARK'S TELESCOPIC VISION REVEALS TO HIM THAT THE MAN IS ALREADY DEAD FROM A CRUSHING BLOW OVER THE HEAD.....

("-ALREADY DEAD! NO USE THEN, TO RISK REVEALING MY IDENTITY!-")

SWIFTLY, KENT SWEEPS LOIS OUT OF DANGER. THEY AVERT THEIR EYES SO AS NOT TO WITNESS THE SICKENING IMPACT.....

DON'T LOOK!

OH, CLARK! HOW-- TERRIBLE!

THUD

THE GATHERING MORBID CROWD IS SWEPT BACK AS SERGEANT CASEY AND HIS MEN ARRIVE.....

HELLO, SERGEANT CASEY!

IT'S POSITIVELY ASTONISHING THE WAY YOU TWO ALWAYS MANAGE TO BE ON THE SPOT WHEN SOMETHING NEWSWORTHY OCCURS!

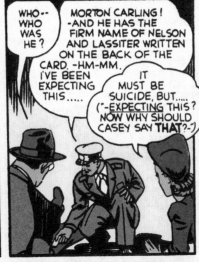

WHO-- WHO WAS HE?

MORTON CARLING! --AND HE HAS THE FIRM NAME OF NELSON AND LASSITER WRITTEN ON THE BACK OF THE CARD. -HM-MM. I'VE BEEN EXPECTING THIS.....

IT MUST BE SUICIDE, BUT..... ("-EXPECTING THIS? NOW WHY SHOULD CASEY SAY THAT?-")

WHERE ARE YOU TAKING US NOW, LOIS?

TO THE TWENTI-ETH FLOOR TO THE LEGAL FIRM OF NELSON AND LASSITER. I BELIEVE CARLING MUST HAVE JUMPED FROM THEIR WINDOW!

MR. LASSITER.... COULD YOU TELL US EXACTLY WHAT HAPPENED, AND WHY CARLING SHOULD HAVE TAKEN THAT-- ER--LEAP?

I SUGGEST YOU SPEAK TO MR. NELSON, MY PARTNER. HE HAS ALWAYS ATTENDED TO CARLING'S AFFAIRS.

THAT'S OKAY WITH US-- JUST AS LONG AS WE GET THE INFORMATION!

PLEASE -- I DON'T FEEL LIKE DISCUSSING IT......

BUT IT'S BEST THAT YOU DO DISCUSS IT, MR. NELSON.

YOU WOULDN'T WANT THE PAPERS TO PRINT A FALSE REPORT.

PERHAPS YOU'RE RIGHT--DURING THE LAST MONTHS, CARLING CONTINUALLY COMPLAINED THAT HE WAS RECEIVING DEATH-THREATS OVER THE PHONE AND FROM STRANGERS WHO PASSED HIM ON THE CROWDED STREET. WE COMPLAINED TO SERGEANT CASEY-- BUT THE SERGEANT, AFTER INVEST-IGATION, DECIDED OUR CLIENT HAD AN OVER-ACTIVE IMAGINATION.

HE WARNED US TO PROTECT OUR CLIENT FROM SUICIDE -- BUT TODAY, HE UNEXPECT-EDLY LEAPED THRU THE WINDOW!

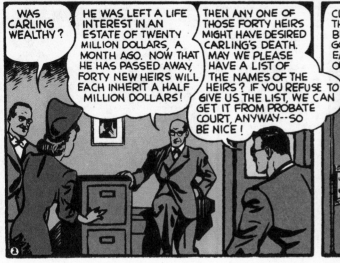

WAS CARLING WEALTHY?

HE WAS LEFT A LIFE INTEREST IN AN ESTATE OF TWENTY MILLION DOLLARS, A MONTH AGO. NOW THAT HE HAS PASSED AWAY, FORTY NEW HEIRS WILL EACH INHERIT A HALF MILLION DOLLARS!

THEN ANY ONE OF THOSE FORTY HEIRS MIGHT HAVE DESIRED CARLING'S DEATH. MAY WE PLEASE HAVE A LIST OF THE NAMES OF THE HEIRS? IF YOU REFUSE TO GIVE US THE LIST, WE CAN GET IT FROM PROBATE COURT, ANYWAY--SO BE NICE!

CLARK--I'M GLAD YOU GOT THAT LIST OF NAMES, BECAUSE WE'RE PERSONALLY GOING TO INVESTIGATE EACH HEIR--YOU, TWENTY OF THEM, AND I. TWENTY!

TWENTY!? LOIS! HAVE A HEART!

THE SURVEY BEGINS......

ER--I BELIEVE YOU'RE ONE OF MORTON CARLING'S HEIRS.....

THAT'S NONE OF **YOUR** AFFAIR!

SLAM!!

AS CLARK CONTINUES ON HIS ERRAND HE ENCOUNTERS ANGER, IRRITABILITY, INDIGNATION......

YOU REPORTERS! A PERSON'S PRIVACY DOESN'T MEAN A THING TO YOU!

I--I ONLY WANTED TO ASK A FEW QUESTIONS....

WHEN, DISCOURAGED, HE LEAVES THE HOME OF THE TWENTIETH NAME ON THE LIST, GEORGE STEELE, HE NOTES.

A CAR-- TRAILING ME THRU TRAFFIC--!

CLARK TURNS INTO AN UNFREQUENTED STREET.....

STILL TRAILING ME!

SUDDENLY, THE TRAILING CAR SWOOPS IN AND FORCES THE REPORTER'S AUTO OFF THE STREET SO THAT IT CRASHES INTO A TELEPHONE-POLE......

YA SAP! WE'RE PAID TO SNATCH THIS GUY-- NOT TO **KILL** HIM!

QUIT SOWAWKIN'! HE'S STILL ALIVE..... JUST UNCON- SCIOUS!

("-I'LL PLAY POSSUM AND LEARN JUST WHAT THEIR GAME IS!-")

THIS GUY IS HEAVY!

ALWAYS COMPLAININ'! GET HIM INTO THE CAR ...AND LET'S CLEAR OUTA HERE!

OFF SPEEDS THE AUTO, WITH THE APPARENTLY UNCONSCIOUS CLARK KENT A NOT-SO- HELPLESS CAPTIVE....!

HALF AN HOUR LATER....THE TWO KIDNAPPERS FORCE THE "REVIVED" CLARK INTO THEIR HIDEOUT......

BUT--!

KEEP WALKIN'! ANOTHER WORD OUTA YOU AND....!

THE DAILY PLANET REPORTER IS TIED TO A CHAIR AND ROUGHLY QUESTIONED.....

TALK, BLAST. YA! WHY WERE YOU QUESTIONIN' ALL THEM PEOPLE?

DON'T HIT ME ANY MORE! I'LL TELL YOU!

SMACK

I HAPPEN TO KNOW-- I'M CERTAIN-- THAT CARLING WAS MURDERED ....DEAD **BEFORE** HE HIT THE SIDEWALK!

FELLA.... THAT'S THE WORST THING YOU COULDA SAID.... FER YOU!

RAISING THE TELEPHONE RECEIVER, ONE OF THE THUGS DIALS A NUMBER......

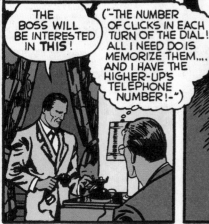

THE BOSS WILL BE INTERESTED IN **THIS**!

("-THE NUMBER OF CLICKS IN EACH TURN OF THE DIAL! ALL I NEED DO IS MEMORIZE THEM.... AND I HAVE THE HIGHER-UP'S TELEPHONE NUMBER!-")

THAT REPORTER KNOWS CARLING WAS MURDERED! WHAT DO YA WANT US TO DO?

THE OBVIOUS THING, YOU FOOL! **KILL HIM!**

WH-WHERE ARE YOU TAKING ME?

FIGURE IT OUT FOR YOURSELF, BUD!

NO QUESTIONS!

YOU'RE TAKING ME FOR A ONE-WAY RIDE! DON'T DO IT! I HAVEN'T MUCH MONEY SAVED UP, BUT.....

WILL YOU SHUT UP??

DISTRACTED BY THE COMMOTION CLARK RAISES, THE CAR'S DRIVER SPEEDS THRU A STOP SIGNAL DESPITE A POLICEMAN'S WARNING WHISTLE.....

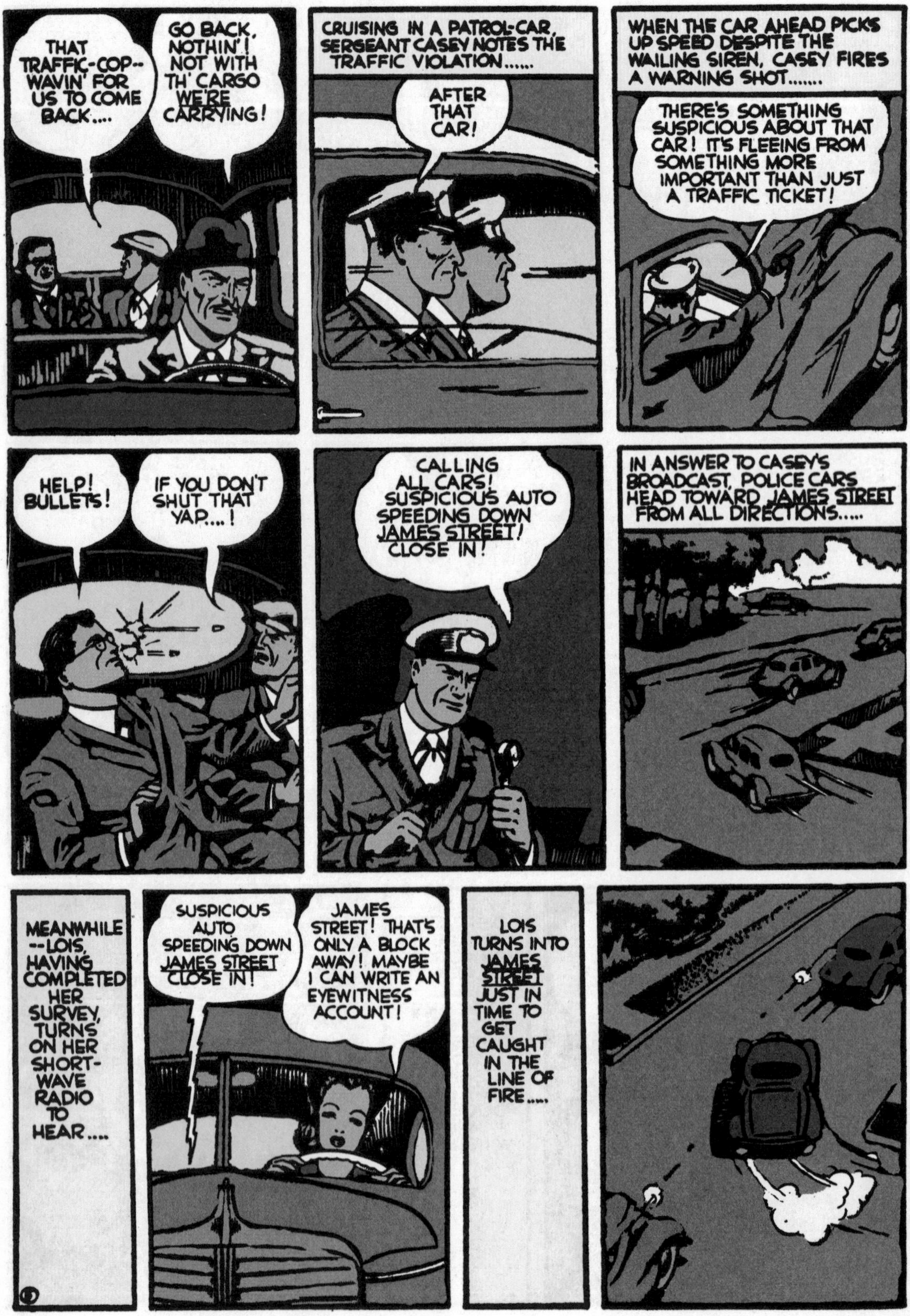
THAT TRAFFIC-COP-- WAVIN' FOR US TO COME BACK....
GO BACK, NOTHIN'! NOT WITH TH' CARGO WE'RE CARRYING!
CRUISING IN A PATROL-CAR, SERGEANT CASEY NOTES THE TRAFFIC VIOLATION......
AFTER THAT CAR!
WHEN THE CAR AHEAD PICKS UP SPEED DESPITE THE WAILING SIREN, CASEY FIRES A WARNING SHOT.......
THERE'S SOMETHING SUSPICIOUS ABOUT THAT CAR! IT'S FLEEING FROM SOMETHING MORE IMPORTANT THAN JUST A TRAFFIC TICKET!
HELP! BULLETS!
IF YOU DON'T SHUT THAT YAP....!
CALLING ALL CARS! SUSPICIOUS AUTO SPEEDING DOWN JAMES STREET! CLOSE IN!
IN ANSWER TO CASEY'S BROADCAST, POLICE CARS HEAD TOWARD JAMES STREET FROM ALL DIRECTIONS.....
MEANWHILE --LOIS, HAVING COMPLETED HER SURVEY, TURNS ON HER SHORT-WAVE RADIO TO HEAR....
SUSPICIOUS AUTO SPEEDING DOWN JAMES STREET CLOSE IN!
JAMES STREET! THAT'S ONLY A BLOCK AWAY! MAYBE I CAN WRITE AN EYEWITNESS ACCOUNT!
LOIS TURNS INTO JAMES STREET JUST IN TIME TO GET CAUGHT IN THE LINE OF FIRE.....

LOWER YOUR GUNS! IT'S THAT DAILY PLANET HOODOO-- LOIS LANE-- IN THE WAY!

LEAVE IT TO HER TO TURN UP AND MESS THINGS!

IN A DESPERATE EFFORT TO THROW OFF PURSUIT, THE THUGS DUMP CLARK'S BODY FROM THEIR HURTLING CAR.....

WE'LL LET THAT DAME FINISH THE JOB FER US!

DESPERATELY, LOIS SWERVES THE CAR SHARPLY TO AVOID HITTING CLARK'S BODY.....

A MAN --IN THE STREET.....!

.....THEN SKIDS TO A HALT-IN THE VERY PATH OF THE POLICE CAR-FORCING IT TO COME TO AN ABRUPT STOP!

CLARK! IT'S A WONDER THAT FALL DIDN'T KILL YOU! HOW DID YOU EVER GET INTO THAT CAR?

THE MEN-- PERFECT STRANGERS-- FORCED ME IN AT THE POINT OF A GUN!

YOU--YOU....! I OUGHT TO TOSS YOU INTO JAIL!

YOU BURN ME UP--BOTH OF YOU! THOSE MEN WERE DESPERATE KILLERS-- IT WOULD HAVE BEEN A FEATHER IN MY CAP TO CAPTURE THEM --BUT YOU--YOU HAD TO SPOIL IT FOR ME!!

I SAID I WAS SORRY!

YOU'RE SORE! WELL, WHAT ABOUT ME? IF YOU TWO HADN'T INTERFERED, I'D PROBABLY HAVE SECURED ENOUGH EVIDENCE ON THOSE FELLOWS TO SEND THEM TO THE CHAIR!

THE CHAIR! IF ANYONE DESERVES IT, IT'S YOU AND LOIS!

LET **ME** GET IN A WORD HERE! --MY QUICK ACTION SAVES CLARK'S LIFE! BUT DOES HE THANK ME? DOES HE APPRECIATE WHAT I'VE DONE FOR HIM? NO! INSTEAD, HE BAWLS ME OUT! VERY WELL! YOU'RE LUCKY--BOTH OF YOU-- THAT I'M A LADY! OTHERWISE....!

THE TWO REPORTERS RETURN TO THE *DAILY PLANET*....

IF YOU'LL ONLY ACCEPT MY APOLOGY, LOIS.....

DON'T YOU SPEAK TO ME, CLARK KENT!

LATER--CLARK DIALS THE TELEPHONE NUMBER HE HAD OVERHEARD. LIFTING HER TELEPHONE, LOIS ACCIDENTALLY OVERHEARS THE CONVERSATION

("--THE JACKSON JEWELRY COMPANY! THEY'VE TOLD CLARK ITS THE WRONG NUMBER....BUT I WONDER!-")

IN PRIVACY, CLARK CHANGES INTO THE DYNAMIC *SUPERMAN*

JACKSON JEWELRY COMPANY, EH? I BELIEVE I'LL GIVE THAT PLACE THE ONCE-OVER!

LOIS ENTERS THE TAYLOR BUILDING, IN WHICH THE JEWELRY COMPANY IS LOCATED, IN TIME TO SEE......

MR. NELSON--ENTERING THE JEWELRY COMPANY'S OFFICE! --THIS CALLS FOR STRATEGY!

CONTACTING THE BUILDING'S SUPERINTENDENT, LOIS SECURES VALUABLE INFORMATION

I WANT TO PLAY A JOKE ON MY GIRL-FRIEND--SHE'S SECRETARY OF THE JACKSON JEWELRY COMPANY. CAN YOU TELL ME THINGS YOU'VE NOTICED ABOUT HER, SO THAT I CAN SPRING THEM ON HER?

YOU MEAN MARJORIE FARNSWORTH? I CAN TELL YOU PLENTY ABOUT HER--!

DOWN OUT OF THE CLOUDS SWOOPS THE *MAN OF STEEL* ONTO THE TAYLOR BUILDING......

THIS DIDN'T TAKE LONG!

LOOKING DOWN THRU THE BUILDING'S ROOF WITH THE AID OF HIS X-RAY VISION, *SUPERMAN* IS STARTLED TO SIGHT......

NELSON--IN JACKSON'S PRIVATE OFFICE!

THIS IS AN EXTREMELY VALUABLE DIAMOND. I'LL HAVE TO ASK #50,000 FOR IT.

VERY WELL. HERE'S MY CHECK FOR THAT AMOUNT!

AS NELSON DEPARTS, HE IS REGARDED BY AN EXTREMELY PUZZLED *MAN OF TOMORROW*....

#50,000 FOR A DIAMOND! --AND I'M CERTAIN IT'S JUST WORTHLESS GLASS ....ITS TRUE VALUE NOT MORE THAN A FEW CENTS!

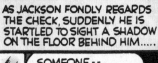
AS JACKSON FONDLY REGARDS THE CHECK, SUDDENLY HE IS STARTLED TO SIGHT A SHADOW ON THE FLOOR BEHIND HIM.....

SOMEONE -- EAVESDROPPING AT THE WINDOW--!

SNATCHING A REVOLVER FROM A DESK-DRAWER HE FIRES!

THIS'LL TEACH YOU IT DOESN'T PAY TO SNOOP!

SLOWLY, LABORIOUSLY, SUPERMAN CLIMBS UP TOWARD THE ROOF, AS THO WOUNDED......

HE'S INJURED! I'LL GET HIM WHEN HE REACHES THE ROOF!

JACKSON EMERGES ONTO THE BUILDING'S ROOF JUST AS SUPERMAN PAINFULLY PULLS HIMSELF UP OVER THE LEDGE......

YOU OVERHEARD EVERYTHING, EH?

PLEASE DON'T SHOOT. I.....

BUT DESPITE THE MAN OF TOMORROW'S PLEAS, JACKSON BLASTS AWAY......

NO! DON'T--

THAT ATTENDS TO HIM!

BUT AS HE STRIKES THE PAVEMENT BELOW SUPERMAN SOMERSAULTS UPWARD --AND AWAY!

HE MUST ACTUALLY HAVE BELIEVED THAT THE BULLETS AFFECTED ME!

SHAKEN BY WHAT HE HAS WITNESSED, JACKSON RETURNS TO HIS OFFICE....

MISS FARNSWORTH-- GET ME NELSON AND LASSITER ON THE TELEPHONE. THEN YOU MAY LEAVE FOR THE DAY.

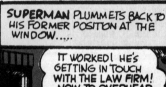

SUPERMAN PLUMMETS BACK TO HIS FORMER POSITION AT THE WINDOW.....

IT WORKED! HE'S GETTING IN TOUCH WITH THE LAW FIRM! NOW, TO OVERHEAR DEVELOPMENTS!

A MAN OF TREMENDOUS STRENGTH--IT MUST HAVE BEEN SUPERMAN--WITNESSED THE DIAMOND SALE! I'M CLEARING OUT OF TOWN BEFORE HE LEARNS MORE!

WAIT, JACKSON! $100,000 IS YOURS--IF YOU ELIMINATE SUPERMAN!

$100,000! FOR THAT AMOUNT, IT MIGHT BE ARRANGED!

DISGUISED BY SHELL-RIMMED GLASSES, LOIS ENTERS THE JEWELRY STORE.....

WHAT CAN I DO FOR YOU?

I CAN SEE THAT MARJORIE IS GONE. I'M HER AUNT JOSEPHINE FROM BRETTVILLE. DO YOU MIND IF I WAIT FOR HER UNCLE? HE'S TO MEET ME HERE.

UNOBSERVED, LOIS SLIPS A LEDGER AND SMALL BLACK BOOK FROM JACKSON'S DESK INTO HER HANDBAG.....

("-IF ONLY HE DOESN'T TURN...!-")

THE TWO HOODLUMS WHO HAD KIDNAPPED CLARK ENTER THE STORE.....

WHAT ARE YOU MEN DOING HERE?

YOU OWE US SOME MONEY--REMEMBER?

AND WE'VE COME TO COLLECT!

WELL, LOOK WHO'S HERE!

MAYBE SHE'D BE BETTER LOOKIN' WITHOUT THOSE GLASSES!

("-ONE OF THOSE MEN. I ONCE SAW HIM IN A POLICE LINEUP. IF THEY REMOVE THE GLASSES HE'S LIABLE TO RECOGNIZE ME!-")

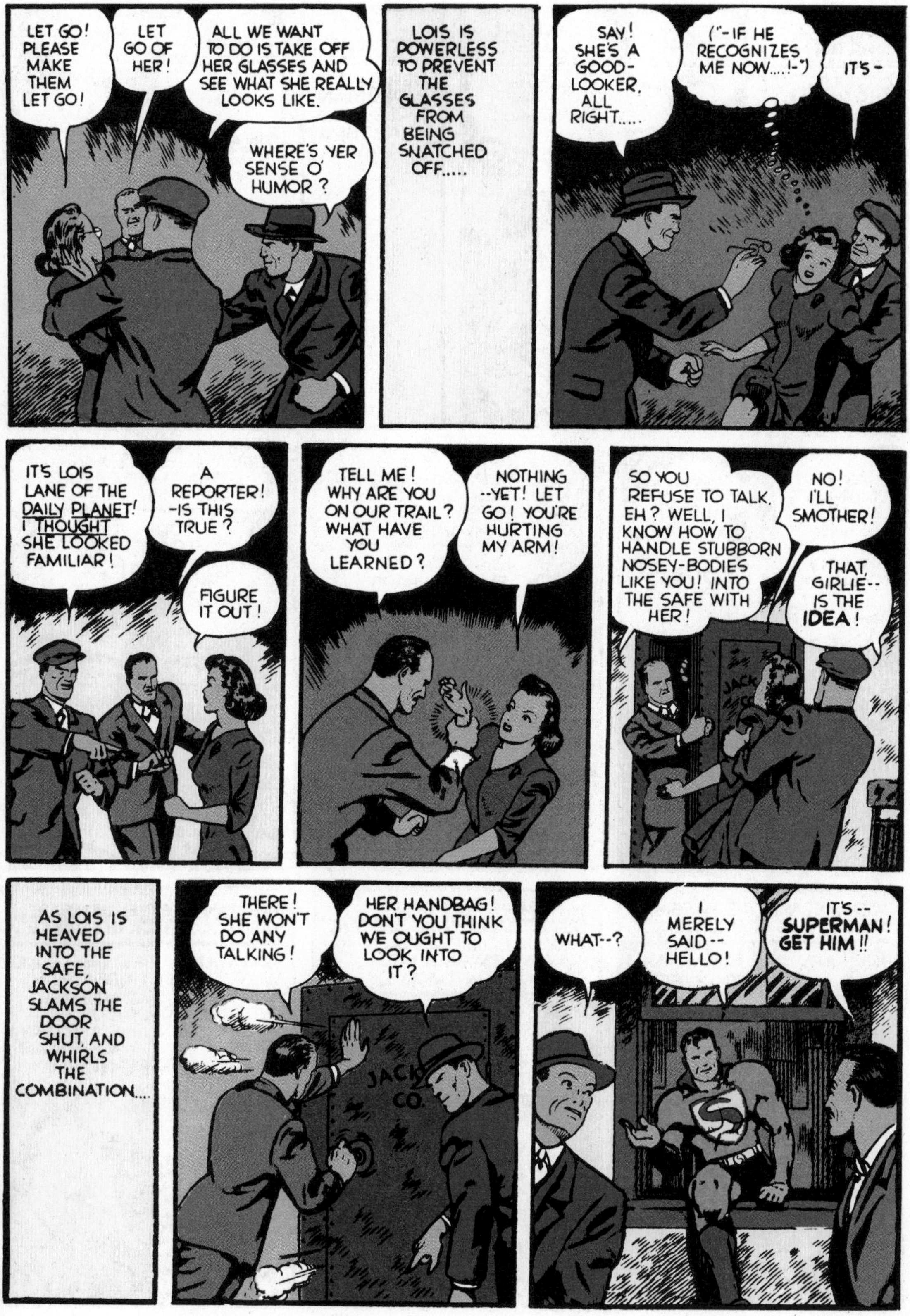
LET GO! PLEASE MAKE THEM LET GO!
LET GO OF HER!
ALL WE WANT TO DO IS TAKE OFF HER GLASSES AND SEE WHAT SHE REALLY LOOKS LIKE.
WHERE'S YER SENSE O' HUMOR?
LOIS IS POWERLESS TO PREVENT THE GLASSES FROM BEING SNATCHED OFF.....
SAY! SHE'S A GOOD-LOOKER, ALL RIGHT.....
("-IF HE RECOGNIZES ME NOW....!-")
IT'S -
IT'S LOIS LANE OF THE DAILY PLANET! I THOUGHT SHE LOOKED FAMILIAR!
A REPORTER! -IS THIS TRUE?
FIGURE IT OUT!
TELL ME! WHY ARE YOU ON OUR TRAIL? WHAT HAVE YOU LEARNED?
NOTHING --YET! LET GO! YOU'RE HURTING MY ARM!
SO YOU REFUSE TO TALK, EH? WELL, I KNOW HOW TO HANDLE STUBBORN NOSEY-BODIES LIKE YOU! INTO THE SAFE WITH HER!
NO! I'LL SMOTHER!
THAT, GIRLIE-- IS THE IDEA!
AS LOIS IS HEAVED INTO THE SAFE, JACKSON SLAMS THE DOOR SHUT, AND WHIRLS THE COMBINATION....
THERE! SHE WON'T DO ANY TALKING!
HER HANDBAG! DON'T YOU THINK WE OUGHT TO LOOK INTO IT?
WHAT--?
I MERELY SAID-- HELLO!
IT'S-- SUPERMAN! GET HIM!!

AS THE CRIMINALS OPEN FIRE, **SUPERMAN** ADVANCES INTO THE HAIL OF BULLETS-- UNHARMED!

THEY-- THEY'RE BOUNCING OFF!

KEEP FIRING!

I CAN'T LET THIS WASTE OF GOOD BULLETS CONTINUE! AND SO.....

SNATCHING AWAY THE WEAPONS, **SUPERMAN** HURLS THEM CLEAR THRU THE WALL.....

--I'LL HAVE TO DISPOSE OF THE GUNS!

L-LOOK AT THAT!

I--I'M LOOKING! BUT I **STILL** DON'T BELIEVE IT!

BACK--I'VE CORROSIVE BULLETS IN THIS GUN! YOU HAVEN'T A CHANCE!

I'LL TAKE MY CHANCES.

AS THE CORROSIVE BULLET STRIKES **SUPERMAN'S** CHEST, IT REBOUNDS...AND PENE- TRATES THE THICK STEEL DOOR OF THE SAFE!

LOIS--WITHIN THAT SAFE! PERHAPS SHE'S INJURED!

JACKSON CO.

LEAPING IN --**SUPERMAN** GRASPS THE SAFE'S FRONT, AND STRAINS.....

FOR-- LOIS--!

WITH A CRASH, THE MASSIVE DOOR FLIES OPEN.....

LOIS! ARE YOU UNHARMED?

A FEW MORE MINUTES AND I MIGHT HAVE SUFFOCATED! STOP THEM-- THEY'RE TRYING TO ESCAPE!

WITH INCREDIBLE SPEED, **SUPERMAN** OVERTAKES THE FLEEING CRIMINALS AND HEAVES THEM BACK INTO THE SAFE'S INTERIOR.....

AWK -STOP!

GET BACK IN THERE!

THE MAN OF STEEL JAMS THE SAFE DOOR BACK INTO PLACE....

THAT WILL MAKE THEM STAY PUT UNTIL THE POLICE ARRIVE!

THEY'LL GET SOME IDEA OF HOW I FELT IN THERE. ONLY YOU, OF COURSE, ARE LEAV- ING SPACE FOR AIR TO REACH THEM!

JACKSO CO.

A GREAT LEAP CARRIES **SUPERMAN** AND LOIS OUT THRU THE CITY....

WOULD YOU MIND DROPPING ME OFF AT THE POLICE PROSECUTOR'S OFFICE?

NOT AT ALL!

WAIT! I ALMOST FORGOT TO THANK YOU!

ANYTHING TO OBLIGE!

BACK IN JACKSON'S OFFICE..... BEFORE THEIR CONCENTRATED EFFORT, THE SAFE-DOOR SWINGS OPEN, SPILLING THEM OUT.....

LET'S BEAT IT!

NO--WAIT 'TILL I MAKE A TELEPHONE CALL!

JACKSON MAKES HIS CALL...

I KNOW OF A WAY WE CAN COVER THE CARLING KILLING. NOW LISTEN......

YES.... YES....

MEANWHILE --AT THE <u>METROPOLIS TOWER</u>......

WELL, WELL! I SEE THAT JACKSON AND HIS FRIENDS HAVE FREED THEMSELVES AND ARE PAYING <u>NELSON AND LASSITER</u> A VISIT!

AND IN THE PROSECUTOR'S OFFICE..

BUT THIS LEDGER ONLY SHOWS TRANSACTIONS OF THE <u>JACKSON JEWELRY COMPANY</u>

HOWEVER, WITH THE AID OF THIS LITTLE CODE BOOK, IT CAN BE SEEN THAT MORTON CARLING WAS MURDERED FOR $50,000 PAID BY GEORGE STEELE, ONE OF THE HEIRS....!

LOIS, SERGEANT CASEY, AND SEVERAL SQUAD-CARS INSTANTLY SET OUT IN A DASH TO THE LAW OFFICE OF <u>NELSON AND LASSITER</u>.....

SO THE <u>JACKSON JEWELRY COMPANY</u> WAS JUST THE FRONT FOR A MURDER SYNDICATE THAT DISGUISED THE TRANSFER OF BLOOD MONEY AS JEWELRY PAYMENTS!

THAT'S RIGHT! --WHILE OTHER POLICE-CARS PICK UP STEELE AND JACKSON, MY SUGGESTION IS THAT WE CLOSE IN ON THE LAW FIRM!

WITHIN THE LAW-OFFICE.... AS THE MEN HOLD A CONFERENCE, UNAWARE OF THE <u>MAN OF STEEL'S</u> SCRUTINY, NELSON NOTES.....

TIME FOR MY MEDICINE!

DON'T YOU FIND TAKING MEDICINE A NUISANCE?

HE HAS TO DO IT AT REGULAR INTERVALS. DOCTOR'S ORDERS!

⑫

UNNOTICED BY NELSON, JACKSON DROPS SOME PILLS INTO HIS MEDICINE.....

OH, YES-- THERE'S ANOTHER IMPORTANT POINT I WANTED TO BRING UP.

YES ?

("-NOW!-")

AS NELSON RAISES THE GLASS TO HIS LIPS....

DROP THAT GLASS!

WHAT--?

AS LOIS AND SERGEANT CASEY ENTER THE OFFICE AT THAT MOMENT.....

SUPERMAN! -WHAT ARE YOU DOING HERE ?

JACKSON PLANNED TO POISON NELSON. YOU'LL FIND MORE PILLS IN HIS POCKET !

JACKSON AND NELSON-- YOU'RE UNDER ARREST FOR THE MURDER OF CARLING !

MY PARTNER-- AN ACCOMPLICE IN MURDER! IF THAT'S **TRUE**, I INSIST HE BE PROSECUTED!

TRYING TO SNEAK OUT AND LEAVE ME IN THE LURCH, HUH ? --WELL, THEN LISTEN TO THIS ! -LASSITER HIRED ONE OF MY MEN TO BASH AND SHOVE CARLING THRU THE WINDOW WHEN NELSON WAS OUT OF THE ROOM. HE HAD NELSON BUY THAT WORTHLESS DIAMOND FOR HIM. AND NOW, HE WANTED ME TO POISON NELSON SO THAT IT WOULD LOOK LIKE SUICIDE -THEN HE WAS GOING TO PIN ALL THE BLAME ON NELSON!

ABRUPTLY WHIPPING OUT A GUN, LASSITER FIRES AT JACKSON......

YOU SQUEALING--!

GOT THE BULLET! CASEY-→ GET NELSON !

.... GAINING HIS CAR, LASSITER BEGINS A GETAWAY DASH.....

THEY'LL NEVER GET ME-- **NEVER** !

STREAKING DOWN BEFORE THE AUTO, **SUPERMAN** FLIPS IT BACK SO THAT IT ALIGHTS UPON ITS ROOF......

YOU'VE ANOTHER GUESS COMING !

LATER...

CLARK, I'M STILL TRYING TO FIGURE OUT HOW YOU COULD HAVE RUSHED THAT MURDER-RING STORY INTO PRINT BEFORE I DID !

MAYBE I HAVE MORE ABILITY THAN YOU GIVE ME CREDIT FOR. ("- SO FAR SHE HASN'T GUESSED AT MY REAL IDENTITY AS **SUPERMAN**. BUT THIS CAN'T GO ON FOREVER. SOME DAY I'LL MAKE A SLIP, AND THEN....!-")

THE END

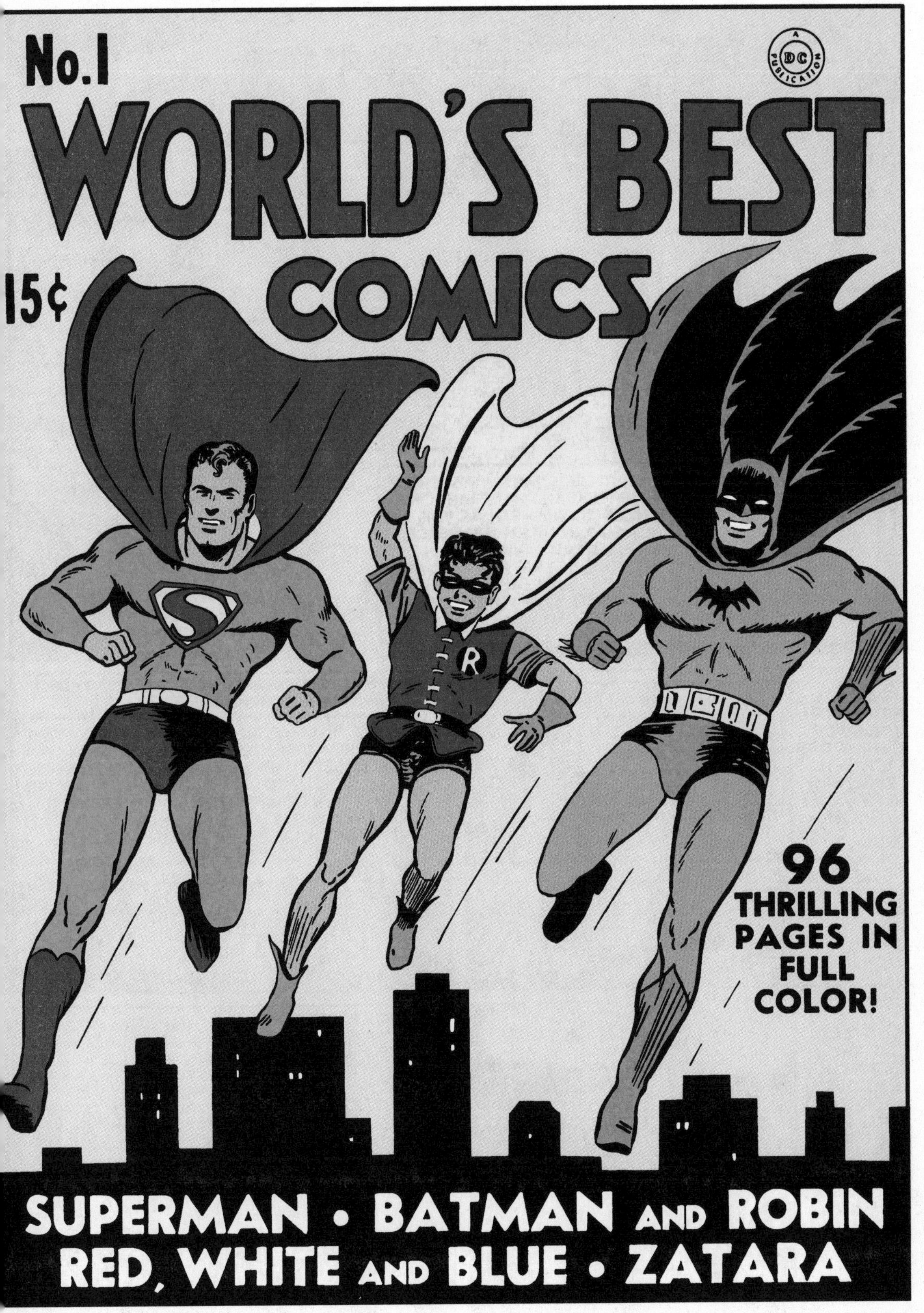
No. 1
A DC PUBLICATION
WORLD'S BEST COMICS
15¢
R
96 THRILLING PAGES IN FULL COLOR!
SUPERMAN • BATMAN AND ROBIN
RED, WHITE AND BLUE • ZATARA

SUPERMAN

by JERRY SIEGEL and JOE SHUSTER

WHEN A CRIMINAL SCIENTIST BECOMES MASTER OF ONE OF NATURE'S MOST BENEFICIAL PHENOMENONS, A BREW OF EVIL COMMENCES TO SIMMER! AS THE GREEDY PLOTTER'S SCHEMES THREATEN THE PEACE AND EXISTENCE OF AN IMPORTANT INDUSTRY, SUPERMAN STEPS IN TO DEMONSTRATE IN HIS OWN INIMITABLE FASHION THAT MIGHT CAN BE ON THE SIDE OF RIGHT—ESPECIALLY WHEN THE AMAZING MAN OF TOMORROW IS ON THE JOB!

B. DREXEL RUTHERFORD, HEAD OF RUTHERFORD UTILITIES, RECEIVES A PUZZLING VISITOR....

YOU MEAN TO SAY YOU'RE TAKING UP MY VALUABLE TIME JUST TO INFORM ME THAT YOU BELIEVE IT'S GOING TO RAIN IN FIVE MINUTES?

YOU MISUNDERSTAND ME—I DON'T BELIEVE IT'S GOING TO RAIN—I KNOW IT IS!

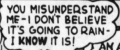

FIVE MINUTES LATER—TO THE SECOND—A DOWNPOUR COMMENCES....

WHAT AN AMAZING CO-INCIDENCE!

CO-INCIDENCE, DID YOU SAY? MAY I DISAGREE! I KNEW THE RAIN WAS COMING BECAUSE I COMMANDED IT TO! YOU SEE, MR. RUTHERFORD, I HAVE LEARNED HOW TO GOVERN RAINFALL—AND UNLESS YOU PAY ME WELL, I'LL SEE TO IT THAT YOUR DAM IN IMPERIAL VALLEY IS DESTROYED!

STARTLED AT THE STRANGE REQUEST, RUTHERFORD CALLS FOR THE OFFICE "BOUNCER", BUT WHEN HE TURNS, HE FINDS.....

WHAT DO YOU WANT, BOSS?

I WANT YOU TO… WHAT?? HE'S GONE!

BUT SHORTLY AFTER....

YOU!

YOU THINK ME A HARMLESS CRANK, EH? YOU WILL SOON LEARN DIFFERENTLY—AT YOUR EMPLOYEES' PICNIC, FOR EXAMPLE!

A WEEK LATER—AT THE OUTING....

IT WOULD RAIN!

UNFORTUNATE, ISN'T IT?

("—HM-MM!—IT'S HARD TO BELIEVE THAT MADMAN'S THREAT—BUT—CAN THIS RAIN HAVE A MORE SINISTER SIGNIFICANCE THAN IS APPARENT?—")

NEXT DAY—ONE OF RUTHERFORD'S MOST IMPORTANT EXECUTIVES IS FOUND—DROWNED!

AND ON THE SUCCEEDING DAY, ANOTHER EXECUTIVE IS SLAIN IN AN "ACCIDENT"....

IT'S TERRIBLE! A TERRIFIC STORM CAME UP WHILE HE WAS FISHING. HE FELL OFF THE YACHT.

I SYMPATHIZE DEEPLY!

("CAN THIS BE MORE 'PROOF' FROM THAT EVIL RAIN-MAKER? WHETHER IT IS OR NOT, I REFUSE TO BE INTIMIDATED BY HIM!—")

SEVERAL DAYS LATER—AS CLARK KENT SAUNTERS DOWN THE STREET, A FIRE ENGINE ROARS BY....

A FIRE!

... HE DEFTLY SWINGS HIMSELF UP ATOP IT!

HAVEN'T CHASED ONE IN YEARS!:

SA-AAY! I DON'T REMEMBER YOU! WHERE DID YOU COME FROM?

ME? I'M CLARK KENT OF THE PLANET! BEEN HERE ALL THE TIME! REMEMBER?

("—WHEW! I MUST REMEMBER NOT TO ABANDON THE ROLE OF TIMID REPORTER! I ALMOST GAVE MYSELF AWAY THAT TIME!—")

WHEN THE FIRE-TRUCK HALTS AT ITS DESTINATION, THE RUTHERFORD MANSION....

TOO HOT FOR THE FIREMEN TO REACH THAT WINDOW ON THE LADDER! BUT IF RUTHERFORD AND HIS WIFE DON'T RECEIVE ASSISTANCE SOON, THEY'RE DONE FOR!

LOOKS LIKE A JOB FOR SUPERMAN!

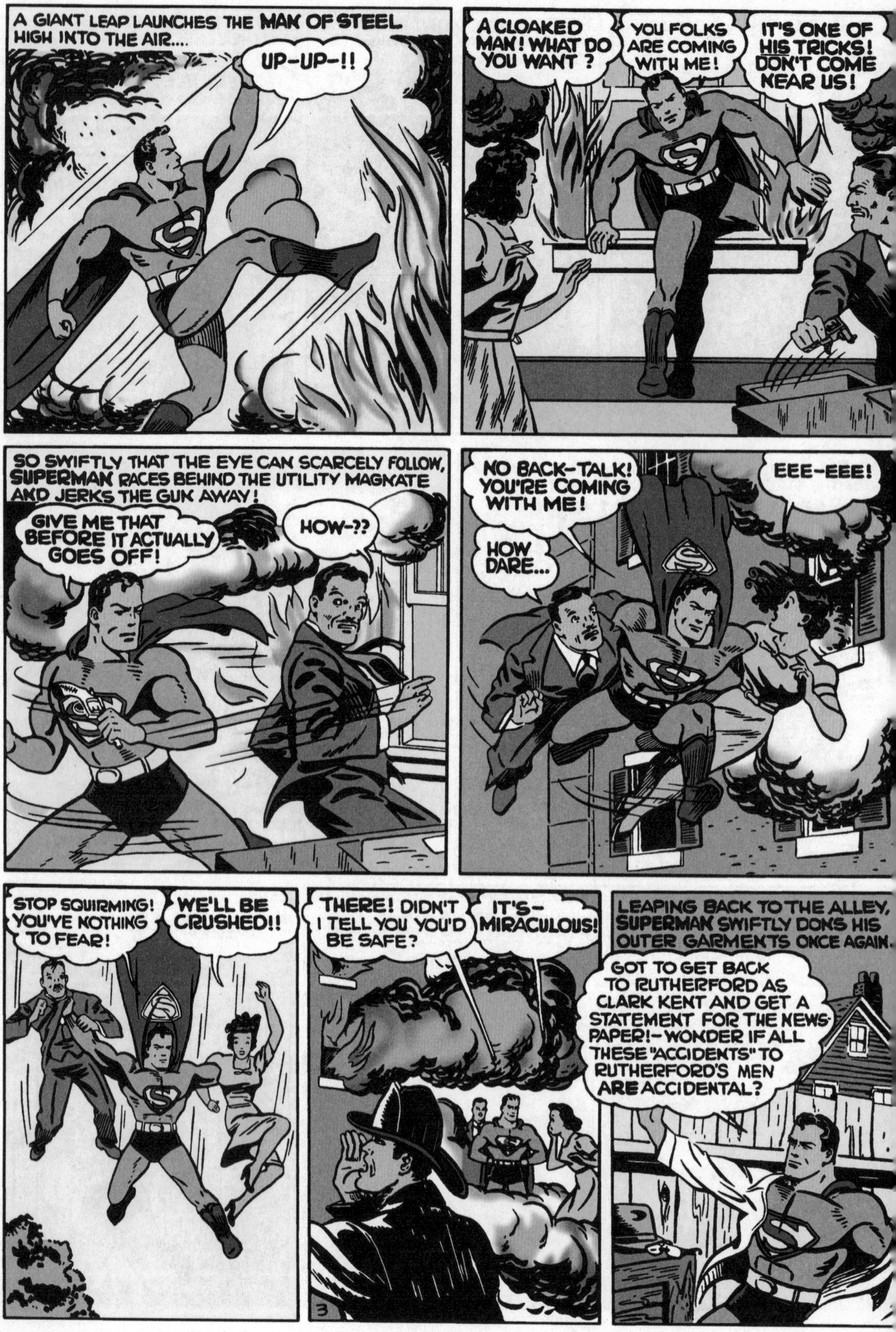
A GIANT LEAP LAUNCHES THE MAN OF STEEL HIGH INTO THE AIR....
UP-UP-!!
A CLOAKED MAN! WHAT DO YOU WANT ?
YOU FOLKS ARE COMING WITH ME!
IT'S ONE OF HIS TRICKS! DON'T COME NEAR US!
SO SWIFTLY THAT THE EYE CAN SCARCELY FOLLOW, SUPERMAN RACES BEHIND THE UTILITY MAGNATE AND JERKS THE GUN AWAY!
GIVE ME THAT BEFORE IT ACTUALLY GOES OFF!
HOW-??
NO BACK-TALK! YOU'RE COMING WITH ME!
EEE-EEE!
HOW DARE...
STOP SQUIRMING! YOU'VE NOTHING TO FEAR!
WE'LL BE CRUSHED!!
THERE! DIDN'T I TELL YOU YOU'D BE SAFE?
IT'S- MIRACULOUS!
3
LEAPING BACK TO THE ALLEY, SUPERMAN SWIFTLY DONS HIS OUTER GARMENTS ONCE AGAIN.
GOT TO GET BACK TO RUTHERFORD AS CLARK KENT AND GET A STATEMENT FOR THE NEWS-PAPER!-WONDER IF ALL THESE "ACCIDENTS" TO RUTHERFORD'S MEN ARE ACCIDENTAL?

I'M FROM THE DAILY PLANET! WAS THIS BLAZE ACCIDENTAL, OR CAN IT BE THAT....?

THE FIRE WAS DELIBERATE! AND I'LL BE ONLY TOO GLAD TO SUPPLY YOU WITH THE DETAILS. I'VE BEEN SILENT LONG ENOUGH!

IT IS BEST YOU TELL EVERYTHING!

I WAS APPROACHED BY AN APPARENT MADMAN WHO CLAIMED HE COULD CONTROL THE FALL OF RAIN. AMONG OTHER THREATS, HE STATED THAT UNLESS I CAME TO TERMS HE WOULD DESTROY THE IMPERIAL DAM!

SOUNDS LIKE A RUTHLESS CUSS!

LATER—AS CLARK HURRIES BACK TOWARD THE NEWSPAPER, HE ABRUPTLY SENSES DANGER!

BEHIND ME!

HE TURNS IN TIME TO SEE A RUNAWAY BUS LOOMING OVER HIM!

WHAT-!?

THE REPORTER BARELY HAS TIME TO FALL BENEATH THE TRUCKS WHEELS....

RAISING IT UPWARD WITH HIS FEET, HE TEARS THE DRIVE SHAFT APART WITH STEELY FINGERS!

THAT OUGHT TO STOP IT!

I WAS UNNOTICED ON THE DESERTED STREET, THANK GOODNESS!—NOW LET'S SEE WHAT'S THE TROUBLE WITHIN THE BUS!

INSTANTLY, CLARK'S SUPER-SENSITIVE NOSTRILS DETECT...

GAS! CARBON MONOXIDE GAS! UNLESS THE AIR IN THE BUS IS CLEARED—AND SWIFTLY—THE OVERCOME PASSENGERS AND DRIVER ARE DOOMED!

METROPOLIS

CLARK RACES 'ROUND AND 'ROUND THE BUS AT SUCH TERRIFIC SPEED THAT GREAT GUSTS OF AIR ARE AROUSED, CLEARING AWAY THE GAS...

AS AMBULANCES ARRIVE ON THE SCENE AND CARRY OFF THE VICTIMS OF THE GAS, CLARK MANAGES TO EXCHANGE A FEW WORDS WITH THE REVIVED BUS-DRIVER....

THIS WAS MY FIRST RUN FOR THE DAY. ONE MINUTE I FELT A HEADACHE, THEN— BLOOIE—EVERYTHING WENT DARK!

("THIS BUS-LINE IS CONTROLLED BY RUTHERFORD AND HIS ASSOCIATES. CAN THE RAINMAKER HAVE STRUCK AGAIN?")

CHIEF, I'VE RECEIVED A TIP FROM RUTHERFORD THAT HE EXPECTS TROUBLE AT THE IMPERIAL DAM. SHALL I INVESTIGATE?

GO TO IT!

WITHIN A STORE-ROOM, THE MEEK REPORTER CHANGES TO MIGHTY SUPERMAN....

NO TELLING WHEN THAT MADMAN WILL STRIKE! AND SO I'D BETTER REACH THE DAM IN A MINIMUM SPACE OF TIME!

OUT THRU THE STOREROOM WINDOW LEAPS SUPERMAN, STREAKING HIGH INTO SPACE....

SORRY—I LOOKED ALL OVER, BUT I COULDN'T FIND CLARK ANY-WHERE!

WHY'D HE HAVE TO RUSH OFF LIKE THAT? I WANT YOU TO COVER THE STORY, TOO. GET GOING!

AND SO, IT OCCURS THAT LOIS TAKES A PLANE TOWARD IMPERIAL VALLEY AT ONCE!

MEANWHILE—SIGHTING AN EXPLOSION AT THE BUSINESS OFFICE OF RUTHERFORD UTILITIES NEAR THE DAM, THE MAN OF TOMORROW SWOOPS DOWNWARD....

WORKING MEN WITHIN THAT BUILDING. I'VE GOT TO HURRY!

SUPERMAN STREAKS INTO THE OFFICE BUILDING TOWARD A COLLAPSING WALL IN A DESPERATE RACE AGAINST TIME!

THE WORKMEN— UNCONSCIOUS!

THERE—THAT SHOULD STEADY THE WALL, IF ONLY FOR A FEW MOMENTS....

SCOOPING UP THE HELPLESS WORKERS, SUPERMAN LEAPS TO SAFETY WITH THEM AS THE WALL COLLAPSES BEHIND THEM!

MADE IT!

WHAT IS IT?

READ!

SO—IT'S A WARNING FROM MY FRIEND, THE RAINMAKER, WARNING ME NOT TO INTERFERE—

AND WHEN THE BOSS SAYS TO LAY OFF—IT AIN'T HEALTHY TO CROSS HIM!

NOTHING WOULD INTRIGUE ME MORE THAN TO INCONVENIENCE YOUR BOSS. NO—I'M AFRAID HE AND I ARE GOING TO BECOME BETTER ACQUAINTED!

SO THAT'S HOW IT IS, EH?

YOU HEARD ME!

("I DID—AN' IT'S YOUR FUNERAL!")

DELIBERATELY AIMING AT SUPERMAN'S BACK, THE COLD-BLOODED ASSASSIN—FIRES!

YOU ASKED FOR IT!!

6

IT—B-B-BOUNCED OFF!

AND I'VE A NOTION TO BOUNCE MY FIST OFF YOUR CHIN!

FOR THAT COWARDLY STUNT, MY FRIEND, YOU'RE GOING TO GUIDE ME TO YOUR BOSS! AND PRONTO!

BUT—HIS LABORATORY IS LOCATED MILES AWAY IN MILLERTON!

THAT'S NO DRAW-BACK! WE'LL BE THERE IN A JIFFY!

AWK!

ALIGHTING NEAR THE LABORATORY, SUPERMAN WALKS OFF FROM THE UNCONSCIOUS FIGURE OF HIS GUIDE, UNAWARE OF A MONSTROUS SHADOW REARING UP BEHIND HIM!

THE RAINMAKER'S LABORATORY—AHEAD! NOW TO....

ABRUPTLY, THE COILS OF A GIANT BOA CONSTRICTOR SEIZE SUPERMAN IN A TERRIBLE GRIP....

TRAINED TO KEEP INTRUDERS AWAY, EH?

AS THE HUGE REPTILE SEEKS TO CRUSH ITS CAPTIVE, SUPERMAN STRAINS AT THE TIGHTENING BONDS....

READY—SET—

—GO!!

THERE—THAT SHOULD KEEP YOU OCCUPIED FOR A WHILE!

NO SOONER DOES SUPERMAN DISPOSE OF OKE FOE THAN HE IS SET UPON BY A DOZEN MORE....

MORE SNAKES!

GET HIM!

RIDDLE HIM WITH BULLETS!

NEXT MOMENT, THE ATTACKERS FLY APART AS THO STRUCK BY A HURRICANE...!

LOOKING FOR TROUBLE? HERE IT IS!

THAT FOR THESE WEAPONS!

SO, RUTHERFORD CHOSE TO DEFY ME! VERY WELL—FOR SENDING YOU AGAINST ME, I WILL DESTROY HIS DAM!

NOT IF I CAN HELP IT!

YOU DO NOT TAKE INTO ACCOUNT MY RADICAL NEW PARALYSIS-GAS!

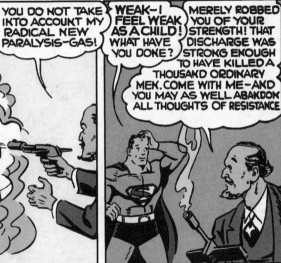

WEAK—I FEEL WEAK AS A CHILD! WHAT HAVE YOU DONE?

MERELY ROBBED YOU OF YOUR STRENGTH! THAT DISCHARGE WAS STRONG ENOUGH TO HAVE KILLED A THOUSAND ORDINARY MEN. COME WITH ME—AND YOU MAY AS WELL ABANDON ALL THOUGHTS OF RESISTANCE

ATTACKED BY A FEELING OF OVER-POWERING WEAKNESS, SUPERMAN QUIETLY FOLLOWS....

BEHOLD—MY RAIN-MACHINE! WITH ITS ASSIST-ANCE I CAN MAKE —OR DESTROY— A WORLD!

YOU MUSTN'T DESTROY THAT DAM! HUNDREDS OF FARMERS IN THE VALLEY WILL HAVE THEIR PROPERTY RUINED—MANY WILL DIE....

DISREGARDING THE MAN OF TOMORROW'S PLEAS, THE RAIN-MAKER TURNS ON HIS FIENDISH MACHINE. IN RESPONSE, THE SKY DARKENS, THUNDER CRACKLES, LIGHTNING STABS OVERHEAD—THEN A DOWN-POUR COMMENCES WHICH STEADILY INCREASES IN FEROCITY.

("—IF ONLY I COULD FREE MYSELF FROM THE GRIP OF THE PARALYSIS-GAS! BUT MY STRUGGLES SEEM IN VAIN!—")

RAIN! HO! HO! HO! —RAIN! RAIN!

("—HE'S MAD!—")

A FINAL, TERRIFIC EFFORT—AND SUPERMAN FEELS HIS STRENGTH SURGE BACK!

("—THAT'S BETTER!—")

LEAPING IN, SUPERMAN KNOCKS THE RAINMAKER UNCONSCIOUS.

OUT—LIKE A LIGHT!

A VERITABLE FLOOD—WITH CONDITIONS EVEN WORSE MILES OVER TOWARD THE DAM! IF THIS KEEPS UP.....

GLANCING BACK AT THE LABORATORY, SUPERMAN'S X-RAY VISION REVEALS TO HIM THAT THE RAINMAKER HAS REVIVED AND IS CONTINUING HIS EVIL WORK....

MORE RAIN! MORE! I'LL SHOW THEM! I'LL WIPE THAT DAM OFF THE FACE OF THE EARTH!

HE INSISTS ON SPREADING DE-STRUCTION, AND SO—

—HERE'S A TASTE OF HIS OWN MEDICINE!

MEANWHILE—OVER THE VALLEY IN A FIERCELY PITCHING AIRPLANE....

WHAT'S THE TROUBLE?

A TERRIBLE STORM! FASTE YOUR SEAT-BELT

HIGH ABOVE EARTH, STREAKING THRU THE DOWNPOUR, SPEEDS SUPERMAN....!

IF ONLY I'M NOT ALREADY TOO LATE.....

BELOW...THE GROUND SHOWS EFFECTS OF THE TERRIBLE RAIN-BLITZKRIEG! TREES ARE BEATEN DOWN.... ROADS FLOODED....

THE DAM-GIVING WAY!

DOWN STREAKS SUPERMAN, BUT BEFORE HE CAN ACT TO PREVENT IT, THE HUGE DAM BLOWS APART BEFORE THE IRRESISTIBLE FORCE OF THE FLOODING WATERS!

TOO LATE!

BUT PERHAPS IT'S NOT TOO LATE TO PREVENT THE SPREAD OF DESTRUCTION!

A DISTANCE AHEAD OF THE TORRENT, SUPERMAN COMMENCES DIGGING A GREAT PIT LEADING THRU A PASS IN THE MOUNTAINS AWAY FROM THE FERTILE LAND AND TOWARD AN ARID DESERT SECTION....

A MATTER OF SECONDS-!

ON RUSHES THE FLOOD-ALMOST UPON SUPERMAN!

LEAPING OUT OF THE PIT, SUPERMAN LABORIOUSLY HOISTS ALOFT A COLOSSAL BOULDER....

-UP! NOW IF THIS GAMBLE DOESN'T WORK, ALL IS LOST!

STRAIGHT AND TRUE, THE MAN OF TOMORROW HURLS THE MASSIVE BOULDER- IT FALLS SQUARELY INTO PLACE....

I'M COUNTING ON YOU!

DIVERTED BY THE PIT AND THE BOULDER, THE RAGING FLOOD TURNS ASIDE FROM THE FERTILE VALLEY AND RUSHES OUT ON TO THE ARID DESERT....

BUT WITHIN THE PLANE WHICH CARRIES LOIS....

EEE-EEE!

WE'RE FALLING-!

FALLING DOWN INTO THE FLOOD!

A MOMENT BEFORE THE PLANE CAN CRASH INTO THE WATER, A LITHE CLOAKED FORM STREAKS TOWARD IT, AND CATCHES THE UNDERCARRIAGE....

BARELY MADE IT!

THRU THE TORRENT SWIMS SUPERMAN, HOLDING THE PLANE OVERHEAD WITH HIS FREE HAND....

TALK ABOUT YOUR TICKLISH JOBS!

AFTER HE PLACES THE PLANE SAFELY DOWN NEAR MILLERTON....

I MIGHT HAVE KNOWN IT WAS YOU WHO SAVED OUR LIVES!

LOIS!

11

ABRUPTLY, A BEDRAGGLED FIGURE CHARGES FROM THE NEARBY BRUSH, SEIZES LOIS...

WHAT~??

BACK! IF ANYONE DARES TO MOVE, THE GIRL DIES! - I'M TAKING THE PLANE, SEE?

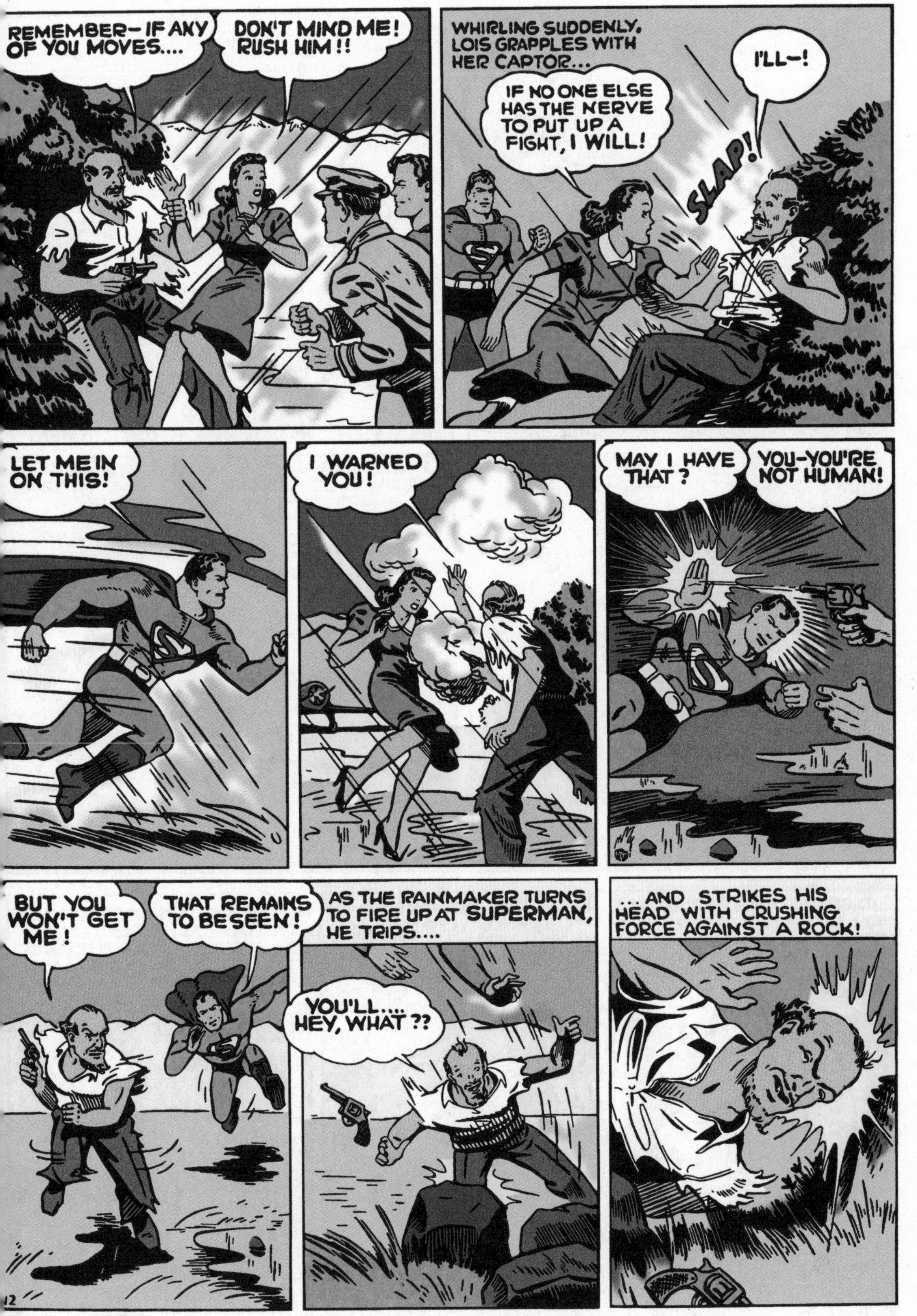
REMEMBER– IF ANY OF YOU MOVES....
DON'T MIND ME! RUSH HIM!!
WHIRLING SUDDENLY, LOIS GRAPPLES WITH HER CAPTOR...
IF NO ONE ELSE HAS THE NERVE TO PUT UP A FIGHT, I WILL!
I'LL–!
SLAP!
LET ME IN ON THIS!
I WARNED YOU!
MAY I HAVE THAT?
YOU–YOU'RE NOT HUMAN!
BUT YOU WON'T GET ME!
THAT REMAINS TO BE SEEN!
AS THE RAINMAKER TURNS TO FIRE UP AT SUPERMAN, HE TRIPS....
YOU'LL.... HEY, WHAT ??
... AND STRIKES HIS HEAD WITH CRUSHING FORCE AGAINST A ROCK!
12

HE'LL NO LONGER MENACE OR BLACK MAIL ANYONE! HE'S—DEAD!

HOW—AWFUL...!

GET BACK INTO THE PLANE!

BUT I'M NOT SURE THE SHIP'S STILL AIR-WORTHY!

YOU'D BETTER DO AS SUPERMAN SAYS!

OFF LEAPS SUPERMAN, CARRYING THE PONDEROUS PLANE OVERHEAD.....

NO DOUBT LOIS IS ANXIOUS TO GET BACK TO METROPOLIS IN A HURRY! THIS SHOULD MAKE IT POSSIBLE!

MINUTES LATER— REACHING HIS DESTINATION, SUPERMAN LOWERS THE PLANE TO A STANDSTILL AT THE AIRPORT, THEN— SPRINGS AWAY!

WAIT!

SORRY—YOU'LL NEVER FIND ME LONG ON ONE SPOT!

RUTHERFORD? MAY I SUGGEST YOU SEE TO IT THAT THE DESERT AREA IS DEVELOPED?

SUPERMAN! I'VE HEARD OF WHAT YOU'VE DONE! LET ME OFFER MY HEARTFELT THANKS!

NOW TO FIND LOIS!

HOW IN THE WORLD DID YOU EVER GET THE DETAILS FOR THIS STORY?

HOW? MERELY BY STICKING ON THE JOB WHILE YOU GO GALIVANTING ABOUT THE COUNTRY ON A JOYRIDE!

THE END

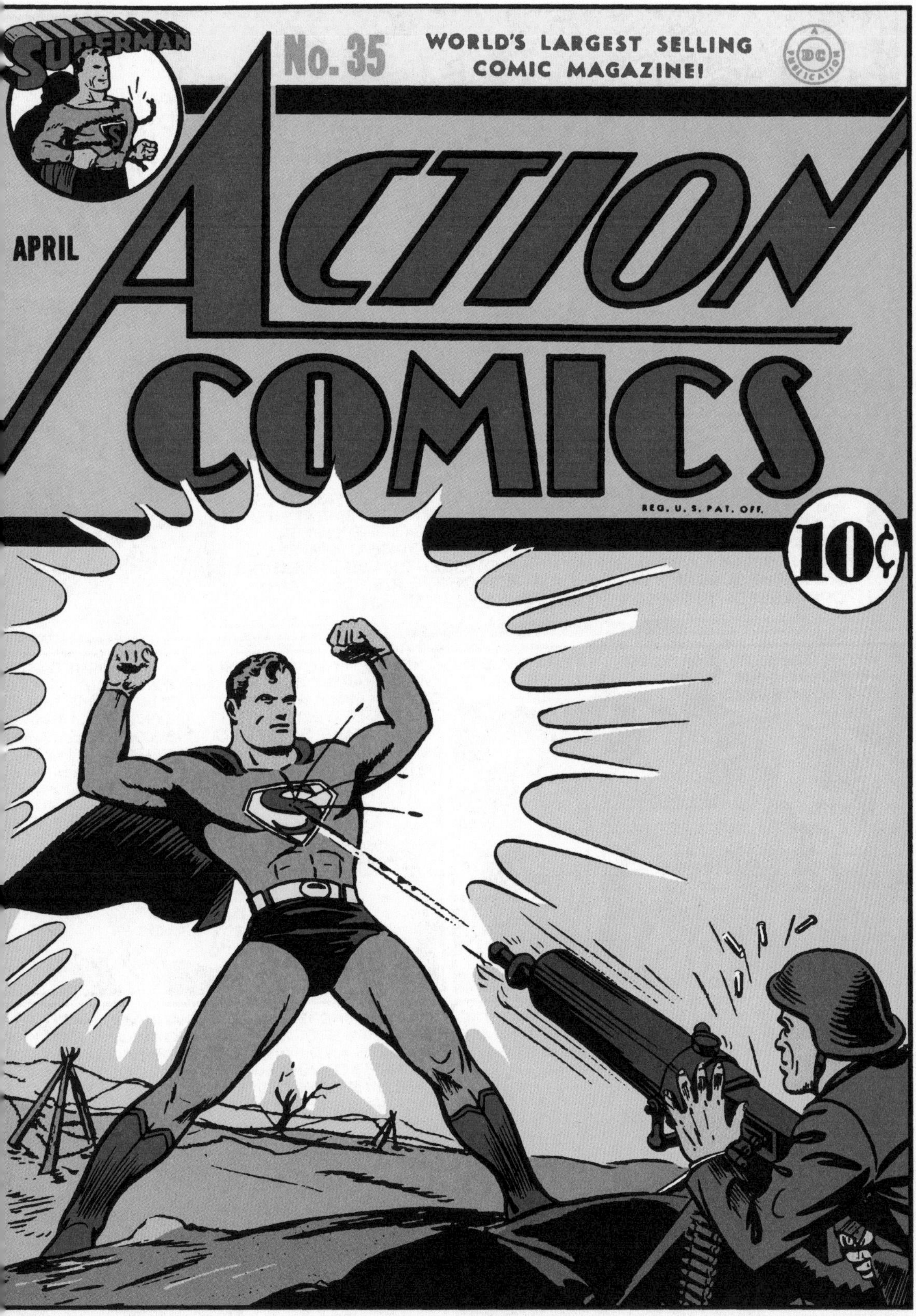
SUPERMAN
No. 35
WORLD'S LARGEST SELLING
COMIC MAGAZINE!
A DC PUBLICATION
APRIL
ACTION COMICS
REG. U. S. PAT. OFF.
10¢

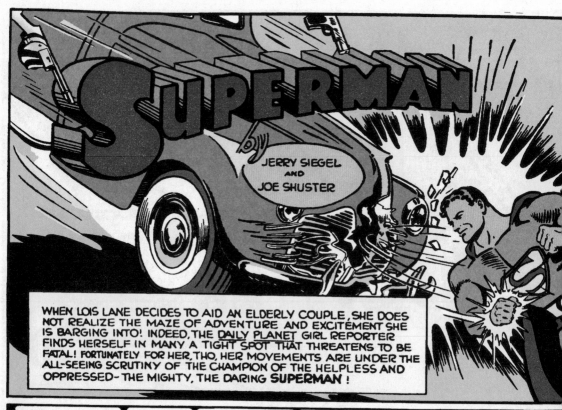

SUPERMAN

JERRY SIEGEL
AND
JOE SHUSTER

WHEN LOIS LANE DECIDES TO AID AN ELDERLY COUPLE, SHE DOES NOT REALIZE THE MAZE OF ADVENTURE AND EXCITEMENT SHE IS BARGING INTO! INDEED, THE DAILY PLANET GIRL REPORTER FINDS HERSELF IN MANY A TIGHT SPOT THAT THREATENS TO BE FATAL! FORTUNATELY FOR HER, THO, HER MOVEMENTS ARE UNDER THE ALL-SEEING SCRUTINY OF THE CHAMPION OF THE HELPLESS AND OPPRESSED— THE MIGHTY, THE DARING SUPERMAN !

WE'VE COME TO THE NEWSPAPER FOR ADVICE AND HELP.

I'M SORRY, BUT—

STEP IN, PLEASE— I'LL SPEAK TO YOU !

NOW WHAT CAN WE DO FOR YOU ?

I'M BENJAMIN SIMS AND THIS IS MY WIFE EMILY. WE USED TO BE WELL OFF, BUT HAVE SUFFERED FINANCIAL REVERSES. WE'RE ABOUT TO LOSE OUR HOME, BUT THERE'S A SLIGHT RAY OF HOPE....

A MAN VISITED US RECENTLY AND OFFERED TO BUY SOME GOLD MINING STOCK WE BOUGHT YEARS AGO. HE OFFERED TO PAY ONLY A DOLLAR A SHARE FOR OUR 500 SHARE THO WE HAD PAID MUCH MORE. SHALL WE ACCEPT HIS OFFER FOR THE GUYBART MINE STOCK

LOIS HAS THE NEWSPAPER'S FINANCIAL EDITOR APPRAISE THE WORTH OF THE STOCK....

HOW MUCH IS IT WORTH?

SORRY, LOIS— IT HASN'T THE SLIGHTEST VALUE. WHY ANYONE SHOULD SEEK TO BUY IT IS BEYOND ME.

DO YOU MIND IF I HOLD ONTO THIS STOCK FOR A FEW DAYS AND INVESTIGATE FURTHER? IT MUST HAVE SOME UNSUSPECTED VALUE IF SOMEONE WISHES TO BUY IT.

THANK YOU SO MUCH FOR BEING SO GOOD TO US!

WE'LL RETURN NEXT WEEK FOR YOUR VERDICT!

1.

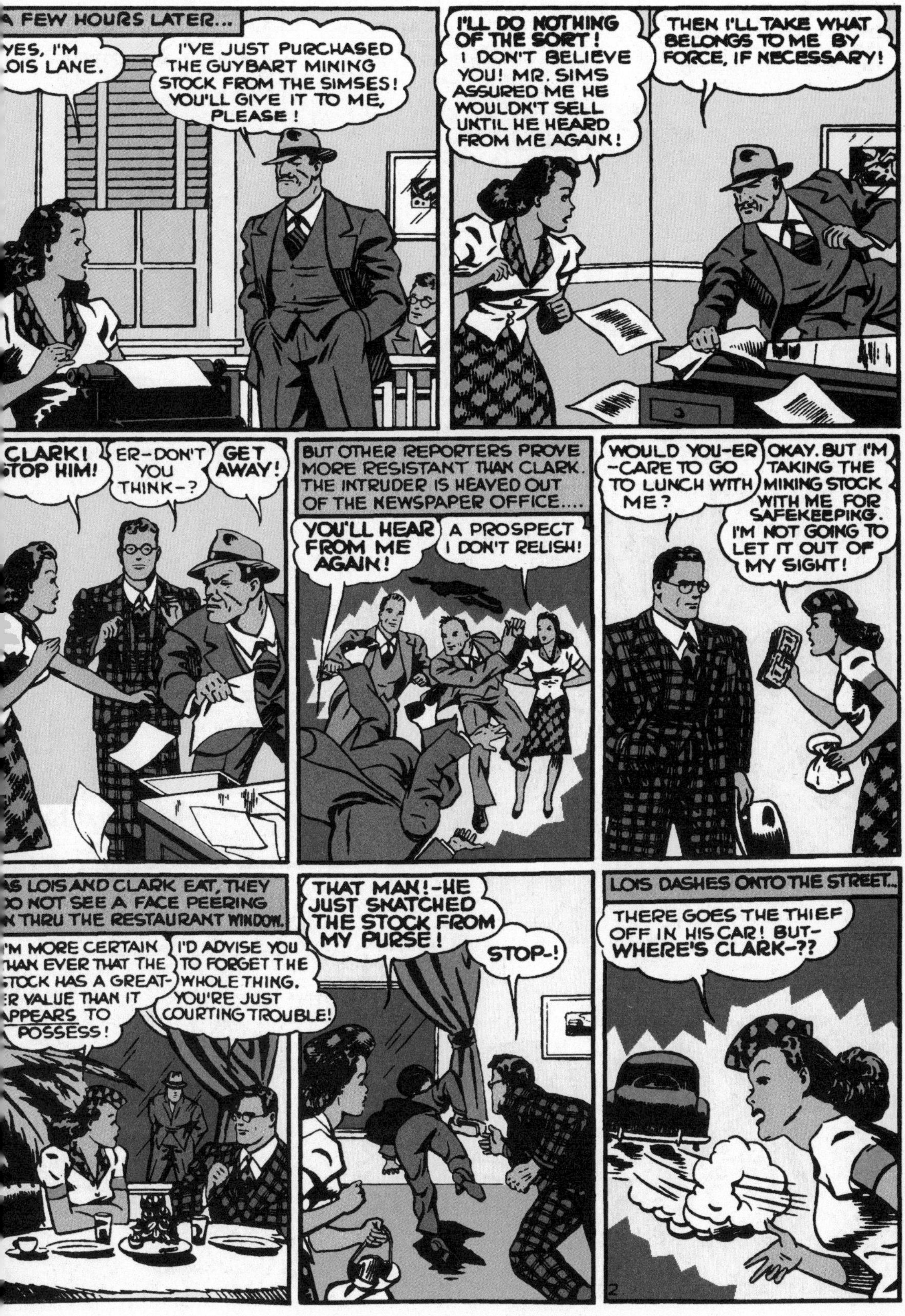
A FEW HOURS LATER...
YES, I'M LOIS LANE.
I'VE JUST PURCHASED THE GUYBART MINING STOCK FROM THE SIMSES! YOU'LL GIVE IT TO ME, PLEASE!
I'LL DO NOTHING OF THE SORT! I DON'T BELIEVE YOU! MR. SIMS ASSURED ME HE WOULDN'T SELL UNTIL HE HEARD FROM ME AGAIN!
THEN I'LL TAKE WHAT BELONGS TO ME BY FORCE, IF NECESSARY!
CLARK! STOP HIM!
ER-DON'T YOU THINK-?
GET AWAY!
BUT OTHER REPORTERS PROVE MORE RESISTANT THAN CLARK. THE INTRUDER IS HEAVED OUT OF THE NEWSPAPER OFFICE....
YOU'LL HEAR FROM ME AGAIN!
A PROSPECT I DON'T RELISH!
WOULD YOU-ER -CARE TO GO TO LUNCH WITH ME?
OKAY. BUT I'M TAKING THE MINING STOCK WITH ME FOR SAFEKEEPING. I'M NOT GOING TO LET IT OUT OF MY SIGHT!
AS LOIS AND CLARK EAT, THEY DO NOT SEE A FACE PEERING IN THRU THE RESTAURANT WINDOW.
I'M MORE CERTAIN THAN EVER THAT THE STOCK HAS A GREATER VALUE THAN IT APPEARS TO POSSESS!
I'D ADVISE YOU TO FORGET THE WHOLE THING. YOU'RE JUST COURTING TROUBLE!
THAT MAN!-HE JUST SNATCHED THE STOCK FROM MY PURSE!
STOP-!
LOIS DASHES ONTO THE STREET...
THERE GOES THE THIEF OFF IN HIS CAR! BUT-WHERE'S CLARK-??
2

DODGING SWIFTLY INTO AN ALLEY AND OUT OF LOIS' SIGHT, CLARK SWIFTLY REMOVES HIS OUTER GARMENTS, TRANSFORMING HIMSELF TO SUPERMAN—!

NOT A SECOND TO WASTE!

THERE'S HIS CAR BELOW! NOW TO THROW AN UNEXPECTED HITCH INTO HIS PLANS!

STOP—OR YOU'LL REGRET IT!

BUT AS THE AUTO CONTINUES WITH INCREASED SPEED—!

SEEING IS BELIEVING, EH?

STILL PLAYING HARD TO GET!

BANG

YOU MIGHT AS WELL HAND OVER THE STOCK RIGHT NOW!

3

HERE! TAKE THESE BLANKETY-BLANK STOCKS! ALL I KNOW IS A GUY GAVE ME A CENTURY TO SNATCH THEM—AND IT'S THE TOUGHEST "EASY MONEY" I EVER LAID HANDS ON!

I SUGGEST YOU INVESTIGATE THE POSSIBILITIES OF EARNING AN HONEST LIVING. BECAUSE IF I EVER FIND YOU ENGAGED IN CROOKED ACTIVITY AGAIN, THERE WILL BE ONE LESS THIEF IN THIS WORLD!

RETURNING TO THE ALLEY, SUPERMAN DONS HIS OUTER GARMENTS.

GETTING THE STOCK BACK WAS EASY, EXPLAINING TO LOIS HOW I GOT IT WILL BE THE TOUGH TASK!

YOU—YOU RECOVERED THE STOCKS! BUT HOW—??

YOU CAN THANK SUPERMAN FOR THAT. HE SWOOPED DOWN OUT OF THE SKY AND HANDED THEM TO ME. BEFORE I COULD QUESTION HIM, HE WAS GONE!

YOU KNOW, LOIS.... EVEN I'M BECOMING CONVINCED THAT PERHAPS THERE IS A STORY BEHIND THIS STOCK!

NOW IF ONLY I CAN MAKE WHITE BELIEVE THAT!

I TELL YOU, THERE MAY BE A BIG YARN INVOLVED. IF YOU'LL ONLY PERMIT ME TO LOOK THE GUYBART MINE OVER

AND IF YOU WANT, CHIEF I CAN ACCOMPANY LOIS AND...

MAYBE YOU HAVE SOMETHING THERE, LOIS! BUT I WANT YOU TO COVER IT ON YOUR OWN. CLARK, YOU REMAIN HERE IN METROPOLIS. I CAN SPARE ONLY ONE OF YOU!

LATER—AT THE AIRPORT....

REMEMBER—BE CAREFUL!

STILL WORRIED, CLARK? WELL, FORGET IT! THIS WILL PROBABLY TURN OUT TO BE TERRIBLY BORING!

("—THE THIEF WHO TRIED TO STEAL THE STOCKS—HURRYING INTO THE TELEGRAPH OFFICE! A LITTLE X-RAY VISION OUGHT TO COME IN HANDY NOW!—")

HE'S WARNING SOMEONE THAT LOIS IS ON THAT PLANE! —NO DOUBT OF IT! LOIS IS IN DANGER!

4.

STEPPING BEHIND A HANGAR, CLARK REMOVES AND HIDES HIS CIVILIAN GARMENTS....

LOIS MENACED! THAT IS THE SIGNAL FOR SUPERMAN TO MAKE HIS APPEARANCE!

LATER—AS THE AIRLINER FLIES THRU FLEECY CLOUDS, A SMALL PLANE ABRUPTLY COMES INTO VIEW AND CIRCLES ABOVE....

THE AIRLINER PILOT RECEIV[ES] AN ASTONISHING MESSAGE..

THAT PLANE ABOVE US—IT DEMANDS WE LAND WITHOUT RADIOING FOR HELP OR WE WILL BE SHOT DOWN!

PIRACY [IN] THE SKY!

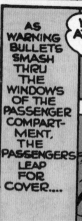

AS WARNING BULLETS SMASH THRU THE WINDOWS OF THE PASSENGER COMPARTMENT, THE PASSENGERS LEAP FOR COVER....

WE'RE ATTACKED!

KEEP DOWN!

DOWN DROPS THE GREAT TRANSPORT PLANE, AND AS IT DOES, THE ENEMY PILOT GRIMLY TIGHTENS HIS FINGER ON THE MACHINE-GUN TRIGGER...

ANOTHER SECOND AN[D] I'LL LET GO WITH A BURST THAT WILL PU[T] IT OUT OF COMMISSION —PERMANENTLY!

JUST AS THE FIGHTING PLANE PUTS THE AIRLINER OUT OF CONTROL, DOWN GOES THE STREAKING FIGURE OF THE MAN OF STEEL AND SMASHES THE MACHINE-GUN WITH ONE SWIFT BLOW OF HIS FIST....

WHAT—!

THAT ATTENDS TO THE GUN!

I'D LIKE TO GIVE THAT MACHINE-GUNNER MORE ATTENTION, BUT RIGHT NOW IT LOOKS LIKE I'D BETTER ATTEND TO THAT PLANE BEFORE IT CRASHES!

5.

SECONDS BEFORE THE GREAT SKY-VESSEL CAN SMASH, SUPERMAN NEATLY DIVES BE-NEATH IT....

THIS CALLS FOR FAST ACTION!

...AND CATCHING ITS GIANT BULK, LOWERS IT SAFELY TO EARTH!

THERE! MAYBE NOW I CAN GET AFTER THAT PILOT!

YOU HEARD ME! DESCEND!!

SO HE CHOOSES TO DISREGARD MY ORDER, EH? THIS WILL PROVE TO HIM THAT I MEAN BUSINESS!

SWIFTLY SUPERMAN TEARS OFF THE OTHER WING....

A FINAL BLOW FROM THE MAN OF TOMORROW AND THE MOTOR FLIES TO FRAGMENTS....

NEXT STOP FOR WHAT'S LEFT OF THIS PLANE—THE JUNK YARD!

AS THE CRUSHED MASS FALLS, SUPERMAN LIFTS THE PILOT TO COMPARATIVE SAFETY....

STICK AROUND! THERE ARE A COUPLE OF QUESTIONS I'D LIKE ANSWERED!

YOU'LL LEARN NOTHING FROM ME—NOTHING!

SUPERMAN SUBJECTS HIS CAPTIVE TO SOME HAIR-RAISING ACROBATICS....

STUBBORN, EH? LET'S SEE IF I CAN FRIGHTEN SOME OF THAT CUSSEDNESS OUT OF YOU!

HEY-!!!

STILL UNCOMMUNICATIVE, EH? THEN I WANT NO PART OF YOU!

EEEEK

BIRDS OF A FEATHER, EH?

HELP! I'LL TALK!

WITH THE COWED PILOT UNDER HIS ARM, SUPERMAN DROPS TO EARTH....

LET'S HAVE IT! WHY DID YOU FIRE ON THAT PLANE?

SOME GUY I NEVER SAW BEFORE OFFERED ME A COUPLE OF HUNDRED IF I'D BRING THE AIR-LINER DOWN AND STEAL SOME STOCK FROM A GIRL NAMED LOIS LANE!

BUCKLE YOUR STRAPS, FOLKS! WE'RE GOING TO ATTEMPT A TAKE-OFF!

BUT THE TERRAIN IS ROUGH! WE NEVER MAKE IT!

THEN LET HOPE FOR THE BEST

ALONG THE ROCKY GROUND SPEEDS THE PLANE, BOUNCING PRECARIOUSLY. IT APPEARS A CRASH IS IMMINENT.....

FORWARD STREAKS SUPERMAN! RAISING THE PLANE BY ITS UNDERCARRIAGE, HE HURLS IT SAFELY UP INTO THE AIR...!

ON YOUR WAY!

SUPERMAN OBSERVES LOIS SAFELY LEAVE THE PLANE AS IT REACHES ITS DESTINATION....

SHE'LL NEVER KNOW HOW REALLY CLOSE TO DISASTER SHE WAS!

COULD YOU TELL ME THE WHEREABOUTS OF THE GUYBART MINE?

BEG PARDON. I COULDN'T HELP OVER-HEARING. I'M BROCK WALTERS, OWNER OF THE WALTERS MINE. I'LL BE GLAD TO DRIVE YOU TO THE GUYBART MINE.

THERE HAVE BEEN NUMEROUS ATTEMPTS TO STEAL GUYBART MINE STOCK. THIS LEADS ME TO THE BELIEF THAT THE STOCK MAY POSSESS UNSUSPECTED VALUE.

SORRY TO DISAPPOINT YOU, BUT THAT MINE HAS BEEN ABANDONED FOR YEARS. IT'S ABSO-LUTELY WORTHLESS!

I HOPE YOU'RE WRONG! LOOK! THERE'S AN ARMOR-ED TRUCK!

THERE HAVE BEEN A NUMBER OF ROBBERIES RECENTLY, AND SO MINERS ARE HAVING THEIR GOLD SHIPPED TO THE BANK IN THAT TRUCK. I'VE BEEN LUCKY SO FAR-ESCAPED ANY ROBBERY ATTEMPT!-DO YOU MIND STOPPING AT MY OFFICE WHILE I SUPERVISE THE TRANSFER OF THE GOLD?

BUT AS WALTERS' GOLD IS RE-MOVED FROM HIS SAFE....

HOLD IT! RAISE YOUR HANDS!

AND NO FALSE MOVES!

WHAT-?

THESE GUARDS-THEY'RE FAKES!!

OUT OF THE MINE OFFICE BACK THE BANDITS, USING LOIS AS A SHIELD....

DON'T MOVE-OR WE SHOOT THE GIRL.

YOU COWARDLY...!

QUICK!

NOW FOR THE GETAWAY!

GOLD ASSAYED CLAIMS RECORDED

TOWARD LOIS' FALLEN FIGURE STREAKS THE PONDEROUS ARMORED TRUCK...

NO!!

8.

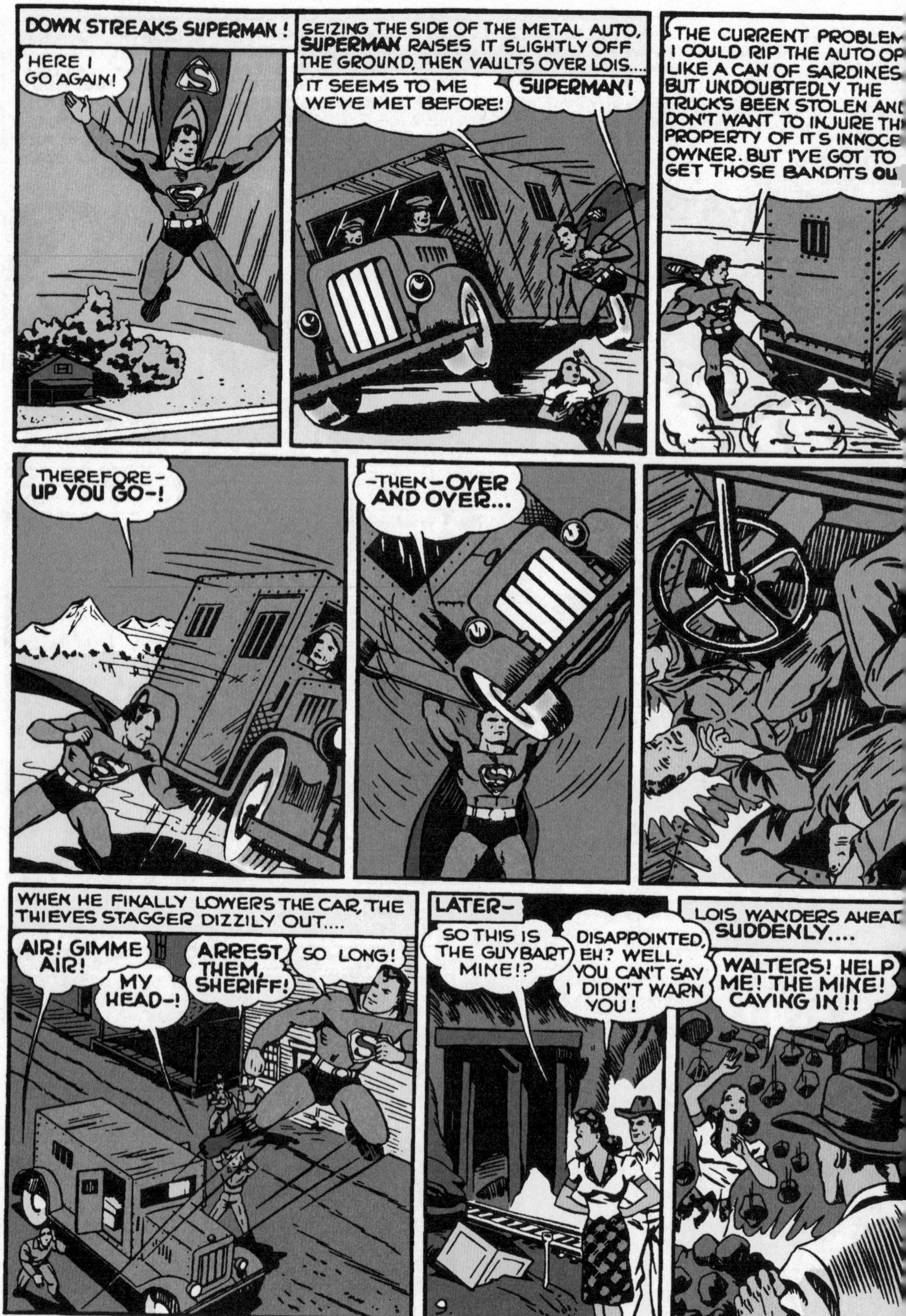
DOWN STREAKS SUPERMAN!
HERE I GO AGAIN!
SEIZING THE SIDE OF THE METAL AUTO, SUPERMAN RAISES IT SLIGHTLY OFF THE GROUND, THEN VAULTS OVER LOIS....
IT SEEMS TO ME WE'VE MET BEFORE!
SUPERMAN!
THE CURRENT PROBLEM I COULD RIP THE AUTO OP LIKE A CAN OF SARDINES BUT UNDOUBTEDLY THE TRUCK'S BEEN STOLEN AN DON'T WANT TO INJURE TH PROPERTY OF IT S INNOCE OWNER. BUT I'VE GOT TO GET THOSE BANDITS OU
THEREFORE- UP YOU GO-!
-THEN-OVER AND OVER...
WHEN HE FINALLY LOWERS THE CAR, THE THIEVES STAGGER DIZZILY OUT....
AIR! GIMME AIR!
MY HEAD-!
ARREST THEM, SHERIFF!
SO LONG!
LATER-
SO THIS IS THE GUYBART MINE!?
DISAPPOINTED, EH? WELL, YOU CAN'T SAY I DIDN'T WARN YOU!
LOIS WANDERS AHEAD SUDDENLY....
WALTERS! HELP ME! THE MINE! CAVING IN!!

BURIED ALIVE!—THE AIR IS BOUND TO BE EXHAUSTED SOON!

BUT WALTERS DASHES FOR HELP....

BACK THERE—A GIRL IMPRISONED IN A MINE CAVE-IN! HELP ME!

AS THE LACK OF AIR BEGINS TO OVERCOME LOIS....

THE AIR—GONE—WHAT'S THAT—BEHIND ME? A SOUND!

PART OF THE DIRT WALL—CRUMBLING...!

NEXT INSTANT...

SUPERMAN!

RIGHT AGAIN!

WH-WHAT WERE YOU DOING IN THE MINE?

THE SAME THING YOU WERE—INSPECTING IT! YOU'D BETTER COME WITH ME!

BUT FIRST—THERE'S THIS LITTLE MATTER TO ATTEND TO!

I NEVER CEASE MARVELING AT YOUR AMAZING STRENGTH!

SHORTLY AFTER...

A SECRET ENTRANCE!

SURPRISED? THEN PREPARE YOURSELF FOR AN EVEN MORE ASTONISHING DISCOVERY!

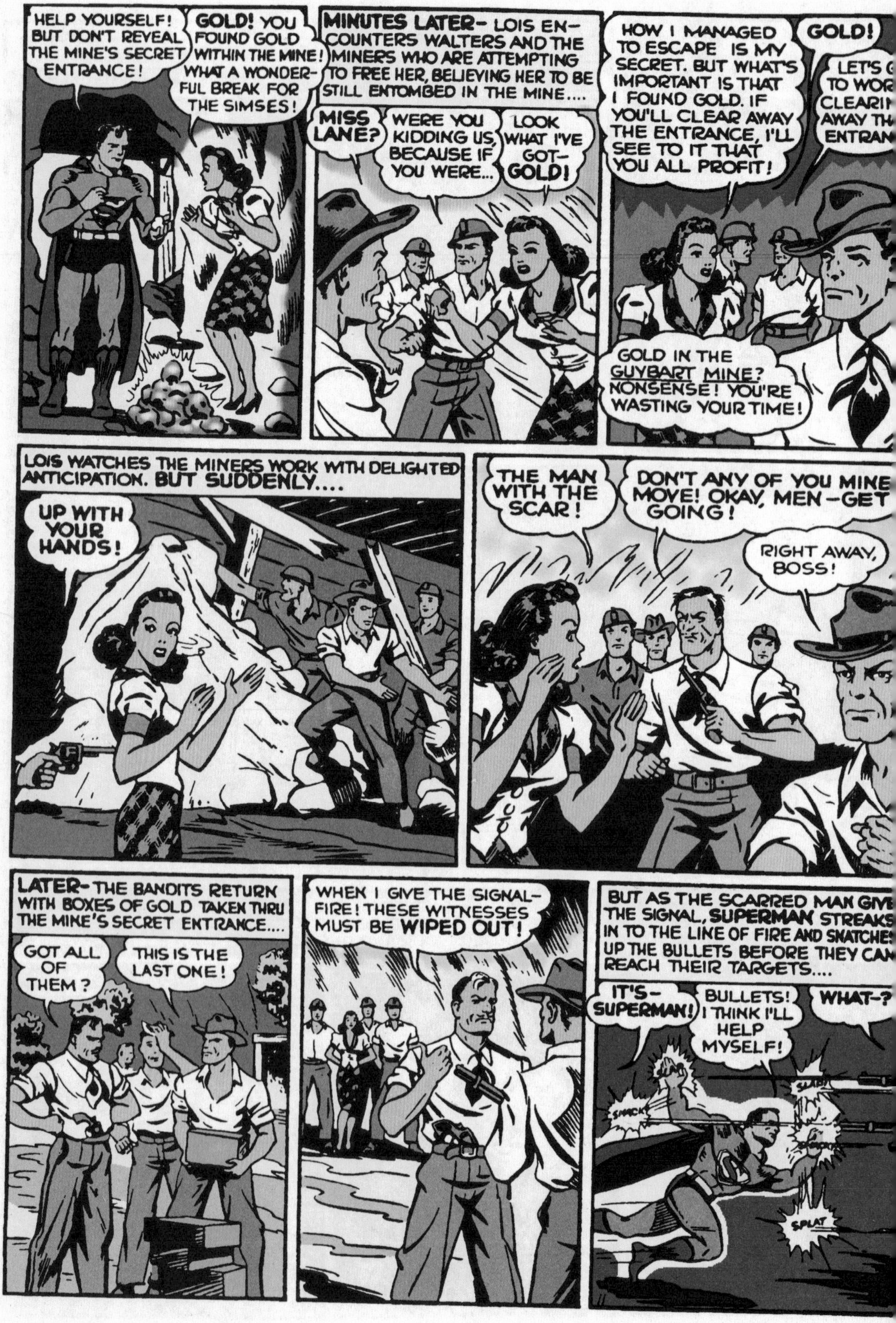
HELP YOURSELF! BUT DON'T REVEAL THE MINE'S SECRET ENTRANCE!
GOLD! YOU FOUND GOLD WITHIN THE MINE! WHAT A WONDERFUL BREAK FOR THE SIMSES!
MINUTES LATER- LOIS ENCOUNTERS WALTERS AND THE MINERS WHO ARE ATTEMPTING TO FREE HER, BELIEVING HER TO BE STILL ENTOMBED IN THE MINE....
MISS LANE?
WERE YOU KIDDING US, BECAUSE IF YOU WERE...
LOOK WHAT I'VE GOT- GOLD!
HOW I MANAGED TO ESCAPE IS MY SECRET. BUT WHAT'S IMPORTANT IS THAT I FOUND GOLD. IF YOU'LL CLEAR AWAY THE ENTRANCE, I'LL SEE TO IT THAT YOU ALL PROFIT!
GOLD!
LET'S TO WOR CLEARI AWAY TH ENTRAN
GOLD IN THE GUYBART MINE? NONSENSE! YOU'RE WASTING YOUR TIME!
LOIS WATCHES THE MINERS WORK WITH DELIGHTED ANTICIPATION. BUT SUDDENLY....
UP WITH YOUR HANDS!
THE MAN WITH THE SCAR!
DON'T ANY OF YOU MINE MOVE! OKAY, MEN-GET GOING!
RIGHT AWAY, BOSS!
LATER- THE BANDITS RETURN WITH BOXES OF GOLD TAKEN THRU THE MINE'S SECRET ENTRANCE....
GOT ALL OF THEM?
THIS IS THE LAST ONE!
WHEN I GIVE THE SIGNAL- FIRE! THESE WITNESSES MUST BE WIPED OUT!
BUT AS THE SCARRED MAN GIVE THE SIGNAL, SUPERMAN STREAKS IN TO THE LINE OF FIRE AND SNATCHE UP THE BULLETS BEFORE THEY CA REACH THEIR TARGETS....
IT'S- SUPERMAN!
BULLETS! I THINK I'LL HELP MYSELF!
WHAT-?
SMACK!
SPLAT

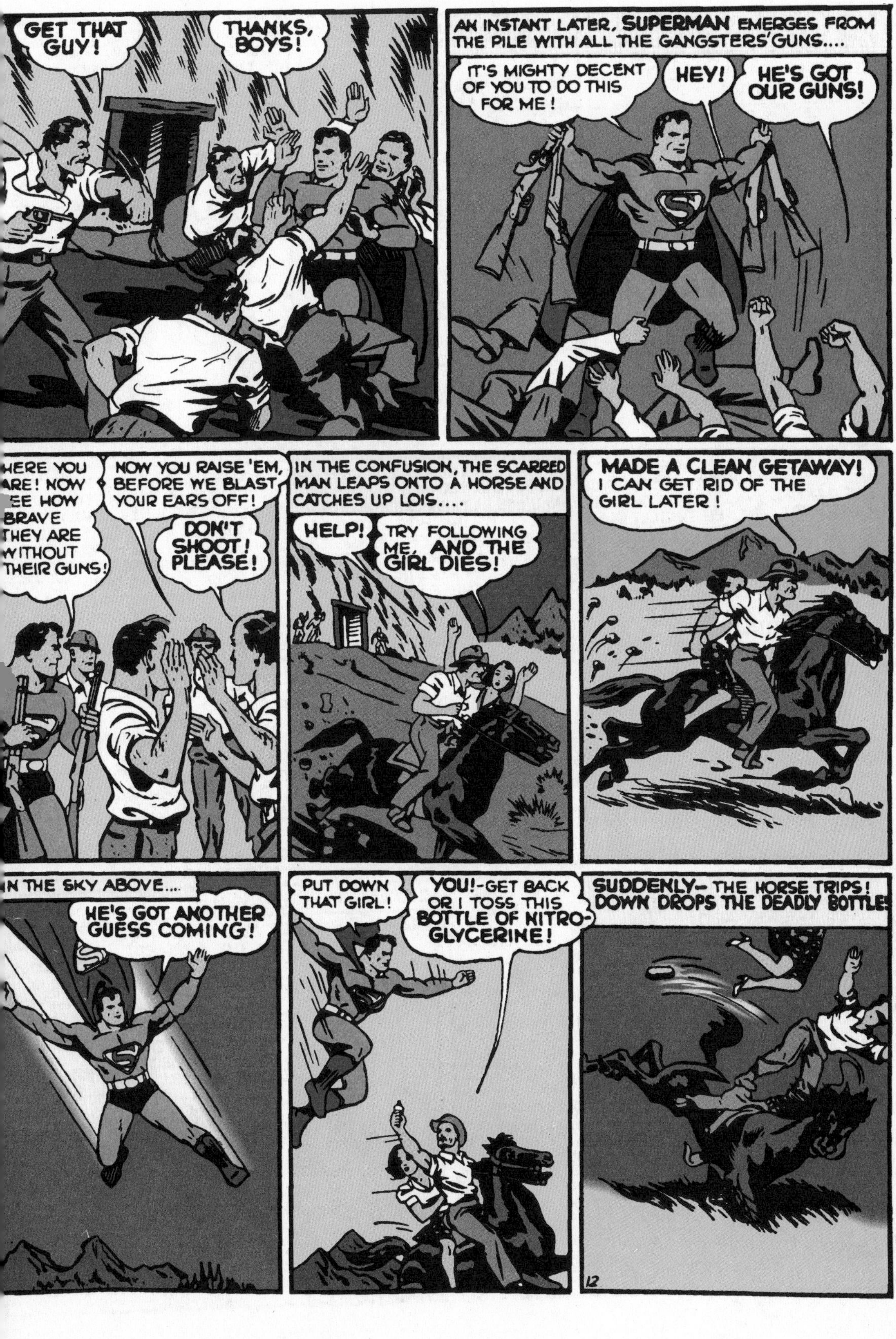
GET THAT GUY!
THANKS, BOYS!
AN INSTANT LATER, SUPERMAN EMERGES FROM THE PILE WITH ALL THE GANGSTERS' GUNS....
IT'S MIGHTY DECENT OF YOU TO DO THIS FOR ME!
HEY!
HE'S GOT OUR GUNS!
HERE YOU ARE! NOW SEE HOW BRAVE THEY ARE WITHOUT THEIR GUNS!
NOW YOU RAISE 'EM, BEFORE WE BLAST YOUR EARS OFF!
DON'T SHOOT! PLEASE!
IN THE CONFUSION, THE SCARRED MAN LEAPS ONTO A HORSE AND CATCHES UP LOIS....
HELP!
TRY FOLLOWING ME, AND THE GIRL DIES!
MADE A CLEAN GETAWAY! I CAN GET RID OF THE GIRL LATER!
IN THE SKY ABOVE....
HE'S GOT ANOTHER GUESS COMING!
PUT DOWN THAT GIRL!
YOU!-GET BACK OR I TOSS THIS BOTTLE OF NITRO-GLYCERINE!
SUDDENLY- THE HORSE TRIPS! DOWN DROPS THE DEADLY BOTTLE!
12

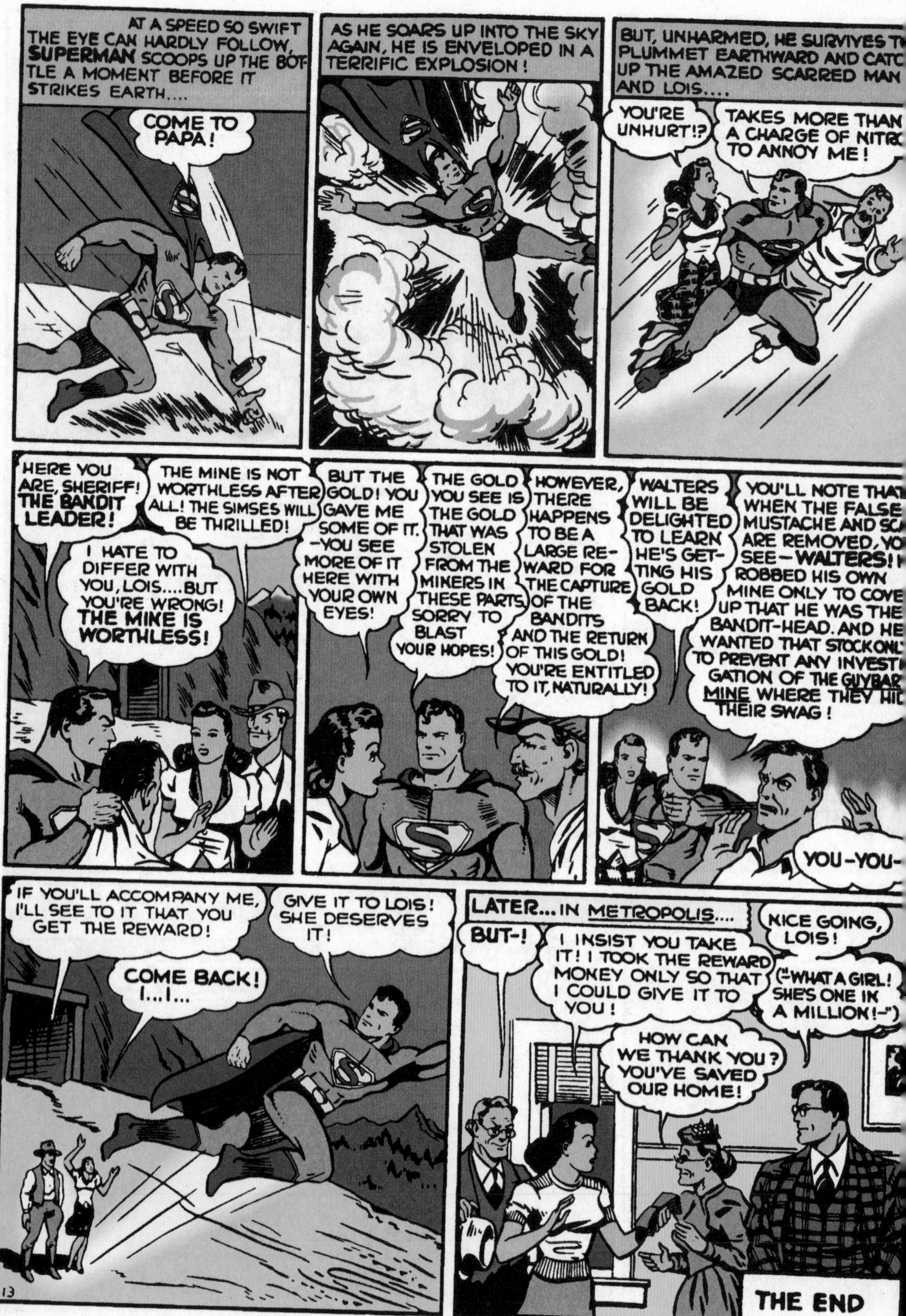
AT A SPEED SO SWIFT THE EYE CAN HARDLY FOLLOW, SUPERMAN SCOOPS UP THE BOTTLE A MOMENT BEFORE IT STRIKES EARTH....
COME TO PAPA!
AS HE SOARS UP INTO THE SKY AGAIN, HE IS ENVELOPED IN A TERRIFIC EXPLOSION!
BUT, UNHARMED, HE SURVIVES TH PLUMMET EARTHWARD AND CATC UP THE AMAZED SCARRED MAN AND LOIS....
YOU'RE UNHURT!?
TAKES MORE THAN A CHARGE OF NITR TO ANNOY ME!
HERE YOU ARE, SHERIFF! THE BANDIT LEADER!
THE MINE IS NOT WORTHLESS AFTER ALL! THE SIMSES WILL BE THRILLED!
I HATE TO DIFFER WITH YOU, LOIS.... BUT YOU'RE WRONG! THE MINE IS WORTHLESS!
BUT THE GOLD! YOU GAVE ME SOME OF IT. -YOU SEE MORE OF IT HERE WITH YOUR OWN EYES!
THE GOLD YOU SEE IS THE GOLD THAT WAS STOLEN FROM THE MINERS IN THESE PARTS. SORRY TO BLAST YOUR HOPES!
HOWEVER, THERE HAPPENS TO BE A LARGE REWARD FOR THE CAPTURE OF THE BANDITS AND THE RETURN OF THIS GOLD! YOU'RE ENTITLED TO IT, NATURALLY!
WALTERS WILL BE DELIGHTED TO LEARN HE'S GETTING HIS GOLD BACK!
YOU'LL NOTE THAT WHEN THE FALSE MUSTACHE AND SC ARE REMOVED, YO SEE—WALTERS! ROBBED HIS OWN MINE ONLY TO COVE UP THAT HE WAS THE BANDIT-HEAD. AND HE WANTED THAT STOCK ONL TO PREVENT ANY INVESTI GATION OF THE GUYBAR MINE WHERE THEY HI THEIR SWAG!
YOU-YOU-
IF YOU'LL ACCOMPANY ME, I'LL SEE TO IT THAT YOU GET THE REWARD!
GIVE IT TO LOIS! SHE DESERVES IT!
COME BACK! I...I...
13
LATER... IN METROPOLIS....
BUT-!
I INSIST YOU TAKE IT! I TOOK THE REWARD MONEY ONLY SO THAT I COULD GIVE IT TO YOU!
NICE GOING, LOIS!
("WHAT A GIRL! SHE'S ONE IN A MILLION!-")
HOW CAN WE THANK YOU? YOU'VE SAVED OUR HOME!
THE END

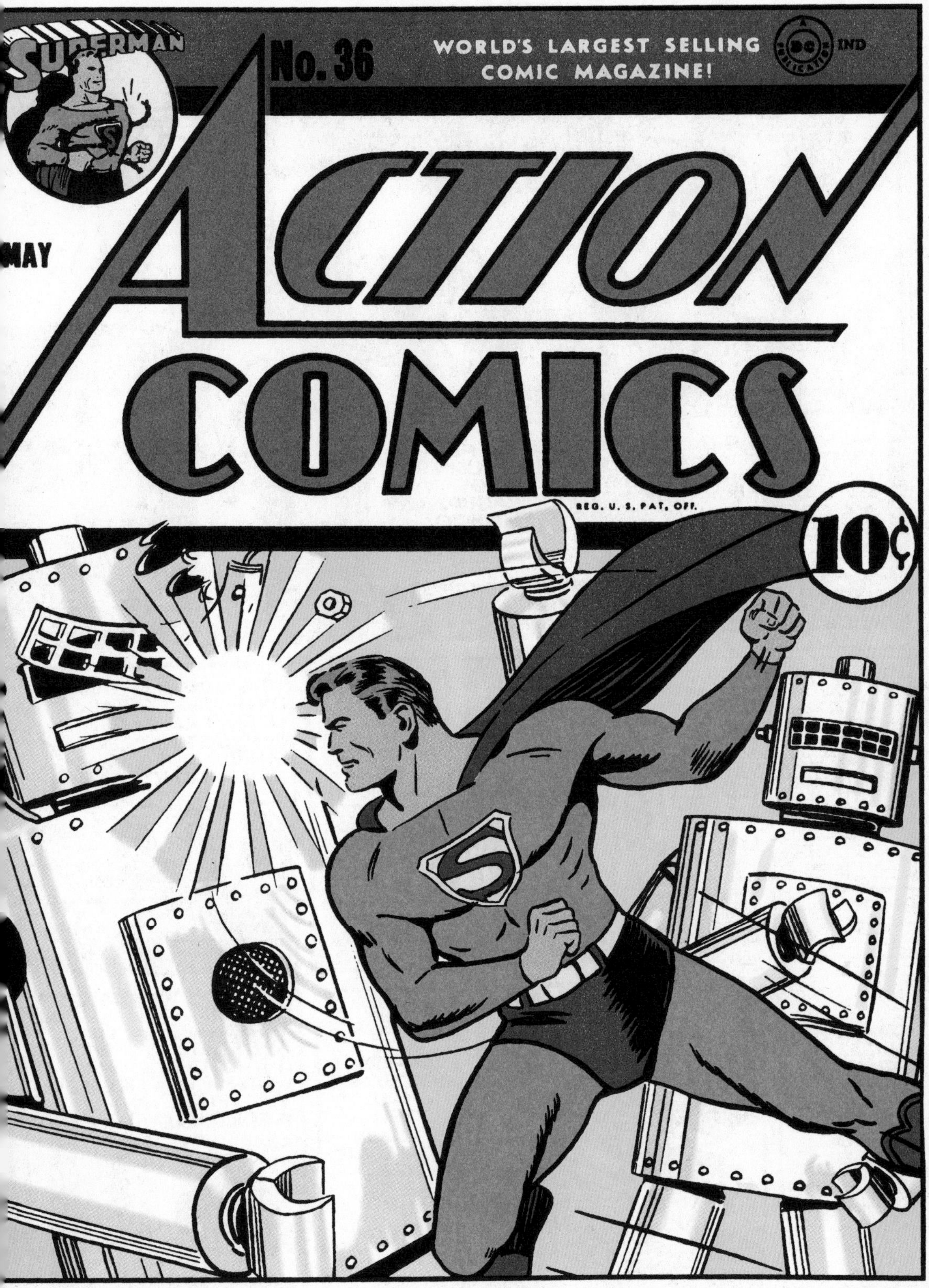
SUPERMAN
No. 36
WORLD'S LARGEST SELLING
COMIC MAGAZINE!
A DC PUBLICATION
IND
MAY
ACTION
COMICS
REG. U. S. PAT. OFF.
10¢

SUPERMAN

by JERRY SIEGEL and JOE SHUSTER

MENACED BY AN ENEMY INVASION AND THE TRAITOROUS ACTIVITIES OF FIFTH COLUMNISTS, THE FATE OF THE UNITED STATES HANGS IN THE BALANCE AS **SUPERMAN**, EXTRAORDINARY *MAN OF TOMORROW*, VENTURES FORTH TO ENGAGE THE FOE IN A GIGANTIC BATTLE WITH THE FUTURE OF DEMOCRACY AT STAKE!

EN ROUTE TO A MEETING OF THE *VOLUNTEERS FOR PEACE* AT *GLADSTONE HALL*, LOIS LANE MUTTERS ANGRILY TO HERSELF....

THAT CLARK! HE BURNS ME UP! JUST BECAUSE THERE'S A FAINT POSSIBILITY THE MEETING MAY BE UNPLEASANT, HE HAS TO BACK OUT!

BUT ATOP THE *DAILY PLANET* BUILDING, AS CLARK KENT REMOVES HIS OUTER CIVILIAN GARMENTS, TRANSFORMING HIMSELF INTO DYNAMIC SUPERMAN...

THIS CRAVEN ATTITUDE ON MY PART CERTAINLY DOESN'T RATE ME HIGH IN LOIS' OPINION, BUT THAT'S JUST WHAT I WANT.

THE *MAN OF STEEL'S* POWERFUL MUSCLES ROCKET HIM OUT INTO SPACE....

SHE MUST NOT SUSPECT THAT I AM, IN REALITY, SUPERMAN!

AS LOIS ENTERS *GLADSTONE HALL*, TED ALLEN CONFRONTS HER....

LANE OF THE *PLANET*, EH? SEE TO IT THAT YOUR WRITE-UP OF THIS AFFAIR IS FAVORABLE!

I'LL WRITE WHAT I PLEASE!

①

NO FIREWORKS YET-- BUT, OF COURSE, LOIS HASN'T BEEN HERE VERY LONG!

AS STUART PEMBERTON, LEADER OF THE *VOLUNTEERS FOR PEACE*, ENTERS THE JAMMED HALL, THE AUDIENCE GOES BERSERK IN FANATICAL APPLAUSE...

I NEVER DID LIKE PEMBERTON'S APPEARANCE-- AND I DISTRUST HIS MOTIVES EVEN MORE!

SH-HH! YOU MAY BE OVERHEARD!

PEMBERTON LOSES NO TIME IN COMING TO THE POINT....

FRIENDS--ONCE AGAIN I URGE YOU TO SHOUT YOUR DISAPPROVAL OF REARMAMENT IN THIS COUNTRY! WE'RE NOT ACTUALLY MENACED BY WAR--THAT'S JUST THE HOGWASH THE GRAFTERS ARE TRYING TO MAKE THE GULLIBLE TAXPAYERS SWALLOW!

I'LL GO FURTHER THAN THAT! I'LL WAGER THAT THE REASON *METROPOLIS* NEWSPAPERS ARE SUPPORTING NATIONAL REARMAMENT IS BECAUSE THEY'RE RECEIVING SECRET PAY-OFFS!

OF ALL THE FILTHY UNTRUTHS--!

DOWN! SIT DOWN, YOU FOOL!

SUPERMAN'S X-RAY VISION AND SUPER-SENSITIVE HEARING HAVE KEPT HIM ACQUAINTED WITH ALL THAT IS OCCURRING BELOW!

THERE SHE GOES AGAIN! --I MIGHT AS WELL PREPARE MYSELF FOR ACTION!

LOIS DASHES TOWARD THE PLATFORM, BUT IS RE-STRAINED BY BRAWNY USHERS....

TELL THEM TO LET GO!

RELEASE HER!--WHAT IS IT, YOUNG LADY?

AS A NEWSPAPER REPORTER, I MERELY WISH TO ANNOUNCE THAT YOU ARE A DELIBERATE LIAR!!

EJECT HER! AND YOU NEEDN'T BE TOO GENTLE ABOUT IT!

DON'T WORRY, WE WON'T BE!

MAY I GET IN ON THIS?

SUPERMAN!!

GIVE THE LADY ROOM!

THAT'S RIGHT! TEACH THEM SOME RESPECT!

SO YOU WANTED HER THROWN OUT, EH?

LET ME GO! LET GO, DO YOU HEAR!?

A FLICK OF **SUPERMAN'S** WRIST AND PEMBERTON GOES SAILING OUT OVER THE AUDIENCE...

③

LET'S SEE HOW **YOU** LIKE IT!

Y//--//!!!

ANGERED AT THE TREATMENT ACCORDED THEIR LEADER, THE MOB RUSHES IN....

WE'LL FIX HIM!

GET THAT GIRL!!

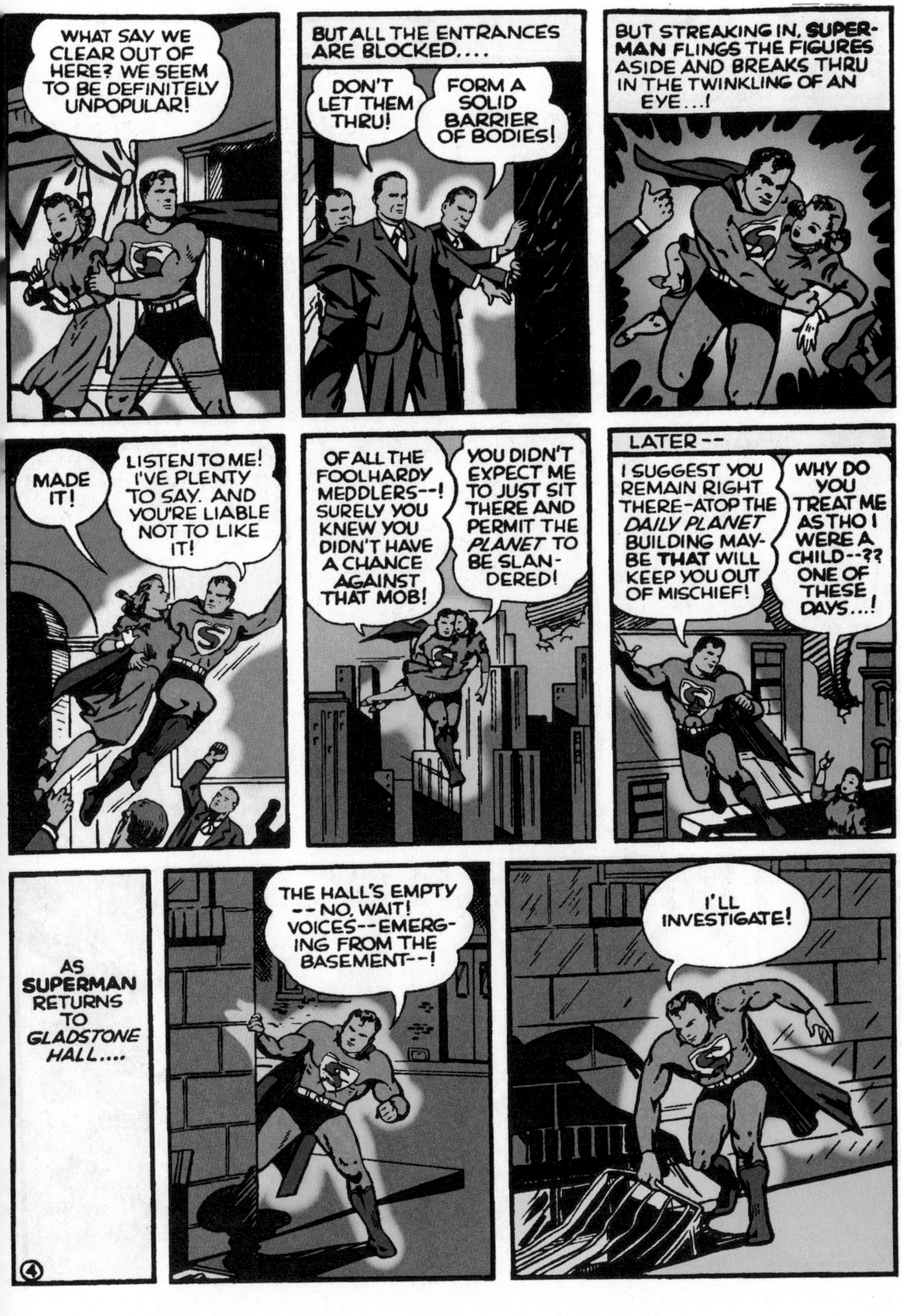
WHAT SAY WE CLEAR OUT OF HERE? WE SEEM TO BE DEFINITELY UNPOPULAR!
BUT ALL THE ENTRANCES ARE BLOCKED....
DON'T LET THEM THRU!
FORM A SOLID BARRIER OF BODIES!
BUT STREAKING IN, SUPERMAN FLINGS THE FIGURES ASIDE AND BREAKS THRU IN THE TWINKLING OF AN EYE...!
MADE IT!
LISTEN TO ME! I'VE PLENTY TO SAY. AND YOU'RE LIABLE NOT TO LIKE IT!
OF ALL THE FOOLHARDY MEDDLERS--! SURELY YOU KNEW YOU DIDN'T HAVE A CHANCE AGAINST THAT MOB!
YOU DIDN'T EXPECT ME TO JUST SIT THERE AND PERMIT THE PLANET TO BE SLANDERED!
LATER--
I SUGGEST YOU REMAIN RIGHT THERE-ATOP THE DAILY PLANET BUILDING MAYBE THAT WILL KEEP YOU OUT OF MISCHIEF!
WHY DO YOU TREAT ME AS THO I WERE A CHILD--?? ONE OF THESE DAYS...!
AS SUPERMAN RETURNS TO GLADSTONE HALL....
THE HALL'S EMPTY --NO, WAIT! VOICES--EMERGING FROM THE BASEMENT--!
I'LL INVESTIGATE!
4

THOSE VOICES ARE FROM THE NEXT ROOM!

WHAT **SUPERMAN** OVERHEARS--!

WE'VE ACCOMPLISHED AS MUCH AS WE CAN, FOOLING THE MEMBERSHIP WITH ANTI-REARMAMENT TALK. THE TIME FOR ACTION HAS ARRIVED! "NATION X" WILL STRIKE IN LESS THAN AN HOUR-- AND IT'S OUR DUTY TO PREPARE THE WAY BY SABOTAGING IMPORTANT STRATEGIC CENTERS, SUCH AS....

SO THAT'S THEIR TRUE GOAL-- WHAT'S *THAT*? SOME ONE APPROACHING!

I'VE GOT TO HIDE!

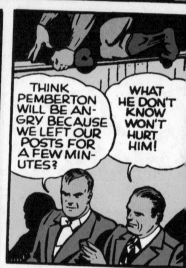

THINK PEMBERTON WILL BE ANGRY BECAUSE WE LEFT OUR POSTS FOR A FEW MINUTES?

WHAT HE DON'T KNOW WON'T HURT HIM!

REACHING DOWN, **SUPERMAN** WHACKS THE TWO HEADS TOGETHER...

⑤

AT THE SOUND OF THE GONG...!

NOW TO RESUME WHERE I LEFT OFF!

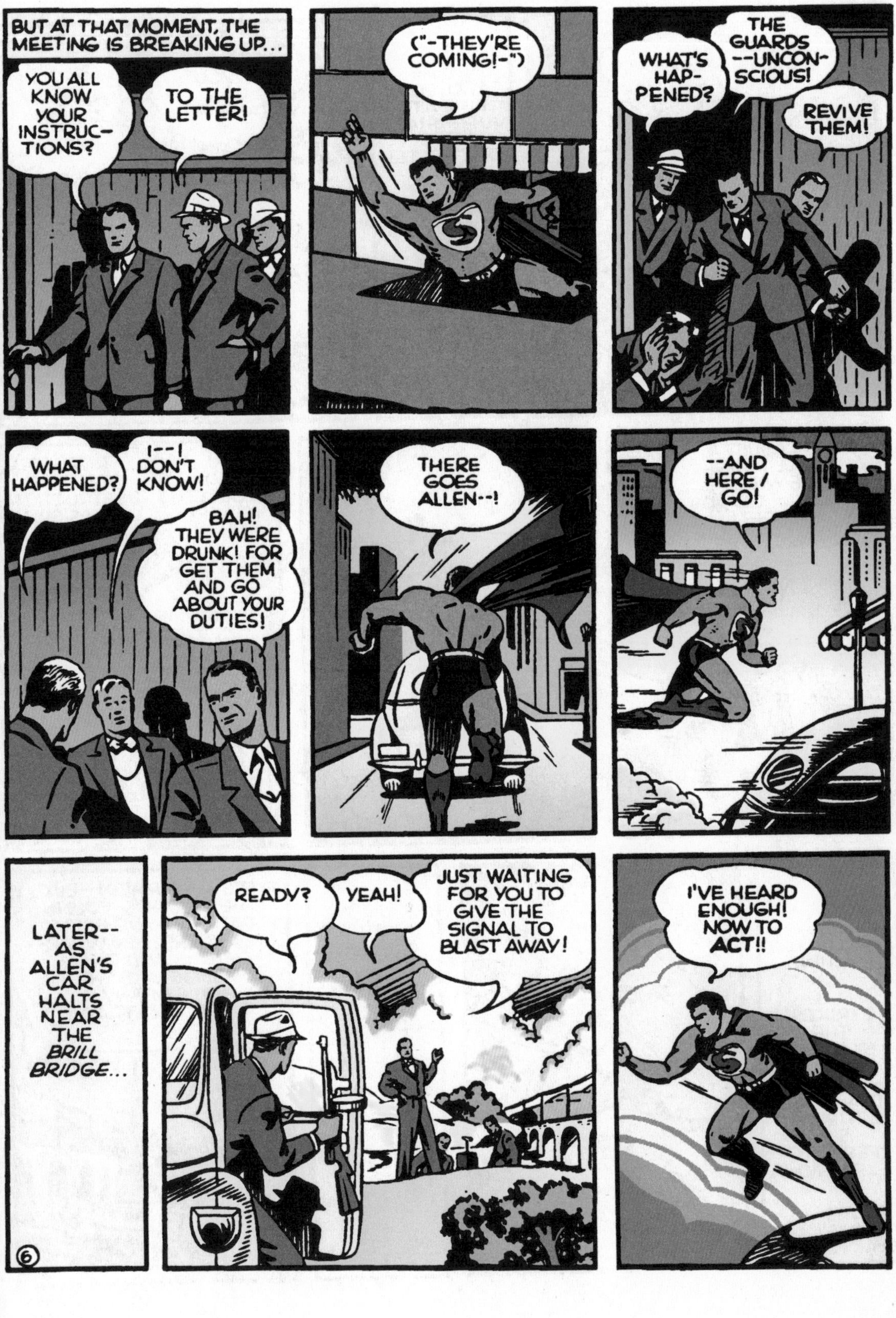
BUT AT THAT MOMENT, THE MEETING IS BREAKING UP...
YOU ALL KNOW YOUR INSTRUCTIONS?
TO THE LETTER!
("-THEY'RE COMING!-")
WHAT'S HAPPENED?
THE GUARDS --UNCONSCIOUS!
REVIVE THEM!
WHAT HAPPENED?
I--I DON'T KNOW!
BAH! THEY WERE DRUNK! FORGET THEM AND GO ABOUT YOUR DUTIES!
THERE GOES ALLEN--!
--AND HERE I GO!
LATER--AS ALLEN'S CAR HALTS NEAR THE BRILL BRIDGE...
READY?
YEAH!
JUST WAITING FOR YOU TO GIVE THE SIGNAL TO BLAST AWAY!
I'VE HEARD ENOUGH! NOW TO ACT!!
6

AS THE SABOTEURS FIRE AT **SUPERMAN**, HE IS UNAFFECTED BY THE BULLETS! BUT HIS PLUMMETING FIGURE SENDS THEM SPRAWLING...

AS ALLEN'S MACHINE-GUN FIRE STRIKES THE STACKED BOXES OF DYNAMITE, THERE IS A TERRIFIC EXPLOSION...

⑦

BUT WHEN THE SMOKE CLEARS...

UP STREAKS SUPERMAN--!

THEN--ALONG THE TRACKS HE WHIZZES...

GOT TO REACH THAT TRAIN-- BEFORE IT'S *TOO LATE!*

AS THE TRAIN COMES ON-TO THE BRIDGE, **SUPERMAN** SEIZES ITS FRONT AND FORCES IT BACK IN A DESPERATE EFFORT....

BACK-- BACK--!

WHAT--? WE'RE SLOWING!!!

327

AND NEXT INSTANT, THE PONDEROUS TRAIN COMES TO A DEAD-STOP!

THAT DID IT!!

BUT NOT SATISFIED, **SUPER-MAN** DISCONNECTS THE LO-COMOTIVE FROM THE REST OF THE TRAIN, THEN....

UP YOU GO--!

TURNING IT, HE LOWERS IT *CROSS-WISE* ACROSS THE RAILS!

THERE! NO WRECK TODAY!

A MOMENT AFTER THE COSTUMED FIGURE LEAPS OFF...

D-DID YOU SEE-- (GULP!)-- THAT DISPLAY OF AMAZING STRENGTH?

I--I DID! AND LOOK AT THE BRIDGE'S FOUN-DATIONS! WE OWE OUR LIVES TO HIM!

8

FORWARD STREAKS THE *MAN OF STEEL* THRU THE AIR! SUDDENLY, HE SIGHTS--

TROUBLE AT THE RESERVOIR!

SABOTEURS ARE ABOUT TO POLLUTE THE CITY'S WATER SUPPLY...

SOMEONE DROPPING DOWN FROM THE SKY!

QUICK! THROW IN THE BOTTLES!

DOWN PLUMMETS THE *MAN OF TOMORROW*--!

DON'T THROW THOSE BOTTLES!

WE'LL DO AS WE PLEASE! GO AHEAD, BOYS-- THROW 'EM IN!

("-I'VE GOT TO THINK FAST!-")

LET ME PROVE YOU'VE BEEN DOUBLE-CROSSED! THE BOTTLES ARE FILLED WITH HARMLESS WATER, NOT DEADLY NARCOTICS! TOSS ME ONE OF THEM AND SEE FOR YOURSELF!

HERE YOU ARE! DRINK, SAP!

THIS OUGHTA BE FUNNY!

SUPERMAN CONSUMES THE BOTTLE'S CONTENTS--!

LOOK AT THAT!

NOW WATCH HIM KEEL OVER!

BUT THEN--

SEE? I FEEL *BETTER THAN EVER!*

YEAH? SAY, LET'S SEE IF THIS *IS* WATER!

WHAT IS PEMBERTON TRYIN' TO PULL?

AS THE THUGS TOPPLE INTO UNCONSCIOUSNESS....

IT WORKED!

WE'VE BEEN-- TRICKED!

⑨

MEAN-
WHILE--
A
GREAT
MASS OF
PLANES
CONVERGES
ON
METROPOLIS...

LOOSING
THEIR
CARGO
OF
DEADLY
BOMBS
UPON THE
HELPLESS
CITY!

NEWS FLASH!--
THE CITY HAS BEEN
ATTACKED BY MYS-
TERIOUS BOMBERS!
DESTRUCTION--
WIDESPREAD-- IS
INCREASING BY THE
MOMENT!

SUPERMAN'S SUPER-SENSI-
TIVE HEARING ENABLES
HIM TO PICK UP THE NEWS
BROADCAST.

PLANES ATTACKING
THE CITY! I'LL HAVE
TO LOOK INTO THIS!

TOWARD
THE GREAT
SKY-
ARMADA
STREAKS
THE LONE
FIGURE
OF THE
MAN OF
STEEL!
SO VASTLY
OUTNUMBER-
ED-- WHAT
CAN HE
HOPE TO
ACCOMPLISH?

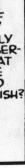

CRASH!
AS THE
MAN OF
TOMORROW
STRIKES THE
V-SHAPED
FORMATION,
HE SENDS
THE
ENEMY
PLANES
WHIRLING
OFF LIKE
BOWLING-
PINS!

THE AIRCRAFT CONCENTRATE THEIR FURY UPON SUPERMAN...

BUT AS HE EXPERTLY DODGES IN AND OUT AMONG THEIR RAINING BULLETS, THEY SUCCEED ONLY IN SENDING THEIR COMRADES DOWN IN FLAMES!

MISSED ME!

I BELIEVE I'LL PAY A CALL ON THE COMMANDER!

WH-WHAT MANNER OF UNEARTHLY CREATURE ARE YOU?

SIGNAL YOUR MEN TO TURN BACK OR I'LL GIVE YOU A TASTE OF YOUR OWN CRUELTY!

TERRIFIED, THE COMMANDER OBEYS--

ABANDON ATTACK!

THAT'S BETTER!

IN RESPONSE TO THEIR COMMANDER'S ORDERS, THE SURVIVING PLANES WING BACK TOWARD THE OCEAN!

AS **SUPERMAN** MOMENTARILY TURNS HIS BACK--!

FOOL! THIS IS THE OPPORTUNITY I WAITED FOR--!

--AND A MOVE YOU'LL SOON REGRET!

THE BULLET REBOUNDS...

SLAIN-- BY HIS OWN BULLET!

MEANWHILE, PEMBERTON PERSONALLY LEADS THE RAID ON RADIO STATION WMET....

LEAVE THAT MICRO-PHONE!

YOU--YOU CAN'T DO THIS!

DO AS HE SAYS!

THE HOUR HAS COME--DEMOCRACY'S DEATH IS AT HAND! EVEN NOW THE PLANES OF THE CONQUERING NATION ZOOM OVER-HEAD! I, STUART PEMBERTON, CALL UPON YOU TO SURRENDER!

CRUISING NEAR THE RADIO STATION, LOIS PICKS UP THE ASTONISH-ING BROADCAST ON HER RADIO....

I KNEW PEMBERTON WASN'T TO BE TRUST-ED! PERHAPS IF I GET INTO THE RADIO STATION IN TIME..!

BUT AS LOIS ENTERS WMET, SHE IS SEIZED BY PEMBERTON'S HENCH-MAN...

LET ME GO!

QUIET! HE HASN'T FINISHED!

OVER-HEARING THE BROAD-CAST **SUPERMAN** STREAKS DOWN TOWARD THE STATION...

SO PEMBER-TON'S COME OUT IN THE OPEN, EH? THAT CALLS FOR OPEN COMBAT!

SUPERMAN!

RIGHT! AND IF YOU'LL KINDLY PERMIT ME TO GET MY HANDS ON YOU!

SWINGING LOIS BEFORE HIM, PEMBERTON USES HER AS A SHIELD...

BACK-- OR THE GIRL DIES!

DON'T MIND ME, **SUPERMAN!** GET HIM!!

I'M SORRY-- I CAN'T SACRI-FICE YOUR LIFE!

TURNING HIS ATTENTION TO THE THUGS, **SUPERMAN** SENDS THEM ALL INTO UNCONSCIOUSNESS IN THE SPACE OF A SECOND FLAT...

PARDON MY HASTE, FELLOWS--!

--BUT I'M IN A HURRY!

DON'T WASTE ANY HOPES! YOU WON'T ESCAPE!

YOU-- TRAITOR!

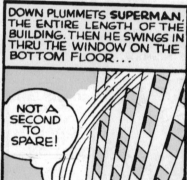

DOWN PLUMMETS **SUPERMAN**, THE ENTIRE LENGTH OF THE BUILDING. THEN HE SWINGS IN THRU THE WINDOW ON THE BOTTOM FLOOR...

NOT A SECOND TO SPARE!

AS THE ELEVATOR DOOR OPENS...

("-IN ANOTHER MOMENT...!-")

NOW!

UH-HH!

GREAT! I KNEW I COULD COUNT ON YOU!

BUT WAIT--!

WHY? I'M NEEDED NO LONGER!

LATER--EDITORIAL OFFICE OF THE *DAILY PLANET*....

LIKE THAT ARTICLE I'VE DASHED OFF? YOU SHOULD TURN GREEN WITH ENVY!

STRANGELY ENOUGH AT THIS MOMENT THE PRESSES ARE RUNNING OFF AN ARTICLE OF MINE--AND IT COVERS THE SAME YARN!

THE END